C.J. Hewitt Jr

1980

NAPOLEON
THE LAST CAMPAIGNS
1813-15

NAPOLEON
THE LAST CAMPAIGNS
1813-15

JAMES LAWFORD

CROWN PUBLISHERS INC./NEW YORK

CONTENTS

*Part I was co-written by James Lawford and Peter Young.
All other chapters are by James Lawford.

LIBRARY OF CONGRESS CATALOGING IN PUBLICATION DATA
LAWFORD, JAMES PHILIP.
  NAPOLEON: THE LAST CAMPAIGNS.
  BIBLIOGRAPHY: P.
  INCLUDES INDEX.
  1. NAPOLEON I, EMPEROR OF THE FRENCH, 1769-1821—
CAMPAIGNS OF 1813-1814. 2. NAPOLÉON I, EMPEROR OF THE
FRENCH, 1769-1821—ELBA AND THE HUNDRED DAYS, 1814-1815.
I. YOUNG, PETER, JOINT AUTHOR.
DC236.L35 944.05'092'4 77-6392
ISBN 0-517-52634-4

MADE BY ROXBY PRESS PRODUCTIONS,
98 CLAPHAM COMMON NORTHSIDE,
LONDON, SW4 9SG

EDITORIAL DIRECTOR MICHAEL LEITCH
ART DIRECTOR DAVID POCKNELL
DESIGN ASSISTANT MICHAEL CAVERS
PRODUCTION REYNOLDS CLARK ASSOCIATES LIMITED
PICTURE RESEARCH MURIEL JEANCARD (PARIS)
AND ANNE HORTON (LONDON)

FILMSET BY REMBRANDT FILMSETTING LIMITED, WATFORD
REPRODUCTION BY COLOUR WORKSHOP LIMITED, HERTFOR
PRINTED AND BOUND
IN BELGIUM BY H. PROOST & CIE, TURNHOUT

FOREWORD

It is probably true that many look upon Napoleon's Russian Campaign of 1812 as the cause of his downfall. Yet Kutusov, the Russian Commander-in-Chief so respected by Tolstoy, advised the Tsar against crossing the borders of his own country, a view in which he was not alone. It cannot be denied that the Russian Campaign marked a turning point in Napoleon's fortunes; but during the struggle for Germany that culminated in the Battle of Leipzig, Napoleon came near to accomplishing a success that would have wiped out the effect of his Russian débâcle. Why did he fail?

Perhaps at last he fell a victim to that nationalism which was to dominate European history for the next century and a half, and which he had done something to foster; or perhaps the vast scale on which he had come to operate had become too much for a single man, even one of his genuis; or he might have so trained his enemy generals in military affairs that they became too good for his own marshals; or perhaps the flower of the French Army had perished and there was nothing with which to replace it; perhaps after years of good fortune his luck had run out. The speculation can be endless, but what is very evident is that the battle for Germany was far from a walkover. Even after he had been driven from Germany and stood at bay within the borders of France, the Allies were still prepared to concede him the Rhine, the Alps and the Pyrenees as his borders. It was not a falling-off in his military powers that betrayed him, rather that he refused to face the political realities of his situation.

His Campaign of 1814 was viewed by many, including that great authority Clausewitz, as one of his most brilliant. The final epitaph that he wrote for himself in the 'Hundred Days' of 1815 is one of the most dramatic in military history. It has been endlessly analysed and criticized. Here it may be enough to quote from that well known military writer of the late 19th century, Prince Hohenlohe-Ingelfingen. In his letter on military strategy he wrote: 'As a young subaltern I learned under clever teachers to laugh at the stupid military mistakes of great leaders, but I cannot say it did me any good. If Frederick and Napoleon made mistakes it only shows us that strategy is not so easy in practice as it may seem. Even with lesser lights, we only learn from their errors that all make mistakes and that they will always be made. For the best is he that makes fewest. What we want is the reason for blunders so as to know what to avoid.'

This book, it will be clear, has no pretensions to be a military treatise. It sets out to tell what occurred, and that is difficult enough. J.P.L.

Chronology

1812

18 December: Napoleon back in Paris after Russian campaign.

30 December: Convention of Tauroggen.

1813

19 March: Prussia and Russia form alliance.

15 April: Napoleon takes the field, reaches Erfurt on 25th.

2 May: Napoleon wins Battle of Lützen.

20–21 May: Napoleon wins Battle of Bautzen.

4 June: Armistice declared.

21 June: In Spain, Wellington wins Battle of Vitoria.

26 June: In conference with Metternich, Napoleon refuses to dissolve Confederation of Rhine.

10 July: Peace Congress in Prague.

10 August: Armistice ends.

12 August: Austria declares war.

23 August: Oudinot loses Battle of Grossbeeren.

26 August: Blücher beats Macdonald at Katzbach.

26–27 August: Napoleon beats Schwarzenberg at Dresden.

30 August: Vandamme surrenders at Kulm.

6 September: Ney defeated at Dennewitz.

9 September: Treaty of Töplitz.

8 October: Bavaria joins Allies.

16–18 October: Napoleon defeated at Leipzig. Defection of Saxons from *Grande Armée*.

30–31 October: Napoleon defeats Wrede at Hanau, returns to France.

PART I
1813

THE STRUGGLE FOR GERMANY

Napoleon prepares for the Battle of Leipzig from his bivouac near the Galgenberg.

CHAPTER 1
AFTER MOSCOW

As in the late autumn of 1812 the snows of Russia disgorged the remnants of his once magnificent army, Napoloen, with only General Caulaincourt and Rustum, his faithful Mameluke servant, left his broken regiments and took sledge and coach for Paris. He knew only too well that the Royalists and Republicans in Paris were honing their blades, ready to stab him in the back. Already an eccentric general called Malet had staged an abortive *coup*.

On 18 December 1812 Napoleon alighted from his coach and strode into the Tuileries while the Guards clanged into their salutes. He seemed

Shattered troops of the *Grande Armée* in Russia.

almost unaffected by the Russian catastrophe, one that would have crushed most other commanders. From an army of half a million disciplined soldiers – numbers that the Western world had never seen before – only some 85,000 demoralized men had managed to stagger out of Russia. Napoleon, however, believed it to have been the forces of nature, hunger, and famine that had defeated him, not the Russians. And indeed at the Battle of Borodino, the great battle of the campaign, the Russians had conceded him victory and abandoned Moscow. Nevertheless he had lost about 400,000 men. It had been a reverse of tremendous proportions; the Napoleonic myth of invincibility had been badly mauled.

But in December 1812 the situation looked far from hopeless. Many Russians, including their celebrated Commander-in-Chief, Field-Marshal Kutuzov, saw no good reason to pursue the war

Charlemagne. His faith in his 'star' remained unshaken. France had remained loyal, Austria would surely stay neutral. He saw no good reason why he should not dictate a triumphant peace on the banks of the River Neman (see map) that would wipe out all recollection of his Russian debacle. Possibly a little trading in territorial advantages would be judicious. Austria might be restored some territory. The Tyrol might be bandied about between Austria and Bavaria, ensuring their mutual hostility. Europe had surely been riven by too many ancient feuds to unite against him.

With amazing resilience Napoleon shrugged off the memories of Russia, and set about organizing a new *Grande Armée*. By the spring of 1813 he proposed to take the field with 600,000 men. Perhaps it would be enough for this great force to do nothing more than to show itself to the rest of Europe. This, however, was not to be. The Tsar

Napoleon retreats by sledge from Moscow.

beyond their frontiers; Frederick William III of Prussia had no desire to sample once again the perils of an armed conflict with the French; many Italians thought of Napoleon as a liberator from Austrian thraldom, and the King of Saxony regarded him as a saviour from the sinister attentions of Prussia. The Emperor Francis I of Austria, Napoleon's father-in-law, considered that the aggressive intentions of Russia and Prussia might threaten him more than the French; to the Poles, ambiguous as his actions might be, he enshrined their one great hope of freedom. Had Napoleon agreed at this stage to withdraw to the natural boundaries of France – the Rhine, the Alps and the Pyrenees – the war would have ended.

The Emperor, however, could not bring himself to abandon either his feud with Britain or his empire, still large enough to rival that of

Alexander I, a chivalrous, idealistic, but somewhat wayward young ruler, was determined to avenge the burning of Moscow. What was more, a strange new spirit, a sense of national identity, seemed abroad in Germany. General Yorck, commanding the Prussian contingent in the *Grande Armée*, a force about 18,000 strong, contrived to get himself cut off by the Russians. On 30 December 1812 he concluded the Convention of Tauroggen, binding his men from carrying out any hostile act against the Russians until 1 March 1813.

When he left Russia, Napoleon had handed over command of the army to Murat; but the Gascon, caring little for his duties, had passed them on to Prince Eugène Beauharnais, Napoleon's stepson and Viceroy of Italy, while he departed without orders for his kingdom of Naples. Prince Schwarzenberg, commanding the Austrians in the

Tsar Alexander I of Russia.

King Frederick William III of Prussia.

Grande Armée, viewed these changes with some disdain: 'We had been transferred from the Emperor to the King; now we are down to the Viceroy.' Soon after assuming his new role, Prince Eugène ordered Schwarzenberg to take up a position on the Vistula, whereupon Schwarzenberg quietly disappeared with his troops into the Austrian Empire. It is perhaps a measure of France's weakness at the time that no immediate breach followed with Austria. Prince Metternich, the effective political ruler of Austria, remained free to wait on events.

Others who did not at this juncture know which way to turn were Bavaria and Saxony. The former knew perfectly well that Austria was bound to try to recover the Tyrol, which Napoleon had given to Bavaria as a reward for support in the Campaign of 1809. Fear of Napoleon was also a strong motive in keeping a Bavarian contingent with the French Army. Moreover Count Maximilian von Montgelas, the Bavarian minister, deeply distrusted the Prussians.

Saxony, too, was torn by doubts, King Frederick Augustus I was well aware of Prussian hostility. Bewildered, the King took refuge at Ratisbon, ordering General Thielmann to keep the Saxon Army out of the way at the fortress of Torgau on the Elbe. Eventually, overriding his people, who favoured the cause of liberation from France, the King of Saxony threw in his lot with Napoleon. So did a dozen other German states, belonging to Napoleon's Confederation of the Rhine. The Scandinavian powers were divided: the Danes supported Napoleon and the Swedes sent a contingent to join the Allies.

It was to be the Tsar, though, who took the decisive steps. He dispensed with the services of the ailing Kutuzov (he died shortly after) and appointed Count Wittgenstein Commander-in-Chief of the Russians. It was a curious appointment, for without having distinguished himself in an outstanding fashion Wittgenstein thus superseded several generals senior to him, men such as Barclay de Tolly, Count Langeron and Mihailovich. At the same time the Tsar intended to keep the reins of power in his own hands when hostilities were resumed.

Soon the Russians began to advance, and Prince Eugène fell back before them. He could do little else. He abandoned the line of the Oder, leaving behind him garrisons at Danzig, Thorn and Modlin near Warsaw – all on the Vistula – and at Stettin, Kustrin and Glogau on the Oder; they were at once blockaded. The Russians surged up to the Elbe, and Cossacks entered Hamburg. Now, as the snows melted and massive new armies emerged from France, it was clear that the decisive battle had yet to be fought.

A Saxon dragoon on outpost duty.
The Saxons were half-hearted allies
of Napoleon for most of 1813,
then at Leipzig on 18 October
the Saxon corps defected.

GERMANY IN SPRING 1813

SWEDEN

DENMARK

NORTH
SEA

BALTIC SEA

Memel

Tilsit

SWEDISH
POMERANIA

HAFF

POMERANIA
(PRUSSIAN)

Danzig

R. Neman

R. Vistula

RUSSIA

Hamburg

MECKLENBURG

Stettin

R. Oder

Thorn

Bremen

R. Elbe

PRUSSIA

R. Weser

HANOVER

Spandau

Berlin

Kustrin

Posen

DUCHY OF
WARSAW

Warsaw

BRUNSWICK

Magdeburg

Grossbeeren

Frankfurt

Harz
Mountains

Wittenberg

R. Bober

Glogau

R. Oder

Kassel

Halle

Torgau

WESTPHALIA

Lützen

Leipzig

SAXONY

R. Spree

Görlitz

Breslau

Erfurt

Chemnitz

Dresden

Bautzen

Liegnitz

SILESIA
(PRUSSIAN)

Königstein

R. Elster

Erzgebirge

GALICIA
(AUSTRIAN)

R. Main

Bayreuth

Würzburg

Prague

BAVARIA

BOHEMIA (AUSTRIAN)

French garrisons

Napoleon's Confederation of the Rhine
comprised most of Central and Western Germany including Bavaria,
Saxony and Westphalia.

CHAPTER 2
THE OPPOSING ARMIES

The *Grande Armée* was Napoleon's creation and he was his own Commander-in-Chief. He alone created Marshals of the Empire or retired them to pastures of varying degrees of lushness. He was absolute, his authority unfettered. He took no one into his confidence, and was beholden to no one. He utterly discredited the old 18th-century concept of lengthy councils of war attended by all the senior officers. It is true that before the Battle of Castiglione (1796) he did hold such a council and accepted Augereau's advice, for which he was ever after grateful, but such occasions were rare. In consequence his decisions had a speed and cer-

The Emperor inspects his Guard.

tainty initially lacking among his contemporaries. The great Duke of Wellington, however, was an exception. He welcomed advice even less than the Emperor.

The *Grande Armée* of 1813 consisted of the Imperial Headquarters, the Imperial Guard, 12 corps and five cavalry corps. The corps were commanded either by marshals or by generals of division, men ranging in age from 35 to 56, the majority being in their mid-40s and therefore well able to sustain the rigours of campaigning. These calculations do not include the Chief-of-Staff, Marshal Berthier, who was 60, or Prince Eugène, who was 33. The former lived a relatively sheltered life at Napoleon's headquarters, while the latter, being Viceroy of Italy, was sent back to his charge in May 1813.

Against these men, in the immense drama that concluded the Napoleonic era, were ranged armies of many nationalities, sizes and abilities. They were commanded variously by Prussian, Saxon, Austrian and British generals and, in Bernadotte, benefited from the strategic advice of a former French marshal who changed sides and in 1810 became Crown Prince of Sweden. Below are brief lives of the principal army commanders in the Campaigns of 1813–15. They are followed on page 22 by an account of the various armies, and how they were organized to fight in the momentous battles of those years.

THE GENERALS

NAPOLEON I
Napoleon Bonaparte,
Emperor of France
(1769–1821)

In 1779 a small, skinny, nervous Corsican child aged nine arrived at the small academy at Brienne in the province of Champagne. He wanted to study to be an officer in the Royal French Army. His classmates tormented him, mocking his outlandish way of speaking French. He called himself 'di Buonaparte'. His father was some poverty-struck Corsican lawyer with pretensions to be called 'Viscount'.

The boy retired into himself, occasionally turning on his tormentors with a fury that surprised them. He spent his days reading and studying his books. He seemed nothing out of the ordinary, although he had a remarkable memory and a decided leaning towards mathematics. Gradually his personality emerged and despite a physique that was far from impressive, he came to be the acknowledged leader of his class. His father died when he was about 16, and he soon experienced grinding poverty, spending his few sous on books rather than food. In due course he was commissioned into the artillery. Then came the Revolution in 1789. He thought it judicious to drop the 'di' from his name and eventually spelt it in the French fashion. In Paris in 1792 he saw the mob attack Louis XVI in Versailles and was furious that the inept Royal Guards did not mow them down with artillery fire. All his life he loathed and feared mobs. When in October 1795 a horde of Parisians, led by the National Guard, sought to overturn the Directory (the Government of France) he followed his own advice. Asked to safeguard the Directory, he sent his friend Murat with his cavalry to ransack the Sablons, the nearest gun park; by dawn he had ringed the Tuileries with cannon, and in the morning as the mob approached, he ruthlessly blew in their head, scattering the remainder.

He was now a man of note. His next chance came when Toulon declared against the Revolution and invited the British to occupy the port. Napoleon became the acknowledged brain behind the siege. He assembled all the cannon he could lay his hands on in the south of France, then established batteries on commanding ground and forced out the British fleet. On 19 December 1794 Toulon surrendered.

He clinched his successes by marrying the beautiful Josephine Beauharnais, widow of a guillotined general and the discarded mistress of Paul Barras, at that time one of the most powerful men in France. Whether it was through 'petticoat influence' or his decisive handling of the guns in Paris and Toulon is uncertain, but the young Napoleon, only 26 years of age, was then selected to take over the Army of Italy from the 61-year-old General Scherer. The latter, driven nearly distracted by advice from Paris, had resigned his command. On 27 March, in Nice, Napoleon met the commander he was relieving and his three senior generals: Sérurier, Augereau and Masséna. They were prepared to laugh at their lean young commander with the intense eyes, newly arrived from Paris, but after a few brief moments his extraordinary air of decision and authority established an unquestioned superiority. Napoleon had with him the intelligent but conceited Marmont, like him a gunner; his earliest friend, Murat, a Gascon and a swaggering cavalry commander who had firmly latched his fortunes to Napoleon's, and the ugly little Berthier, the first great Chief-of-Staff. In 1796 Napoleon invaded Italy. His outstanding victories at Lodi, Arcoli and Rivoli revealed him as already probably the greatest military commander of the age.

In 1798, having subdued Italy and routed the armies of Austria, he cast around for new fields to conquer. France had meanwhile proved herself an uncertain and dangerous place in which to live. He had already been gaoled twice on trumped-up charges of conspiring against the state and been released shortly afterwards; another term of imprisonment might easily end on the guillotine.

Napoleon devised a glorious scheme for invading the East. With the Directory's approval he proposed to seize Egypt, then advance to Persia and so cut the route to India. An expedition was launched through the Mediterranean, now once again occupied by the British. At first Nelson missed Napoleon's great convoy, but then caught up with his fleet and destroyed it at Aboukir Bay (The Battle of the Nile, 1798). Locked in Egypt, Napoleon sought escape along the coast road to Constantinople, but Sidney Smith with the help of the Turkish garrison firmly barred his passage at the old Crusader stronghold of Acre.

Meanwhile France had experienced disaster. Both in the north and the south invasion threatened. Only Masséna stood firm in Switzerland. In Paris the Directory, ever more discredited, hung on to power. The Abbé Sieyès planned to overthrow it, but needed a soldier to lead the way. Bernadotte would neither accept nor refuse the task. Then Napoleon suddenly appeared, having threaded his way past Nelson's cruisers. He at once accepted, but then at St Cloud, when dispersing the Chamber of Deputies, he uncharacteristically panicked. In the gathering darkness the deputies flourished their knives and menaced him. Then Murat appeared with a column of grenadiers. 'Throw me out these rascals,' he ordered. His soldiers obeyed, and Republican France disappeared for close on 50 years. Napoleon was named one of three consuls. He thought this two too many, and made himself first consul with two colleagues as deputies.

Now for the first time Napoleon set about raising an army. Aided by good fortune, he routed the Austrians at the decisive Battle of Marengo (1800), and France was saved. In 1802 the Treaty of Amiens restored peace throughout Europe. But with Britain it was no more than a truce. Nothing had been decided. War again broke out in 1803. Now Napoleon made his great effort at sea, only for Nelson's guns to blow his fleet apart off Cape Trafalgar. In 1804 he became Emperor of an embattled nation. Austria and Russia, at the instigation of Pitt, then prime minister of England, combined against him. In perhaps his finest battle, Austerlitz (1805), he beat both. Then at the end of 1806 he smashed Prussia at the twin Battles of Jena and Auerstädt. At the Treaty of Tilsit (1807), signed on a raft in the middle of the River Neman, he made peace with the Russians, virtually giving himself a free hand west of the river.

Encouraged by a French disaster at Baylen in the Spanish Peninsula, Austria again went to war, only to be finally crushed at the Battle of Wagram (1809). Napoleon at that juncture seemed like a visitor from some other planet, without human weakness. His armies had penetrated to the uttermost ends of Spain and Italy, Prussia lay crushed and dismembered, and Austria trembled at his presence. The German states rushed to obey his slightest whim. Only one country still defied him: Britain. An assault by sea was unlikely to succeed, so Napoleon planned to hit his most resilient enemy where it would hurt most, in the pocket. In a fatal moment he launched his 'Continental System', banning trade between Britain and Continental Europe. To establish his supremacy beyond question, he divorced Josephine, who had borne him no heir, and married Marie-Louise, the daughter of Francis I, Emperor of Austria. But this could not offset the hardships his System caused. There was evasion on a large scale, particularly in Russia, and the Tsar refused to satisfy Napoleon's demands that he put his house in order. In the summer of 1812 Napoleon invaded Russia with the most splendid army he had ever assembled, including contingents from Prussia and Austria. The French occupied Moscow, then the city was fired by the Russians. The French, poorly provided for a Russian winter, had to retreat, and the retreat turned into an appalling disaster. Now, in 1813, with a resilience almost past belief, Napoleon had re-created his *Grande Armée*. He might yet dictate his terms on the banks of the Neman. But he would have to strike soon.

The Old Guard marches past the Emperor, probably at Montmirail.

Uniforms of a marshal of France and his *aide-de-camp*.

BLÜCHER
Gebhard Leberecht von Blücher
Prince of Wahlstatt
(1742–1819)

Essentially Blücher was a simple man with simple convictions. He was Napoleon's implacable enemy, and wanted to see him dead. Physically Blücher was very strong and in character as immovable as a rock. He was a warm man, jovial if somewhat foul-mouthed, fond of hunting and gaming and a passionate gambler. He was shrewd enough to recognize that his intellect was not the equal of his other talents and, unlike his great enemy, he would accept advice, but once his mind was made up nothing would move it.

A Mecklenberger, he drifted into the Prussian Army and early showed his mettle. He overstepped the mark when questioning a Polish priest, and his superiors passed him over for promotion. Blücher, furious, characteristically took the matter up with his monarch, Frederick the Great. Frederick told him that he 'might go to the devil', and cashiered him. He saw some talent in the angry young Mecklenberger, but thought him too intractable ever to make a good officer.

The Prussian Army was barred to him while Frederick lived. He took up farming in Pomerania with some success, but immediately the old monarch died (in 1786) Blücher applied to his successor, Frederick William II, to take him back. The King not only did so, he restored to him all the seniority that he had lost. Blücher was at this time aged 45 and had become a man of some consequence in Pomerania. He threw it all aside to wear uniform once again.

He learned his basic soldiering under the Duke of Brunswick. When in 1794 he was made a major-general, he proclaimed that he had 'achieved the goal of all his desires'. He earned a reputation for energy and integrity, and in 1806, when Napoleon trounced Prussia at Jena and Auerstädt, Blücher refused to be discouraged and was one of the last to surrender. He survived, in consequence, when almost all the other Prussian generals were disgraced. He loved his men and treated them as his 'children', and they rewarded him with unswerving devotion. Scharnhorst, the Prussian Chief-of-Staff, believed he was the only man who could lead a renascent Prussian Army.

The French occupation of Prussia after the Treaty of Tilsit (1807) was anathema to him. He became seriously ill and began to suffer from delusions. On one occasion he thought himself pregnant and about to be delivered of an elephant, on another that his head was a ball of stone. Scharnhorst, however, remained unshaken in his belief and was heard to declare that Blücher should still lead the Prussian Army, even if he thought he had a hundred elephants inside him. Fortunately, Blücher recovered with his zest undiminished. After the French debacle in Russia he implored his sovereign (Frederick William III) to attack the French; even so, whatever his feelings, he would never act against the wishes of his king; his loyalty to the throne was as unqualified as his hatred of the French. In the next three years he probably did more than any other man to ruin his great enemy, the humiliator of Prussia. In 1813, at the age of nearly 71, he was to reach his greatest heights.

SCHWARZENBERG
Prince Karl Philipp of Schwarzenberg
(1771–1820)

It had beeen trenchantly observed that the Holy Roman Empire was neither holy, Roman, nor an empire. When Napoleon abolished it, Austria emerged as the dominant power in Germany – though she looked a little nervously at the rising power of Prussia. When in 1813 Austria once more took up arms against Napoleon and the German states started to change their allegiance, it seemed natural that the Commander-in-Chief of the Austrian Army should be elevated to the position of supreme commander under the Council of Monarchs who established the Allies' long-term policy. The job was given to Prince Schwarzenberg.

Born in Vienna, Schwarzenberg joined the Imperial cavalry in 1788 and fought against the Turks under Marshals Lacy and Loudon, and was already a major in 1792. He won the Maria Theresa Order for a famous charge at Cateau Cambrésis (1794): at the head of his regiment and 12 British squadrons, he routed a French corps, causing 3,000 casualties and taking 32 guns. Promotion came fast. In 1796 he was made a major-general and in 1799 lieutenant-field-marshal. His promptitude and courage saved the Austrian right wing in the disaster at Hohenlinden (1800), and when Mack surrendered Ulm (1805), Schwarzenberg was one of the few who cut their way out.

In 1808 Schwarzenberg, who was *persona grata* with the Russians, was a special envoy to the Court of St Petersburg. Returning in time for Wagram (1809), he won the highest Austrian

honour, the Golden Fleece. It fell to Schwarzenberg to negotiate the marriage between Napoleon and the Archduchess Marie-Louise, and the Emperor greatly esteemed him. He commanded the Austrian contingent in 1812. Early in 1813 he was promoted field-marshal and was, therefore, the senior officer serving with the Allied armies in 1813 and 1814.

He had a task of astonishing difficulty. The Council of Monarchs followed him about, and the Tsar in particular was constantly pressing advice on him. Schwarzenberg's own Emperor was by no means clear how much he desired the fall of Napoleon, and he himself had none of the virulent hatred that distinguished Blücher. He was fighting to preserve the existing *status quo,* not to usher in some 'brave new world'. He has been accused of excessive timidity both by his contemporaries and by subsequent historians. Although he would not have reached his rank by being timid, he accepted it as self-evident that if he confronted Napoleon on level terms, Napoleon inevitably would win. If he was to give battle he had to possess some significant advantage; in the meantime he sought to confine Napoleon within a reasonable compass rather than to destroy him.

WITTGENSTEIN
Ludwig Adolf Peter,
Count Wittgenstein
(1769–1843)

When the Tsar dismissed the dying Kutuzov, he selected Wittgenstein to replace him. It was a curious choice since he was junior to such generals as Barclay de Tolly, Count Langeron and Mihailovich, and although his service had been distinguished there appeared to be no outstanding feat that justified his early promotion. He was a compromise candidate. The Tsar resented Kutuzov appearing as the 'saviour of Russia', and the independent attitude he had on occasion adopted. Barclay de Tolly had pursued an energetic feud with Prince Bagration, probably the most competent of the Russians. Nevertheless the feud had scarcely been in the interests of Russia, and when Bagration fell at Borodino the Tsar looked elsewhere for his next commander.

Wittgenstein was the son of a Westphalian nobleman settled in Russia. He had distinguished himself in the Polish War (1794–95) and afterwards served in the Caucasus. He fought at Austerlitz (1805) and Friedland (1807), and in 1812 he com-

manded the Russian right wing which fought the Battles of Polotsk; in addition he concluded the Convention of Tauroggen with the Prussian General, Count Yorck. The Tsar eventually split Wittgenstein's forces between the Allied armies, and he himself became little more than a corps commander under Schwarzenberg; Count Langeron with his army served in Blücher's newly formed Army of Silesia and Barclay de Tolly came to command the Reserve, which included the Russian Guards.

Count Langeron generously wrote of the junior who had superseded him, 'Of all the secondary generals he was the most distinguished and had the most brilliant success against Oudinot and Saint-Cyr.' It was no disgrace not to be outstanding in the company in which Wittgenstein served in the Campaigns of 1813 and 1814.

WELLINGTON
Arthur, Duke of Wellington
(1769–1852)

In 1813 Wellington, the British Commander-in-Chief in Spain who had been quietly nibbling away at the French with markedly inferior forces, achieved the culmination of his five-year campaign and drove the French out of the Spanish Peninsula, except for a small stretch on the east coast still held by Marshal Suchet. However, not until the Hundred Days of 1815 were Wellington and Napoleon to meet on the battlefield. Before 1815, therefore, Wellington's effect on Napoleon's fortunes, although considerable, was indirect.

Wellington was arguably the greatest British general there has been. Born in 1769, the same year as Napoleon, Soult and Ney, he was in his prime when he met Napoleon at Waterloo. He was one of the younger sons of an impoverished Irish peer. The young Wellington, or Wesley as he then was (he progressed by easy stages to Wellesley and then to Wellington) enjoyed the social round in Dublin and showed a certain affection for playing the violin. However, younger sons had to make their way in the world, and he joined an infantry regiment.

He was chased by his creditors out to India. There he threw away his violin and found that serious soldiering appealed to him; he also paid off his creditors. His elder brother, the then Lord Mornington, also went to India, as Governor-General; this was, obviously, no handicap for an aspiring soldier, but Wellington soon showed that he had no need of such influence. By his brilliant victories at Assaye and Argaum he did much to break the hold of the powerful Mahrattas. He came home to England and in 1808 forced Junot out of

Portugal. At last here was a British general able to fight the French on equal terms. His lack of numbers forced him on to the defensive and the French generals, while admitting his skill in defence, doubted his ability to launch an offensive. Then in 1812 at the Battle of Salamanca he made a sudden surprise attack and destroyed an army under the able Marshal Marmont. French power in Spain was rocked, but it recovered and Wellington had to winter in north-eastern Portugal. The next year, he drove the French out of Spain and took the British up to the outskirts of the Pyrenees.

He was a general after the typical British model. Contemptuous of flamboyance or the carefully rehearsed gesture, he had a cool analytical mind that was never carried away by success. He possessed a determination of steel and could be a tiger on the battlefield, but never allowed his judgment of a situation to be influenced by personal considerations, however unpalatable the result might be. He kept his own counsel, asking advice from no one, and was harsh with any who sought gratuitously to offer it.

BERNADOTTE
Carl Johan (Bernadotte)
Crown Prince of Sweden
(1763–1844)

He was numbered among Napoleon's enemies in 1813, but it had not always been so. He was born in Béarn, the son of a French notary with a liking for soldiering. He enlisted in 1780 and by a careful application to his duties achieved the rank of sergeant-major in the Régiment Royale Marine.

Bernadotte was deferential towards those likely to help him and treacherous towards those who stood in his way. He was considerate to his men and made a particular point of looking after his wounded and prisoners. Of his ability as a soldier than can be no question. He served initially with the Army of Italy in 1780, and there encountered Napoleon, who from the beginning appears to have disliked and mistrusted him.

He married Desirée-Clary, the sister-in-law of Napoleon's brother Joseph. His first great opportunity occurred when Napoleon was in Egypt and the Abbé Síeyès approached him to lead the *coup d'état* against the Directory. He vacillated and temporized and lost the opportunity. He would not reveal his sympathies in the *coup* that followed. Napoleon at one point offered to arrest him on behalf of the Directory, but men of his ability were rare and Napoleon promoted him among the first flight of his marshals; in 1806 he made him the Prince of Ponte Corvo.

Bernadotte commanded I Corps in the *Grande Armée* at Austerlitz (1805) and in the Campaign of 1806. On the day of Jena and Auerstädt (1806) he remained between the two battlefields without intervening in either. This remarkable lack of initiative, whatever its motive, infuriated the Emperor, who came near to ordering a court-martial. Perhaps it was for the sake of Desirée, whom he himself had loved, that Napoleon forbore. He was to regret his leniency. In the pursuit that followed, Bernadotte displayed considerable energy, and it was he who compelled Blücher to surrender at Schwartau. A curious episode followed. A Swedish contingent under Count Moerner had landed at Lübeck with the object of supporting the Prussians. Bernadotte went out of his way to be pleasant to them, and permitted the grateful Swedes to depart.

During the Campaign of 1807 he was wounded on two occasions and compelled to give up command of his corps. In 1809 he was in command of IX (Saxon) Corps which was routed at Wagram. Napoleon relieved him of his command on the spot. But if he was in disgrace with the Emperor, the Swedes still thought kindly of him, and, seeking to reconquer Finland, were not unmindful of his skill on the battlefield. On 21 August 1810 their States-General elected him Crown Prince. Napoleon, albeit reluctantly, consented to his accepting. Bernadotte now became more Swedish than the Swedes. He abjured Catholicism, and was adopted by King Charles XIII.

When in March 1812 Napoleon seized Swedish Pomerania, the Crown Prince allied himself with the Tsar and the following year brought Sweden into the Sixth Coalition. His new Allies were to lean heavily upon him as a strategist, although he was to display no great zeal in attacking his old master. In 1814 he intrigued for the crown of France, but too many opposed him. In Sweden, however, he was more successful, and there founded a new dynasty.

Among Napoleon's marshals were some whose names have come down through the years with their brilliance undimmed, however unfortunate their end. Murat, like Bernadotte, was to become a king, but he was to found no dynasty.

MURAT
Joachim Murat
King of Naples
(1767–1815)

Joachim Murat was a big, handsome Gascon who early linked his career with that of Napoleon. His horsemen brought up the guns to the Tuileries for the famous 'whiff of grapeshot' of 1795, and in the following year he accompanied Napoleon when the latter went to command the Army of Italy. He was a vain man, a peacock who loved bright colours and astonishing uniforms, and on one occasion Napoleon compared him to the circus rider Signor Franconi. But Murat was a magnificent rider and a daring horseman who set a pattern for the French cavalryman. When young, he was a gay and attractive rogue ready for any challenge. He was quick-tempered and fast-moving, particularly where there was a chance of loot. As a cavalryman he tended to be in the lead during any advance, stripping places bare before the slower-moving infantry could arrive.

He had a wonderful eye for country and a genius for leading large-scale cavalry charges. It was typical of his ostentatious, extrovert nature that he liked to lead a charge merely flourishing a whip over his head. At Jena (1806) he led the final, decisive charges in that fashion. Then in the pursuit after the battle the disputatious side of his nature came to the fore. He quarrelled with Ney, claiming to have captured fortresses taken by that Marshal. He entered into a dispute with Bernadotte and complained bitterly about the conduct of Marshal Lannes. Such outbursts were typical of the man and recurred with some frequency. During the advance on Moscow in the summer of 1812 he reached such a pitch of exasperation with Marshal Davout that he had to be restrained from going after him with a sabre. Nevertheless Murat's achievements as a commander were considerable. In 1806, after Jena, it was he who pursued the Prussians to Prentzlau and there compelled 10,000 to surrender. On the following day at Stettin, his subordinate, General Lasalle, with 5,000 horsemen, wheeled up an empty ammunition wagon opposite the town, as though it were a breaching battery, and bluffed the garrison into surrender.

Murat was the ideal *beau sabreur* of the cavalry, dashing, courageous, quarrelsome, hard-riding. General Savary summed him up with these words: 'It would have been better if he had been endowed with rather less courage and rather more common sense.' When the French held Moscow, for example, Murat had his troops deployed on the Motsha River some 50 miles to the south. He established very friendly relations with the Cossacks – and was not the first to find this an unwise move. They suddenly turned on him near Vinkovo, and he had to cut his way out to rejoin the main body, about to begin the long and disastrous trek back to the Vistula and beyond.

In Russia Murat's faith in Napoleon seems to have been shaken. In 1813 he deserted the *Grande Armée* for Naples, departing without permission and giving command of the army to Prince Eugène. In 1814, under the impression that he was serving his own best interests, he deserted his old master and joined his enemies on the assurance that he could keep his kingdom. His treachery must have weighed on him. In 1815 he suddenly threw in his lot with Napoleon. To the Emperor his act in joining the Allies had been unpardonable. He contemptuously refused to give Murat a command. The wretched Murat went his own way, was defeated by the Austrians at Tolentino, and in due course was seized and executed for treason by the Allies. It was a sad end to a glittering career.

NEY
Michel Ney, Duke of Elchingen
Prince of the Moskva
(1769–1815)

If not the best of Napoleon's marshals, he is the most readily remembered. Napoleon christened him 'the bravest of the brave', and there has been no one to question the justice of this title. He was born in Saarlouis, then French, and when later he was tried for treason he scorned to plead that he was not a Frenchman. He came of a long line of soldiers who, lacking in noble blood, carried the pike or musket rather than the sword. His father intended him for the law, a profession offering him a chance to rise in the world. But when he saw the garrison riding by, and heard some of his father's tales, the musty atmosphere of books did not appeal. In 1788 he enlisted in the Duke of Chartres's Regiment of Hussars.

He was strong, active, a first-class shot and rider, something of a swordsman, and a pleasant, good-natured man. He was always being criticized for being lax in his discipline, but was nevertheless almost certainly the greatest leader of men serving under Napoleon. From his red hair he received the soubriquet *le rougeaud*. His legendary courage (it was a sentence of death for a horse to carry him in battle) has tended to obscure his other great qualities, and to create the impression of a great-hearted man without much intellect. But he was no fool and could be a sound administrator. If not a great disciplinarian, he never experienced any difficulty in having his wishes carried out.

He served initially in the north with the Army of the Sambre and Meuse, receiving rapid promotion. He did not meet Napoleon until 1800. He was then appointed to command VI Corps, and his courage and solicitude for his men quickly made him their idol. His finest moment, and also the beginning of his disillusionment with his master came to him in Russia in 1812. At Borodino, Napoleon, sitting on his charger a mile behind the battle line, refused to send in the Old Guard to clinch the success. Ney saw his herculean exertions about to be wasted, and burst out, 'If he is no longer a general, let him go back to France and leave us to do the commanding for him.' Nevertheless, during the fearful retreat from Moscow Ney commanded the rearguard with a courage and determination that has become immortal. Napoleon drew strength from his fiery spirit and thereafter never let him stray far from his side.

THE SECONDARY COMMANDERS

The strategic plans of the generals profiled on the preceding pages were in due course passed for execution to their immediate subordinates. Some of the outstanding secondary commanders of both sides are reviewed below. Most spent the years 1813–15 commanding at corps level, but on occasion they exercised separate commands. For the French, with vast territories and scattered garrisons to protect, this was a necessity, but one that turned to disaster as the Allies began to enact their winning strategy. This, in the words of Prince Schwarzenberg's Chief-of-Staff, Count Radetzky, was 'to avoid any unequal struggle and so to exhaust the enemy, fall upon his weakened parts with superior strength, and to defeat him in detail'.

THE ALLIES

BÜLOW

Friedrich Wilhelm, Count Bülow of Dennewitz (1755–1816), was Governor of East and West Prussia before, in 1813, as a lieutenant-general in Bernadotte's Army of the North, he defeated Oudinot at Grossbeeren and Ney at Dennewitz, victories that early endorsed the Allied plan to erode Napoleon's strength by beating his lieutenants. Bülow served under Blücher in 1814–15, leading the Prussian IV Corps at Waterloo.

YORCK

Hans David Ludwig, Count Yorck of Wartenberg (1759–1830), led Napoleon's Prussian contingent in the Russian Campaign of 1812. After Moscow, he boldly extricated his corps from French control and signed a neutrality pact with the Russians. He fought in Germany and France in 1813–14. An independent man, Blücher said of him, 'He does nothing but argue, but when he attacks, he gets stuck in like nobody else.'

GNEISENAU

August, Count Neithardt of Gneisenau (1760–1831), was a Saxon who fought with the Prussian Army from 1786, rising to become Blücher's Chief-of-Staff. After the Peace of Tilsit (1807) he worked with Scharnhorst to reorganize the Army. His critical moment came after Ligny when, with Blücher injured, he took the decision to withdraw on Wavre, so creating the circumstances for the decisive battle at Waterloo.

THE FRENCH

MACDONALD

Jacques Macdonald, Duke of Taranto (1765–1840), was the son of a Scots Jacobite exile and the only one of Napoleon's marshals to be promoted on the battlefield itself – after Wagram (1809). Entrusted with a separate command, he was defeated on the Katzbach in 1813 but served with distinction in France the following year.

DAVOUT

Louis Nicolas Davout, Duke of Auerstädt and Prince of Eckmühl (1770–1823), was a fine tactician and administrator. In 1813 he retook and successfully defended Hamburg, but was unable to link with the *Grande Armée,* as Napoleon had hoped. During the Hundred Days he served as Minister of War.

OUDINOT

Nicolas Charles Oudinot, Duke of Reggio (1767–1847), commanded a corps in 1813 and 1814. As an independent commander he was defeated by Bernadotte's Army of the North at Grossbeeren. Much scarred by combat, he sustained over 20 wounds during his service, and retired rather than fight again in the Hundred Days.

MARMONT

Auguste de Marmont, Duke of Ragusa (1774–1852), was an artillerist, like Napoleon. He commanded a corps in 1813, and in 1814 was posted with Marshal Mortier to guard the approaches to Paris. Unable to prevent the fall of the city, he was later vilified for negotiating independently with Schwarzenberg.

SOULT

Nicolas Jean de Dieu Soult, Duke of Dalmatia (1769–1851), achieved his greatest success at Austerlitz (1805). Napoleon called him 'le premier manoeuvrier d'Europe' but in Spain he was defeated several times by the British. In 1813 he fought at Lützen and Bautzen, and in 1815 Napoleon appointed him Chief-of-Staff.

A French soldier grabs a mug of soup on the march.

THE SOLDIERS

The successful general, provided he escaped death or mutilation, might expect honours and riches, the soldier little but hardship and a pittance. Why then did he enlist or fight? It was true that those ready to soldier were always too few, and that their numbers had to be supplemented by persuasion and often coercion. But why then did they fight?

The penalty for desertion in almost every army was death, and savage punishments, particularly in the Prussian Army, were meted out for lesser crimes. But no articles of war could make a soldier fight wholeheartedly if he did not want to, especially if his non-commissioned officers, that backbone of any army, were discontented. Indeed in some armies the men were generally unwilling to fight with enthusiasm; in consequence their contemporaries referred to them mockingly as cowards, although the individual men might be courageous enough.

It was one of the most powerful motives for behaving well that if a regiment or army failed to do so, this was regarded as a slur on the courage of its members. In addition to the pressures of public opinion upon him, the soldier was clad in colourful uniforms, involved in the splendours of military pageantry, and instilled with a reverence for regimental tradition; patriotism might also play a part, but at that time nationalism, except in England and France, lay largely dormant.

In the 18th century, battles were fought in accordance with well-established rules; it was accepted that where a man of sense saw no prospect of ultimate success it was reasonable for him to surrender. Wars were fought not to a finish but to achieve some strictly limited aim. Then came the wars against Revolutionary France. The young untrained soldiers of France, fighting with the fervour of those pursuing an ideal, overthrew the massed veterans of Europe. It was demonstrated unmistakably that an army fighting to establish an idea enjoyed an immense superiority over any other, irrespective of its weapons and the standard of its training.

By 1813 the old gladiatorial contests were giving way to the bitter national conflicts of the 19th and 20th centuries. The year 1812 marked the watershed. After the invasion of Russia, the Russian soldier fought not solely from national or regimental pride: he fought, and more ferociously, to avenge the wrongs the French had done to him personally and to his country. In Germany, where initially Napoleon had come as a liberator from petty tyranny (or so he claimed), now he was detested as a foreign oppressor. The European monarchs, not entirely to their delight, were dragged along by a great tide of nationalism that the more far-seeing realized might eventually overwhelm them. Before, the rulers of the many small German states had dreaded the power of Austria and viewed with apprehension the rise of Prussia. Now their subjects insisted that they combined against the French despoiler – a viewpoint quite alien from that of former times. This spirit of nationalism gave the contending armies a new purpose that Napoleon was slow to recognize.

An officer of the Imperial Russian Guard.
In general the Guard preferred not to soil their uniforms
by indulging in fighting, and kept well to the rear with the reserve.
Such reticence was one of the counter-productive aspects
of military pageantry.

THE RUSSIAN ARMY

Normally the rank-and-file joined the Army for the rest of their working days. Military life was not a particularly disagreeable alternative to serfdom. However he lived it, the life of a Russian peasant was almost invariably frugal and hard. Sir Robert Wilson, serving with the Russian forces in 1812, noted that the Russian soldier was small but stocky, hardy and strong, 'inured to the weather and hardship . . . ferocious but disciplined'. Surprisingly, Wilson observed that punishments were less severe than in other armies, and that the officers treated their men kindly and thought of them as human beings rather than machines. The officers, however, were inclined to indolence, courageous enough in battle but careless and indifferent about training. The Russian soldier was probably the worst trained and armed of the Allies, relying on the bayonet rather then gunpowder. He would contest a battlefield obstinately, if unskilfully, and served his officers cheerfully and loyally – accepting, it seems, their rather casual approach to human life without resentment.

The infantry comprised regiments of Guards (who rather resembled personal toys of the Tsar), light infantry, grenadiers, and infantry of the line, each composed of two battalions of 700 men. Six regiments, including one or two of light infantry, went to form an infantry division. Two or more divisions might be grouped together to form a corps – which had no cavalry component. Authorized strengths were seldom kept up, and at Montmirail, for instance, Sacken's five infantry divisions only amounted to 18,000 men, an average of fewer than 3,500 men to a division.

The Russian artillery, perhaps to compensate for poor standards of musketry, was organized in 12-gun batteries and included a proportion of heavy and cumbersome pieces. Technically the Russian gunner lacked skill, but he fought his guns with great stubbornness.

As for their cavalry, the Russians followed the current European fashion of having cuirassiers, carabiniers, dragoons and hussars, and keeping them massed in cavalry corps perhaps 2–3,000 strong; in addition they had the Cossacks, fierce bands of tribal freebooters who owed no allegiance except to their chiefs. Not at this time amenable to discipline, they were of little use on the battlefield, but were excellent for patrolling and controlling the countryside. Their barbaric behaviour, their thieving and plundering were always likely to provoke the French peasantry to rise against the invaders rather more effectively than did Napoleon's decrees.

A genial group of Austrian cavalry officers 'coffee-housing' by the ante-room of a general.

THE AUSTRIAN ARMY

This Army had a proud tradition, but the Emperor Francis I, ruling a multi-national Empire, distrusted nationalism. After the Battle of Austerlitz (1805) the Archduke Charles reorganized it on the lines of the French Army (see below). But it was still an 18th-century army and lacked any greater driving force than its pride in its own past and traditions. There was a reluctance to decentralize into corps and divisions. Army headquarters enjoyed writing voluminous instructions, laying down in great detail what should be done in almost every conceivable circumstance – except, usually, those that occurred. In outlook at this time the Austrian Army was rather defensive-minded.

THE PRUSSIAN ARMY

Under Frederick the Great, by dint of probably the most rigid and inhumane discipline in the world, the Prussian Army had scored many notable successes. The men were treated as automatons and cruelly punished if they showed any signs of wanting better. With Frederick in command, they had triumphed many times over numerically superior enemy armies. In the Napoleonic Wars, early reverses against the French were attributed to bad luck. Then in 1806 came the Battles of Jena and Auerstädt, after which French soldiers swaggered through the streets of Berlin. The army of automatons fell apart and Prussia was dismembered.

Now came a bitter analysis. The army was old-fashioned, its tactics out of date. Worse, its officer structure was hopelessly rigid. Only proud and often ignorant members of the aristocracy were admitted. General Müffling, serving with the Prussian Army, noted that the junior officers of the *Grande Armée* marched with their men and carried packs on their backs, while a Prussian officer would think it beneath his dignity to dismount from his horse.

A small, dedicated group led politically by Baron Stein and composed militarily of such officers as Gneisenau, Grolman and Clausewitz, the latter group being led by General Scharnhorst, at that time Chief-of-Staff to the Army, set about a political and military regeneration. The middle classes, hitherto forbidden to be officers and re-luctant to become privates, had to be inveigled into the Army. Political stratification had to be broken down. Every man should be proud to serve in the Army. The reforms met with considerable opposition. The King felt his own position might be threatened. Nevertheless Scharnhorst pressed on with his concept of a nation-in-arms.

The reforms had one unexpected result. When Scharnhorst was mortally wounded at the Battle of Lützen, in May 1813, his followers and would-be successors were mostly high-ranking staff officers, not field commanders. The finest commander in the field, the man the soldiers would follow anywhere, was undoubtedly that splendid ex-hussar, Blücher. Blücher had long ceased to trouble himself about politics: he thought all politicians rascals, and had scarcely more time for military theory. He became the commander in the field, Gneisenau the Chief-of-Staff. He described their relationship thus: 'Gneisenau reports to me on the manoeuvres that need to be done. Once convinced I never stop until the objective is achieved.' The peculiar position of authority later held by Chiefs-of-Staff in the Prussian Army may well have developed from these circumstances.

After its overthrow by Napoleon, the rump of Prussia had been permitted an army of only 42,000 men. Scharnhorst had then inaugurated a system of short-term enlistments to build up a reserve of trained manpower; even so, the Prussian Army that was born anew in 1813 went through a period of bewildering change. The Army was only semi-trained and had yet to build up its self-confidence. A short time before the Battle of Waterloo, Blücher confided to Wellington that his men, deployed in line, could not yet be trusted to stand up to a French column. However, a new spirit was abroad and the Prussians desired passionately to take their revenge on the French.

The Army was organized in army corps, but at that time had not adopted a divisional organization. Prussian infantry brigades usually con- sisted of three three-battalion regiments, each battalion being about 800 strong. With regiments at their full strength of approximately 2,400 men, a brigade might total nearly 7,500 men, as opposed to the French infantry division which by 1814 seldom much exceeded 4,000. Two cavalry brigades, each nearly equivalent to a French cavalry division, were integral to each corps. No cavalry was held centrally. The artillery was organized in eight-gun batteries composed of six guns and two howitzers. It was held centrally at a scale of about one battery per regiment and one per cavalry brigade.

An NCO and a soldier of the Prussian Guard.
The headgear was clearly impractical for anything but the fairest weather,
and like the Russian Guard these warriors were mainly for show
and to protect the person of the monarch.

A Highlander of the 42nd or Black Watch
and another of the 92nd or Gordon Highlanders.
A piper is encouraging them in the background.

THE BRITISH ARMY

The British Army, like the Austrian, was composed of men serving long periods of regular service. They came from a variety of sources. Some were offered the army as an alternative to gaol, others were apprentices or employees fleeing from intolerable employers, and yet others enlisted as an alternative to destitution. A few enlisted from a sense of adventure, and a significant number felt that Napoleon, 'the Ogre', had to be checked.

Whatever their original motives, they almost all nourished a keen sense of patriotism and developed a fierce pride in themselves and their regiments. Under Wellington they were confident that they were the finest soldiers in the world, and were happy to have a chance to prove it. Their chief, in a moment of exasperation, described them as the 'scum of the earth', a phrase which unfortunately was recorded. His true opinion of his soldiers was that they were magnificent in battle, splendid on parade, but almost uncontrollable off it. He regarded the use of the lash as essential for his men, but thought that the French could forego it because conscription, drawing from all levels,

brought a superior type of man into their ranks.

While his infantry was organized in divisions of two to three brigades, he kept his cavalry in brigades with a supreme cavalry commander living at his headquarters. He had suffered at the hands of some eccentric divisional commanders of cavalry in the Spanish Peninsula, and disliked the divisional system of organization – as he disliked the army corps, for he was not fond of decentralization. His artillery he parcelled out to divisions, normally at a scale of one battery per division, and a proportion of light artillery was placed in support of the cavalry brigades as might be advisable. Against Napoleon in the Low Countries he increased his scale of batteries to two per division. Müffling, the Prussian who served with Wellington as a liaison officer, left this description of the British soldier: 'It was not the custom in this Army to criticize or control the Commander-in-Chief. Discipline was strictly enforced . . . Our infantry does not posses the same bodily strength as yours [the British] . . . The greater mass of our troops are too young and inexperienced.'

The French Army initially fought to preserve and then to spread the Revolution. Gradually the ideal faded, but the men remained intoxicated by their undreamed-of success on the battlefield. Like the British, the French felt a national pride, and, unlike the British, every soldier could believe that he carried a field-marshal's baton in his knapsack. By 1813 some of the best men in the French Army had perished, but an intense professional pride remained. In 1813 Captain Leith Hay, serving with Wellington, had been taken prisoner by the French. King Joseph's French army was retiring on Vitoria, and Leith Hay left this description of it.

The discipline of the troops seemed not of the strictest description, nor did the regimental officers apparently preserve that control so necessary for its support. The same line of distinction between officers and man was not so sedulously observed as in the British Army . . . occasionally the private or non-commissioned officer was of a superior grade of French society from that of the officer placed over him. But with all this apparent laxity, it was impossible to see the French armies without being impressed with the perfectly *au fait* manner in which the duties were performed; ever in readiness, the soldier was instantaneously put in motion when occasion demanded celerity of movement. Under the most unenviable conditions custom had inured him to the practice of endeavouring, as far as possible, to provide for diminishing the want of comfort that prevailed, and instead of staring about to discover all the miseries of his bivouac, he had probably already half unroofed the nearest habitation for the purpose of composing his fire . . . In marching the French infantry appeared indefatigable: their progress was equally remarkable for the rapidity with which they passed over the ground or the distance performed.' A picture emerges of a flexible, highly trained army in which discipline was almost instinctively observed.

In 1814 organizations were pared to meet with diminished resources. Battalions were around 600 strong and were composed of about six line companies and possibly one *tirailleur* (light infantry) and one grenadier company. The *tirailleur* company would throw out a screen of infantry in extended order (skirmishers) if the battalion had to advance. There were specific light infantry regiments called *voltigeurs* or *tirailleurs,* but by now most French infantry of the line could act as light infantry. There were no riflemen. The army was organized in twos; there were two battalions in a regiment, two regiments in a brigade, and two brigades in a division, which normally numbered between 4–5,000 men, or two-thirds the strength of a British division or Prussian brigade in 1815.

An army corps was generally composed of several infantry divisions, a light cavalry division and eight-gun batteries at a scale of one per division, one in reserve and a horse artillery battery to support the cavalry. The powerful artillery of the Guard was kept as a reserve of firepower to meet the needs of a particular situation. The cavalry had an organization somewhat similar to the infantry. Two heavy cavalry regiments, 4–500 strong, formed a brigade, two brigades a division and two divisions a corps. Light cavalry might be farmed out or held centrally.

A French camp.
An officer smokes his pipe and wanders round his men's bivouacs before nightfall.

BATTLE TACTICS

The infantry battalions of all armies, except on occasion those of the British, used columns for movement. The French rarely deployed into line, but a brigade or division launching an attack might have some battalions in line, others in column. Battalions were subdivided into companies. A French company, averaging 70–80 men, formed in three ranks, a British company, normally about 50–60 strong, in two. A British battalion had 10 companies at this time, a French one about six.

Both sides screened their battle lines with skirmishers in open order. An attacker would drive in the enemy skirmish line, then start a brief but deadly musketry duel at a distance of 100 yards or less. One side might waver, and the other would clinch its success with the bayonet. For an attack in column, the attacker would generally rely more on supporting artillery fire and, ultimately, the bayonet to bring him success rather than on his own musketry.

The artillery fired shells and roundshot at ranges over 300 yards, canister at ranges below. Roundshot and shells were unpleasant but canister, often called grape, was more so: each round of

A diagrammatic illustration of various formations adopted during a corps attack. In the left foreground dragoons in open order are covering the right flank, while to their left hussars in column of route are fording a rivulet at the approaches of a village. On the far side of the hussars, and fording the main river, are the infantry. Formed in what appears to be an open column of double companies, they are about to attack the church and scale the bluff to their front. On their left guns are supporting the advance and in the distance a regiment or brigade is attacking along the far bank. In the centre background the skirmishers of both sides have clashed near the church. In the background the enemy is deployed in line to dispute the river crossing. Faced with all this, the simple villagers in the foreground seem gripped by an understandable panic.

canister, holding up to 100 bullets, broke up and sprayed its contents in a lethal pattern rather like shot from a shotgun. In musketry or artillery fire, although higher rates might be obtained under peacetime conditions, about two round a minute was the most that could be achieved in the field.

Cavalry in theory attacked 'boot to boot', but in practice they kept a rather looser order and generally attacked in considerable depth. Except in the British Army, heavy cavalry were armoured and were reserved for shock action.

Napoleon claimed to fight each battle ac-cording to its individual characteristics, and he valued surprise above all else. He invariably attacked. In his later years a recognizable style had begun to appear. He would first mass his artillery against selected points, then launch his infantry columns, preceded by clouds of skirmishers, against the enemy position. Later attacks might be supported by heavy cavalry. When his enemy had committed all his reserves, Napoleon would strike with his Guard at the decisive point. The sight of their bearskins was a signal to the enemy that he would be wise to depart.

CHAPTER 3
THE BATTLE OF LÜTZEN

Blücher had gone to the castle and estates in Silesia given to him by the Prussian King, and Breslau, the capital of that province, had become a centre of anti-French activity. Early in January 1813, chafing at Prussia's inactivity, he wrote to Scharnhorst, now the head of the commission set up to reform the Prussian Army: 'I am itching in every finger to grasp the sword. If His Majesty the King, if all the other German Princes, if the German nation as a whole do not now rise and

A French sergeant resumes the march.

sweep off from German territory the entire rascally French brood together with Napoleon and his following then it seems to me that no German is any longer worthy of the name.'

He besought his monarch to lead Prussia against the French. Frederick William III paid him no attention; he merely relieved General Yorck of his command for negotiating without consent the Convention of Tauroggen. Then Hardenberg, the King's chief minister, took a hand. He told his monarch that his secret police had reported a French plot to kidnap or kill the Royal family. The plot probably existed only in Hardenberg's fertile imagination, but it was enough. Greatly alarmed, Frederick William left Berlin hurriedly for Breslau. There, surrounded by the enemies of France, he eventually succumbed to their entreaties. On 13 March he officially declared war on France. Protesting that it was a waste of time since no one would respond, he issued a proclamation calling every able-bodied man between the ages of 18 and 24 to the colours. To his amazement his loyal subjects flocked in their thousands to enlist.

The French seemed meanwhile to have lost their nerve. The garrison in Hamburg, faced by a few Cossacks, withdrew. The French garrison in Berlin, spat on and reviled by the people, also departed, although there was no direct military threat. It looked as if the French would be howled out of Germany. Then, from the west, came the long columns of French troops and, more important, Napoleon himself. Many of his men were raw recruits, his cavalry lacked chargers, his marshals wanted nothing more than to retire to their estates in peace. But Napoleon himself was in the field and suddenly everything was changed.

The Allies – Russia and Prussia – planned to hold the line of the River Elbe and try to persuade Saxony to join them. Scharnhorst and the more fiery of the Prussians wished to continue the advance to the Rhine, summoning all Germans to throw off the French shackles as they advanced. But Kutuzov, still at that stage Commander-in-Chief of the Russians, had only been persuaded with difficulty to come as far as the Elbe. He adamantly refused to cross the river and maintained that if the Germans wished to liberate themselves they were welcome to do so, but it was no concern of the Russians. The Tsar disagreed strongly with this point of view, but he had to be cautious about opposing the aged 'saviour of Russia.'

The Allies planned to hold the river with three armies. One, under Yorck and Wittgenstein, was to take up a position west of Berlin; Blücher, with his newly formed Army of Silesia, composed of Russians as well as Prussians, was to hold Dresden while Kutuzov had his army between the two, ready to aid either. The latter also exercised a general suzerainty over all three armies.

The Russian concentration was slow and dilatory. Kutuzov with his central army had only reached Kalisz when Blücher was hammering on the gates of Dresden. Kutuzov fell ill on the line of march and died on 28 April. The Tsar nominated Wittgenstein as Commander-in-Chief with authority over Blücher, but as the other two Russian corps commanders, Tormassov and Barclay de Tolly, were senior to Wittgenstein, they received their orders direct from the Tsar. The Tsar, however, was not to act without consulting Scharn-

horst or General Toll; as a system of command it was clumsy in the extreme.

Meanwhile Prince Eugène with his regiments of gaunt spectres from the old *Grande Armée* gave back whenever he was pressed, sheltering his men behind the walls of fortresses commanding the main routes along which the Allies were likely to advance. Reinforcements were arriving from the old garrisons in Germany and from France, and his army began to increase in size and efficiency. The Allies, using only second-line troops, proceeded to blockade the fortresses without wasting time trying to reduce them. They screened their front with a host of Cossacks and tried to guess what Napoleon intended to do next.

The Emperor, after his appalling loss of horses in Russia, was very short of cavalry and advanced forward blindly. Breslau seemed the centre of disaffection, and so, while never fettering himself with a rigid plan, he proposed in general terms to advance towards Breslau by Leipzig and Dresden. He hoped to force the Allies to give battle. When he had won the victory that he regarded as inevitable, he expected the Prussians would retreat northwards to guard their homeland while the Russians withdrew to the east across the Vistula and Neman. He could then turn north on Berlin. Davout was separately organizing an army of five divisions with which to retake Hamburg. From there he would descend on Berlin from the northwest while Napoleon swung up from the south-east. The Prussian Army would be crushed between the hammer of Napoleon and the anvil of Davout.

Wittgenstein, unaware of the true strength of the French but knowing that Napoleon was steadily accumulating superior numbers, resolved to strike first before the French were fully assembled. He ordered General Kleist with his corps to cover Leipzig while he concentrated his army in the area of Pegau. On the next day, 2 May, he planned to strike northwards and cut the main road to Leipzig at Lützen. His orders for the move were verbose and his staff arrangements bad; however, he had undeniably secured the greatest of all tactical advantages, surprise.

Napoleon was aware that there were some enemy to the south of him but he had no idea how strong they were. He planned to continue his advance and seize Leipzig on 2 May. He issued his orders. Lauriston (V Corps) from Prince Eugène's army was to seize Leipzig itself with the assistance of Latour-Maubourg's cavalry corps. Macdonald from the same army was to descend with his XI Corps on Markranstädt, about seven miles west of the city on the main road. Reynier (VII Corps) would close up to Marseburg on the Elster, about 15 miles farther west. Bertrand with his IV Corps was to come up from the south and position his leading troops in Tachau, on the western edge of the low feature south of Gross Görschen. Oudinot was at Naumberg and unlikely to arrive in time for a battle. The Imperial Guard were to be in reserve behind Ney. Ney's III Corps held the area about Lützen, guarding the route forward.

Included in Ney's area were, to the west, the empty village of Starsiedel; at the edge of the low plateau south of Gross Görschen was Rahna; in the centre of his position, where Ney had his headquarters, was Kaja, and Gross Görschen and Klein Görschen were a little way to the east. The small village of Eisdorf lay about one and a half miles

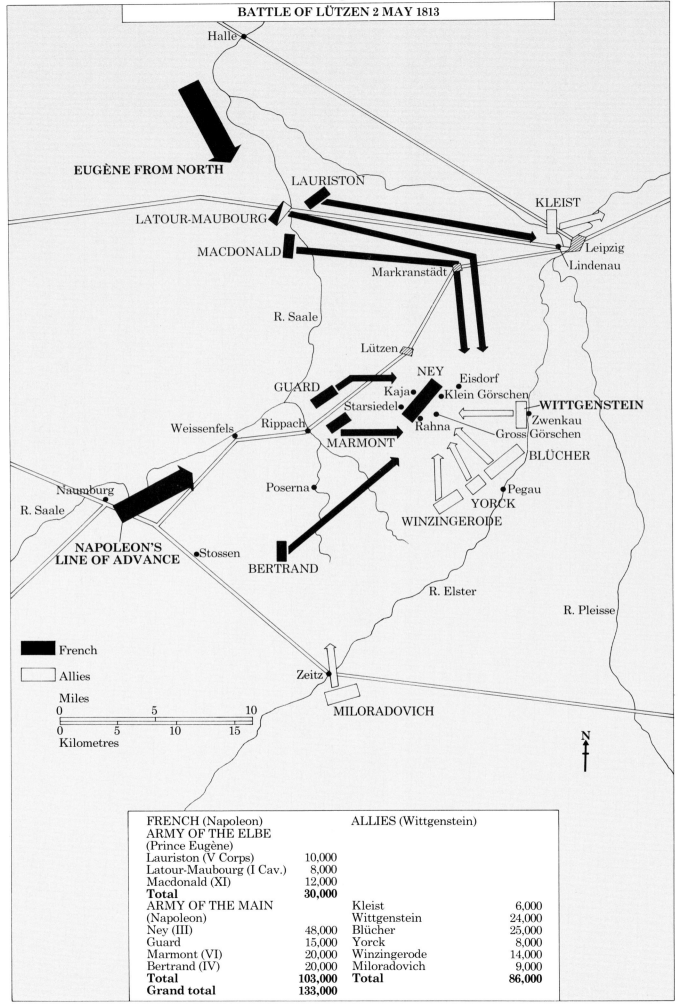

BATTLE OF LÜTZEN 2 MAY 1813

Halle

EUGÈNE FROM NORTH

LAURISTON

LATOUR-MAUBOURG

MACDONALD

Markranstädt

KLEIST

Leipzig

Lindenau

R. Saale

Lützen

NEY

Eisdorf

GUARD

Kaja

Klein Görschen

Starsiedel

WITTGENSTEIN

Weissenfels

Rippach

Rahna

Zwenkau

Gross Görschen

MARMONT

BLÜCHER

Poserna

YORCK

Pegau

Naumburg

WINZINGERODE

R. Saale

NAPOLEON'S
LINE OF ADVANCE

Stossen

BERTRAND

R. Elster

R. Pleisse

French

Allies

Zeitz

Miles

0   5   10

MILORADOVICH

0   5   10   15

Kilometres

N

FRENCH (Napoleon)		ALLIES (Wittgenstein)	
ARMY OF THE ELBE			
(Prince Eugène)			
Lauriston (V Corps)	10,000		
Latour-Maubourg (I Cav.)	8,000		
Macdonald (XI)	12,000		
Total	**30,000**		
ARMY OF THE MAIN		Kleist	6,000
(Napoleon)		Wittgenstein	24,000
Ney (III)	48,000	Blücher	25,000
Guard	15,000	Yorck	8,000
Marmont (VI)	20,000	Winzingerode	14,000
Bertrand (IV)	20,000	Miloradovich	9,000
Total	**103,000**	**Total**	**86,000**
Grand total	**133,000**		

Napoleon at Lützen urges his troops forward.

north-east of Klein Görschen, nearer to Leipzig. The country was flat and open with only slight gradients and would make excellent going for the cavalry – in which the Allies were so markedly superior. Only the houses and enclosures of the villages offered any security to Ney's infantryman. The guns, in which the Allied superiority was equally marked, had splendid fields of fire.

Ney's function was to guard the army's right flank, and he anticipated no trouble on 2 May. At 4 am that morning Napoleon had dictated a letter to Berthier, his Chief-of-Staff, in which he gave orders for Ney to concentrate his five divisions and to send two strong reconnaissance forces to the south and towards Pegau. It is clear that Ney did not do so. Indeed, he let his men disperse to do some discreet foraging. Some of his soldiers were digging up potatoes in Starsiedel, and Ney himself was with Napoleon near Markranstädt, possibly querying his morning orders, when suddenly they heard the sound of gunfire to the south. It was about 11.30 am and upon Ney's corps was to fall the full weight of the Allied attack.

Earlier, to the north, the first fighting of the day had occurred when Lauriston (V Corps), heading for Leipzig with General Maison's division in the lead, had attacked General Kleist's bridge-head at Lindenau. The bridge over the Elster between Lindenau and Leipzig caught fire, but some light infantry found a ford and dashed across. There were still two Prussian guns in the highway firing on the French infantry, but a battalion of the 153rd of the Line rushed upon them and pursued the enemy into the city. Lauriston supported them with the rest of the regiment and with the 151st. Kleist thereupon withdrew to Paunsdorf, a village

situated three miles east of Leipzig.

The second phase of the battle – that on Ney's front – began when Blücher rode up to Wittgenstein on the plateau about one and a quarter miles from Gross Görschen on the road to Pegau. The Prussian commander saluted and asked permission to attack. 'With God's help,' replied Wittgenstein, and Blücher launched his men north-wards towards Kaja and Gross Görschen, with Klix's brigade leading. Leiutenant-Colonel (later General) Karl von Müffling, who had reconnoitred the villages round Kaja, had reported that there were only about 2,000 French troops in the area. It came, therefore, as a rude surprise to the Allies when they discovered that they were opposed by a whole division. Even so, had they pushed on with the bayonet they might have carried the villages at the first rush. In the event, Wittgenstein halted the attack 800 yards short of Gross Görschen.

The Allies opened a terrible cannonade of 45 guns, which is said to have lasted 40 minutes, in which time they could easily have got off 4,000 rounds. Souham, commanding the 8th Division of Ney's corps, replied as best he could with his 12 6-pounders and four howitzers, but his batteries were enfiladed and three of his guns were hit. The French gunners were compelled to withdraw. De-prived of artillery support the French fell back behind Gross Görschen, which was taken by Klix's Prussians. Souham's division was now in position between that village and Kaja, along with Lamour's brigade. Here they sustained a frontal attack by the Prussians, while two Russian col-umns sought to turn the flanks of their position. Supported only by the remains of their divisional artillery, the two brigades held out for more than

an hour, but were eventually obliged to retire behind Kaja. Help was to arrive, but it would be a long time coming. The Allied attack had had no part in Napoleon's calculations, and for a considerable time the Emperor remained unconvinced of its seriousness.

Thus, having reviewed Macdonald's XI Corps near Markranstädt soon after 11 am, Napoleon had then watched from afar Lauriston's attack on Lindenau. Macdonald in his *Recollections* describes the sequence of events. 'The Emperor, believing that all the enemy's forces were collected at Leipzig, sent thither General Lauriston (V), who commanded the left. He came up to me, and gave me orders to support him if necessary; but at that moment he received intelligence that the allies, who had debouched from Pegau, were advancing towards us. The Emperor would not believe it, because he was firmly convinced that their main force was at Leipzig. Marshal Ney, who was with him, confirmed him in that idea, and declared he had noticed nothing unusual on the Elster.' Napoleon could see powder smoke and distant columns, but he was convinced that the Allies could not mount a serious attack until the next day, and said to Ney, 'Go. You will see it is no more than a reconnaissance.' However, as the firing increased in violence Napoleon ordered Ney

to hasten back to his corps, and soon afterwards followed him.

Ney galloped off, flat out, to Starsiedel. It was 10 miles, but even if he stopped briefly to give orders to his divisions in Lützen he was probably there by about 1 pm. General van Dedem, a brigade commander, saw him examine the enemy and then, closing a telescope with a snap, heard him say to one of his ADCs, 'Go and tell the Emperor that it really is a battle, and a battle such as he has never seen before.' In due course the Emperor gave out his orders and placed himself behind Girard's division of III Corps on the plateau which dominates Kaja and Starsiedel.

The Emperor's plan, rapidly formulated, was that III Corps, with the Guard in reserve, should hold Kaja and the surrounding villages, whilst the corps on the flanks should close in and crush the Allies in a hastily improvised double envelopment. Macdonald and Lauriston were ordered to come up on the left of Ney. The Emperor went himself to the head of the Guard in rear of the centre of the army, supporting Ney's right. Marmont (VI Corps) with his three divisions was to come up on Ney's right, and Bertrand (VI Corps) was ordered to debouch on the rear of the Allied army from the south-west.

Excellent though these dispositions were, they needed some time to develop. It was vital that

Ney's corps in the centre held its ground. Ney lost no time in launching a counter-attack. At the very outset his horse was killed by a cannon-ball, and he himself was hit in the leg by a musket-ball. These misfortunes did not prevent his exercising command. Girard's division moved off to support Souham's retreating infantry, whose flanks were now threatened by the Prussian reserve cavalry. Saluted with grapeshot, these last elected not to charge at this juncture. Girard, leading his division forward, was soon dismounted and wounded twice. Covered with blood, he seized the eagle of a regiment and led its grenadiers towards the Prussian batteries crying, 'It is here that every brave Frenchman must conquer or die!' A third bullet pierced his thigh. 'Take command,' he said to General van Dedem, 'I can do no more.'

Grape spewed on all sides; the Prussian cavalry charged several times, but could make no impression. The French divisional artillery ran out of ammunition and van Dedem had to send the guns to the rear. An engineer, Colonel Simon Bernard, one of the Emperor's ADCs, galloped up amidst a terrible fire and reconnoitred gun positions for the artillery of the Guard, which did marvels. Bernard also brought van Dedem orders to hold on at all costs. By this time the infantry had run out of cartridges; resorting to the bayonet, they advanced

Deployed near the village of Kaja, the Imperial Guard have begun to advance on Rahna, middleground centre. On the left, Drouot's great battery is shrouded in smoke. In the centre, an officer carrying a captured colour and flanked by a disconsolate column of prisoners, is about to present his prize to Napoleon, mounted on the grey horse.
Painting by M. Beaume.

against the Prussian guns. Meanwhile Brenier's division had come up, debouching to the left of the village of Kaja, but was repulsed. By now Ricard's division was also in action, but it too was checked, and the survivors of Girard's men were carried backwards by the withdrawal of the other two divisions. The Prussians had reinforced their attack by sending in Ziethen's brigade (equivalent to a French division), and at about 2 pm the end of the second phase of the battle found Ney's III Corps just hanging on to Kaja, with the Allies in possession of Gross Görschen, Klein Görschen and Rahna. In murderous fighting some of these villages had changed hands several times. By then not only had Ney and Girard been wounded, but in the 8th Division Souham, his Chief-of-Staff, de Contamie, and both brigadiers had been hit. On the Allied side Scharnhorst, the Prussian Chief-of-

Staff, had been wounded (he died on 28 June).

Ney's cavalry brigade, weak in numbers though it was, distinguished itself. At the beginning of the action several squadrons of Cossacks came slipping in between Kaja and the 10th Division, now commanded by van Dedem, and fell upon the park of the corps artillery and baggage to the right rear of the village. They had already carried off three guns and some caissons when a squadron of the 10th Hussars charged and routed them, recovering the Cossacks' trophies. During the rest of the day Ney's cavalry brigade was to make several more successful charges.

The situation in the French centre was still far from encouraging when Marmont's VI Corps, some 20,000 strong, came up into the line on the right of Ney. At this juncture the Prussian infantry had taken Klein Görschen for the second time, and Rahna. Several brilliant charges by the Prussian cavalry had contributed to this success, and the

Marmont (ignoring, evidently, Toulon and Lodi), 'was probably the day, of his whole career, on which Napoleon incurred the greatest personal danger on the field of battle. He exposed himself constantly, leading the defeated men of III Corps back to the charge.' Certainly Napoleon's personal leadership had not lost its magic. The cry of 'Vive l'Empereur!' was heard on every side. The Saxon Odeleben wrote that 'hardly a wounded man passed before Bonaparte without saluting him with the accustomed *vivat.*'

Some time was still to pass before the two corps of Macdonald (12,000 strong) and Bertrand (some 20,000) were in a position to make themselves felt. Bertrand, indeed, alarmed by the approach of Miloradovich from Zeitz, in the south, halted from about 1 pm until after 3 pm, and it took some prodding to make him resume his advance.

Much, therefore, depended on Marmont's VI Corps, which was now in the line in and around

'Vive l'Empereur!'
His soldiers cheer as Napoleon sweeps by.

Prussian Guards had followed up by hurling the French back beyond Kaja, which the latter had set on fire. It was in this desperate fighting that, at about 4 pm, Blücher had his horse shot under him, and was wounded in the side by a bullet. He sent orders to Yorck to take over, and rode to the rear to find a surgeon.

Napoleon supported Ney with Bonet's division of VI Corps and with part of the Young Guard, who had followed Marmont along the Weissenfels–Lützen road. Numbers of the conscripts of III Corps, unnerved by the fearful cannonade, had taken to their heels. Major Chlapowski of the 1st Regiment of Light Horse (Old Guard) later recalled that his unit was 'halted between the road and the village of Kaja, and deployed on a line facing the village in a field where the remnants of Ney's green troops were still in flight. The Emperor ordered us to bar their passage between our squadrons . . .' This done, Napoleon rode amongst his shattered infantry, exhorting them to rally. 'This,' wrote

Starsiedel. Captain Barrès of the 47th Regiment of the Line related, 'At last we moved forward; our division was on the extreme right. In close column we went along the road and moved straight on the village, to the right of Starsiedel.' On their left they passed the monument to King Gustavus Adolphus, who had fallen there in 1632. 'In front of Starsiedel we were saluted by the whole artillery of the enemy army and horribly cut up. Threatened by the cavalry we formed square, and . . . received incessant charges which we always successfully repulsed.'

Meanwhile Macdonald's XI Corps was beginning to make an impact. According to him, his men went forward at the double. It was high time. Ney's III Corps had lost much ground, and some Allied cavalry had got round their left flank. Seeing the approach of XI Corps, the Allies turned to retire, but not before Macdonald had time to get 30 guns into position, and they had to gallop back through his grape.

During this phase of the fighting Marmont's corps on the right took a heavy battering. In Barrès's words, 'At last, after three and a half to four hours of stubborn fighting, having lost half our officers and men and had our guns dismounted and ammunition caissons blown up, we retired in good order . . . as on parade.' They fell back behind Starsiedel, Major Fabre conducting the movement with admirable coolness and presence of mind. Barrès, himself hit twice, found that his company had suffered 44 casualties. By then it must have been nearly 6 o'clock, and Winzingerode's Allied corps had come up into line on Blücher's left.

Macdonald continued to press in upon the Allied right and 'forced them into a position covered by a little artificial canal used for floating wood'. They crossed a little valley, not without loss, and, crowning the height, saw the whole plain outstretched before them, 'but without cavalry it would have been unsafe to venture there'.

The Allies for their part were short of infantry, and if they managed to hold Marmont, and Bertrand when at last he came up into line, it was by murderous cannonades, interspersed with brave and energetic cavalry charges, which cost the French thousands of casualties. Prince Wilhelm of Prussia executed several charges against French infantry squares posted near Starsiedel. The Prussian cavalry are credited with breaking two squares and taking several guns.

It was approaching 6 pm when Count Wittgenstein threw in his last reserves. Outnumbered though he was, he ordered Eugen of Württemberg with his Russian infantry to advance against the French left. But it was all the Russians could do to hold their more numerous opponents at bay. Macdonald's approach was fiercely greeted. 'Suddenly,' he wrote, 'the fire ceased all along the front of the enemy, and was directed at us; the enemy sent forward their cavalry reserves, composed of the Guards of the sovereigns of Russia and Prussia. Thrice they attempted to break our squares, but in vain; each time they were driven back with loss, and the third time in such confusion as must have given great advantage to our cavalry had we possessed any.' General Latour-Maubourg, with a few squadrons, was on Macdonald's left, but Prince Eugène remained mindful of Napoleon's orders to husband his cavalry and did not wish to hazard them, despite Macdonald's entreaties; so a good opportunity slipped away. Prince Eugène eventually got as far as Eisdorf, but not before 9 pm, when the fighting had died down.

In the French centre, meanwhile, the climax of the battle was reached between 6.30 and 7.30. An hour or so earlier the corps of Macdonald and Bertrand, pressing in on the flanks of the Allies, had compelled them to redouble their efforts against the French centre. The village of Kaja had been carried once again and several battalions had fled in disorder. Once more it was the Emperor himself who had rallied them.

Napoleon now decided that the moment of crisis had arrived. He ordered Mortier to take 16 battalions of the Young Guard and storm Kaja. At the same time he ordered his ADC, General Baron Antoine Drouot, to build up a battery of 80 pieces in order to support the French centre. Deployed behind Drouot's guns would be the six battalions of the Old Guard drawn up like four redoubts, and all the cavalry, some 3,000 sabres. Drouot and two

other artillery generals, Desvaux and Dulauloy, went off at the gallop, and soon their guns were thundering forth cannon-balls at a rate amounting to 160 rounds a minute.

The Emperor then led forward his Young Guard. They did not show much *élan* at first, and van Dedem heard him say, 'Know that our Fate is decided; if we are destined to die, perish we must. En avant!' At about 6.30 pm the columns of the Young Guard, 10,000 strong, carried Kaja and pushed on, drums beating the charge, towards Gross Görschen. Joseph Dufraisne of the 1st Fusilier-Grenadiers (Young Guard) tells us that cannon-balls and shells fell like hail on their column. He was horrified when one dismounted Mortier, took off two legs in the first company and his lieutenant's arm – the wound proved mortal – before killing a comrade at his side. Still, the casualties of the Young Guard (1,069) were few indeed compared with those of Ney's III Corps (more than 17,000).

Mortier's success was followed up with a general advance by the French. The movement of the Young Guard on Gross Görschen had disengaged Ney's left and he ordered General Ricard to attack the little wood beyond Kaja where the enemy was still showing a bold front. The tired troops set off at some speed, but after a few hundred paces were held up by musketry and artillery fire. Five successive attacks were made in vain. Then Ricard collected all the officers in one platoon, and placing them at the head of his disordered troops, made them swear upon their swords that they would get to the wood or perish. They rushed forward with cries of 'Vive l'Empereur!' The Allies were routed and pursued for two miles. By this time it was night and Ricard's exhausted regiments bivouacked in squares.

The advance of the Young Guard, brilliant though it was, left Gross Görschen in the hands of the Prussians. As darkness fell the battlefield was lit by burning villages. The cannonading continued, albeit spasmodically; the musketry gradually died down. The Allied sovereigns, who had watched the fighting from a small hill near Werben, eventually quit the field at about 9 o'clock. But as late as 10 pm the Allied army was still in position with its right situated at Gross Görschen and its left near Muschwitz.

Both armies were in considerable confusion. The debris of Ney's 8th and 10th Divisions spent the night in front of the village of Kaja, the 39th Regiment taking up a position before Klein Görschen. In Lützen Captain Coignet had formed a wagon laager with his horses inside and a garrison of the Gendarmerie d'Élite (Old Guard). The Emperor at this time was composing his *Bulletin de la Grande Armée*, in which he tells us that this 'brilliant day . . . like a thunderclap, has pulverized the chimerical hopes and all the calculations of the destruction and dismemberment of the Empire. The shadowy dreams nursed at the Court of St James throughout the winter find themselves undone in an instant as was the Gordian Knot by the sword of Alexander.' To a staff officer he remarked, 'I am once more master of Europe.'

Although it looked well enough in the *Bulletin,* Lützen was far from being the decisive victory which Napoleon had sought. The Allies, though greatly outnumbered, had attacked him with astonishing vigour, had badly mauled III Corps and

A grenadier of the Imperial Guard.

given VI Corps a severe fight. Threatened by a skilful if slow pincer movement, they had extricated themselves and departed in generally good order, having inflicted a great many more casualties than they had suffered themselves. The reborn Prussian Army had done particularly well. 'These animals have learned something,' was Napoleon's own comment, while Count Nesselrode, the Russian statesman, wrote, 'The Prussian troops have covered themselves with glory; they have become once more the Prussians of Frederick.'

The Allied losses may have amounted to 15,000 men, the majority being Prussian. Blücher and Yorck had 8,400 casualties, and Prince Eugen of Württemberg had 1,600. The French losses were in the region of 25,000, the great majority being in III Corps, which according to the parade states had 17,633 fewer men on 5 May than on 25 April.

The Battle of Lützen left Napoleon Leipzig and battalions of corpses. The Emperor had reason to be satsified with Marmont, Macdonald and Mortier. To an ADC of Lauriston he said on 3 May, 'What were you doing yesterday, when we were fighting here? You were warming your bottoms in the sun.' This was hardly fair. With orders to take Leipzig, Lauriston had done so by about 3 pm and had redeployed to intervene at Lützen if necessary.

Bertrand's overcaution has already been mentioned. Prince Eugène had prevented Latour-Maubourg's 1st Cavalry Corps from charging the Allied right, but as Napoleon had given him strict written orders to husband the cavalry, he cannot be blamed for this.

In reviewing the conduct of the various marshals, it is particularly difficult to account for the way Ney handled his corps. There can be no question that on the morning of the 2nd he received orders in writing to concentrate his corps. But he did no such thing. Had Wittgenstein seen 48,000 foot drawn up around Kaja at noon, would he even have launched his attack? It seems highly improbable. Ney was certainly the bravest of the brave, but to disregard the Emperor's orders completely was a thing so extraordinary that it demands some explanation. The clues are perhaps to be found in Ney's character and in his relations with the Emperor. He was one of those men whose courage and energy were apparent only when he was in action. Otherwise he was inclined to be guided by his entourage. He was also retiring and uncommunicative. He got on well with Macdonald, but none of the other marshals. He was on bad terms with Napoleon's Chief-of-Staff, Berthier, which must have led to confusion. Moreover, deep down,

A French captain of dragoons.

he detested the Emperor. That, at any rate, is the picture that General van Dedem paints of his chief, and though it may be too sombre, he knew the Marshal well. One suspects that Ney went off on the morning of the battle to find the Emperor and question his orders. He thought that there was not going to be any action that day, and he did not wish to harass his tired troops. Scattered about the countryside, they would find more potatoes than if they were concentrated at Kaja. Ney was no great disciplinarian and was unlikely to discourage his men from a little marauding.

On the other hand, it was Ney's refusal to concentrate his forces that had encouraged Blücher to attack with such vigour. This in turn had caused Napoleon to devise his neat pincer movement. The latter had not quite come off, but the account of it looked very well in the *Bulletin*. The Emperor had good cause to be pleased with the Prince of the Moskva: he had done the right thing, but for the wrong reason.

To a commander-in-chief and a private soldier a battle may appear in a somewhat different light. Napoleon announced Lützen as a victory. Francois-Joseph Dresse of Herve, near Liège, thanked God that he had managed to survive when his battalion in Ricard's division of III Corps had suffered heavy losses. He does not scruple to describe Lützen as a defeat.

The people of Lützen were generous. Captain Coignet saw some 60 young girls and boys go out from the town and carry in the French wounded. Baron Larrey, whose flying ambulances arrived from Merseburg at midday, wrote, 'Dead and dying covered the battlefield. We gathered up the enemy wounded as well as our own. After the battle, the inhabitants of Lützen gave welcome aid to our casualties. They brought linen, lint, and food on to the field and provided means of transport. They then received these men into their town and spared no effort in caring for them.' In the next 48 hours Larrey performed or supervised 365 operations.

Napoleon wrote of Lützen, 'This is like the battles in Egypt. Good infantry supported by artillery must suffice.' Faced by the superior Allied cavalry, the French infantry was compelled to keep forming square. In square, however, it offered marvellous targets to the numerous Allied guns. For once it was the French who were outnumbered in artillery. Tormassov and Miloradovich arrived too late to take part in the battle. But their eventual presence, as well as a lack of cavalry, prevented Napoleon from taking full advantage of his slender victory.

CHAPTER 4
BAUTZEN AND DRESDEN

Not until two days after the Battle of Lützen did Napoleon discover that the Allies had gone back to Dresden. Although he had not obtained the decisive success that he had been hoping for, he planned his next moves with confidence. Davout was presently gathering an army with which to retake Hamburg, and Vandamme's corps was near Magdeburg. The Emperor disbanded the Army of the Elbe and despatched Prince Eugène back to Italy to reorganize the army there in case the Austrians declared war. He then formed a new army under Marshal Ney that comprised Ney's own corps and those of Lauriston, Reynier and

The Emperor plans his moves at Bautzen.

Victor, and Sébastiani's cavalry, in all a force of about 84,000 men.

Ney marched some 60 miles north to cross the Elbe at Torgau. At that time the town was occupied by General Thielmann with his Saxon Army. Thielmann personally sympathized with Blücher and protested that Saxony was neutral. Napoleon pressed the Saxon King to admit his men. The King personally admired Napoleon and ordered Thielmann to stop obstructing Ney. Thielmann, disgusted with such conduct, disappeared to join the Prussians. His troops, who disliked their predatory northern neighbours more than they did the French, happily joined the latter. On 10 May Ney started to cross the river.

Meanwhile Napoleon skilfully forced a crossing by Dresden. With Ney at Torgau, a prolonged resistance by the Allies would have been useless. Napoleon paused while he organized a vast administrative base in Dresden. The city was situated dangerously far to the east if things went wrong, but the Emperor refused to consider any such eventuality. He now heavily outnumbered the Allied army, but he was handicapped by his lack of cavalry and the difficulty of obtaining information in a hostile country. The Allies had retreated, but where? He wrote on 13 May to Ney in Torgau: 'I still do not see clearly what the Prussians have done; it is enough that the Russians are retreating on Breslau . . . Have they [the Prussians] gone towards Berlin as seems natural?' He ordered Ney to march on Berlin, but on 15 May Miloradovich fought a rearguard action with Macdonald, who forced a passage over the Spree. To Macdonald, who could see the enemy camps beyond Bautzen, it was evident that the Allies were not going back without a fight.

Napoleon joyously prepared this time to crush them. He cancelled the orders to advance on Berlin. Ney turned about, but his four corps were somewhat scattered. Wittgenstein, considering that Lauriston's corps was dangerously exposed, sent Yorck and Barclay de Tolly to break him. They had a sharp brush with the French near Hoyerswarda, about 20 miles north of Bautzen, but found Ney close at hand and withdrew before they could suffer serious damage. By this move, however, Wittgenstein had hazarded a substantial part of his army on an ill-timed diversion; the Allies' faith in their Commander-in-Chief, never high, sank lower.

The Allies, outnumbered as they were, had nevertheless decided to fortify a defensive position by the little town of Bautzen in the hope that Napoleon would shatter himself to pieces against it. If they continued to retreat, they considered they would lend colour to Napoleon's extravagant claims for his victory at Lützen, undermine further the morale of their men and discourage the other German states from joining them. For the underlying battle was for the allegiance of Germany as a whole. If the various states turned against Napoleon, the French were doomed – but those states were scarcely likely to link their fortunes with an army that seemed anxious only to run away.

The position they selected, with its left only six miles from the Austrian border and astride the main road to Breslau, suffered from two defects. It was rather too long for the troops available, and it was intersected by the narrow valley of the Blöserwasser, which flowed into the Spree. The Allied defensive position was organized in two parallel lines. The first, along the heights between the Spree and the Blöserwasser, was held from north to south by the corps of Tchaplitz, Kleist, Württemberg and Saint-Priest. The second line was much stronger. To the south it was behind the Blöserwasser, but on the right it was north-west of that river. From north to south the second line was held by Barclay de Tolly, Yorck, Blücher, and Gortchakov. The Russian Guard was in reserve behind Baschutz. The Allied sovereigns had their HQ at Nechern. Wittgenstein was still nominally the Commander-in-Chief, but in practice the Tsar Alexander had assumed the direction of affairs.

Napoleon with his army of 115,000 men intended to fix the Allies' attention on their left flank in the south and on their centre. He then planned that Ney with his army of 84,000 should attack well to the east of their right flank, after which the two combined armies would drive the enemy up against the hills on the Austrian border and annihilate them. The Allies numbered roughly 100,000. If Napoleon could induce them to hold their positions long enough, he could win that devastating victory which he needed to bring the war to a successful conclusion.

About noon on 20 May the French began their attack on the line of the River Spree. Whilst Oudinot (XII Corps) moved on Singwitz, Marmont (VI Corps) and Macdonald (XI Corps) advanced respectively north and south of Bautzen. Reiset's cavalry brigade linked Macdonald with Oudinot in the south. At about 1 pm Oudinot crossed the Spree by the bridge and a ford at Singwitz, driving the Russians back until he was halted by their cavalry. His right-hand division under Lorencez, meeting but feeble opposition, pushed forward in the direction of Mehlteuer. Meanwhile Macdonald not only secured the bridge to the south of Bautzen, he had two more constructed there.

Marmont, having massed 60 guns on the heights above Bautzen, got Compans's division across the Spree and by about 3 pm won a foothold in the north-western outskirts of Bautzen. Captain Barrès (47th of the Line) wrote that the attack began at about 10 am; that they had the town of Bautzen opposite them, and that they crossed by bridges 'thrown across the trestles'. Before they crossed the river Compans asked Barrès for a sergeant, a corporal, and 14 men, and led them himself to the foot of the walls of the town. He showed them a breach, and told them to climb over and open a gate which he pointed out. The sergeant, leading the way up to the breach, was killed, but the corporal took over and pulled his men up. They fired a volley and, for the loss of two or three men, got the gate open.

The Russians in the town of Bautzen, threatened by Macdonald on the one flank and Marmont on the other, withdrew. To the south Miloradovich retired before Oudinot lest he should be cut off, and the advancing French reached, roughly speaking, the line Binnewitz – Nadelwitz – Basankwitz – Pleifskowitz before fighting died down. The French fought well, and the advance of Lorencez in particular had convinced the Tsar that Napoleon's aim was to interpose between the Allies and the Austrians. In fact his object was the precise opposite. Alexander's reserves were already weak, but he now sent part of them to reinforce the troops facing Oudinot. The Tsar at this stage of the battle

was playing into Napoleon's hands.

During the day Ney had advanced against some opposition and bivouacked in the area of Särchen in the north. His army of four corps consisted at this stage of only his own III Corps, and Lauriston's V Corps. At about 4 pm on 20 May, orders signed by Berthier were sent to Ney. Although they were carried by one of Ney's own staff officers, they did not reach him until 4 am on the 21st. They ordered him to drive the enemy from Drehsa, about three miles to the south-east, and then march on Weissenberg and surround the Allied right.

At about 7 am on the 21st Napoleon was on the heights to the east of Bautzen when one of Ney's staff rode up. The Emperor explained the situation further, and sent him back with a pencil note. 'The intention of the Emperor is that you should follow constantly the movement of the enemy. His majesty has shown your staff officer the positions of the enemy, which are defined by the redoubts which he has constructed and occupies. The intention of the Emperor is that you should be on the Blöserwasser about six miles south-east of Särchen. You will be on the extreme right of the enemy. As soon as the Emperor sees you engaged at Preititz we shall attack vigorously at all points. Have General Lauriston (V) march on your left so as to be in a position to turn the enemy if your movement decides him to abandon his position.'

Oudinot (XII Corps) advanced at daybreak and took Rieschen. Still convinced that Napoleon meant to cut him off from Bohemia, the Tsar drew on his reserves until Miloradovich had 20,000 men to oppose Oudinot's 15,000. By 11 o'clock Oudinot, back on the heights east of Binnewitz, was asking for reinforcements. Characteristically Napoleon did not even trouble to reply. Macdonald (XI Corps) moved forward to the heights near Baschutz to the north of Oudinot and opened a heavy bombardment. Marmont (VI Corps) contented himself with holding the heights of Burk, with infantry in Nadelwitz, Nieder Kaina and Basankwitz. The Guard in squares crowned the heights to the north-east of Bautzen. Soult with Bertrand (IV Corps) made much slower progress than he had expected, but by 2 pm had Bertrand's 21,000 men and 30 guns on the plateau east of the Spree near Doberschutz.

Ney moved off early, between 4 and 5 am, and drove Barclay de Tolly back until about 10 am. His men were soon on the heights of Gleina, and Lauriston was on his left. It was now that Napoleon's message reached Ney. Jomini, the clever Swiss theoretician who was now his Chief-of-Staff, urged the Marshal to advance at once on Preititz. Perhaps this was not very tactful, but Ney pointed out that the Emperor intended him to be there at 11 o'clock. He would stand fast for an hour. He took this decision even though he had four divisions up, and with their 23,000 men he could no doubt have wolfed Preititz in a mouthful.

In 1823, long after the Marshal was in his grave, Jomini wrote, 'When Ney saw the fine heights of Klein Bautzen (Kreckwitz) he was carried away by the idea that they were the key to the position.' He thought he ought to wait until Reynier (VII Corps) came up, and then storm the heights. At 11 o'clock he sent in Souham's division which drove two battalions of Barclay's corps from Preititz. As F. Petre observes in his book on Napoleon's German campaigns, 'Had he had his whole corps there, and been on the move towards Hochkirch, as Jomini urged him, Blücher could hardly have held on to the Kreckwitz heights, and, the pressure in front of Soult being removed, that marshal also would have got forward.' Ney's

Russian officers of the period:
on the left is a Cossack, next to him a general of brigade and, in white, an officer of dragoons;
those on the right are infantry officers.

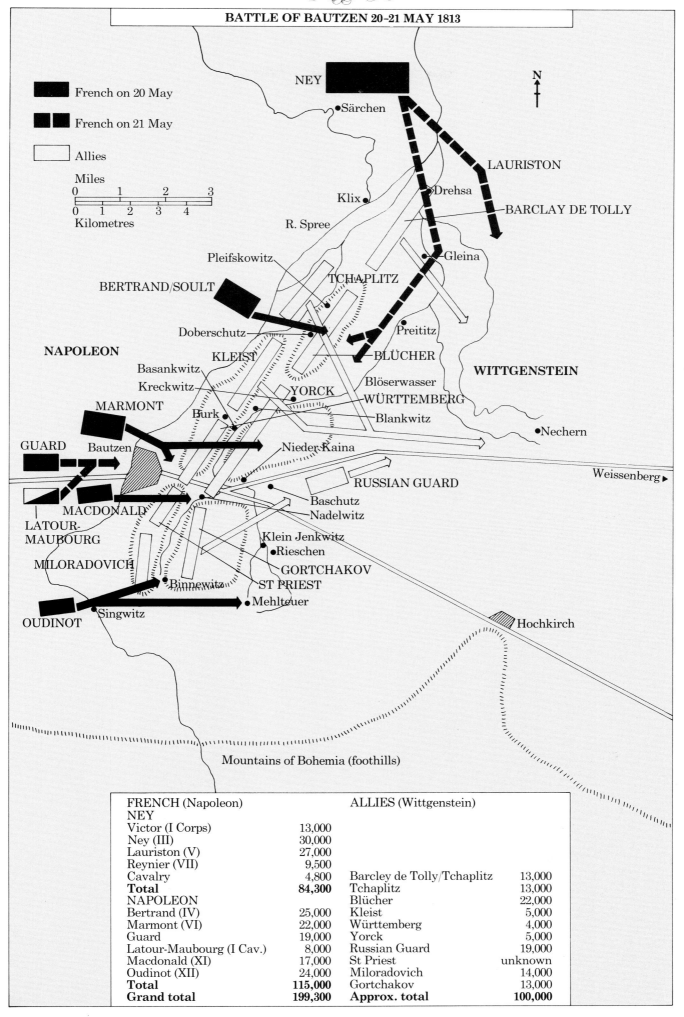

BATTLE OF BAUTZEN 20-21 MAY 1813

N

French on 20 May

French on 21 May

Allies

Miles
0   1   2   3
0 1 2 3 4
Kilometres

NEY

●Särchen

LAURISTON

Klix● ●Drehsa

BARCLAY DE TOLLY

R. Spree

●Gleina

Pleifskowitz

TCHAPLITZ

BERTRAND/SOULT

Doberschutz

●Preititz

NAPOLEON

KLEIST

BLÜCHER

Basankwitz

WITTGENSTEIN

Kreckwitz

Blöserwasser

YORCK

WÜRTTEMBERG

MARMONT

Burk

Blankwitz

●Nechern

GUARD   Bautzen

Nieder-Kaina

RUSSIAN GUARD

Weissenberg ▶

MACDONALD

Baschutz

LATOUR-
MAUBOURG

Nadelwitz

MILORADOVICH

Klein Jenkwitz

●Rieschen

GORTCHAKOV

Binnewitz

ST PRIEST

OUDINOT   ●Singwitz

●Mehlteuer

Hochkirch

Mountains of Bohemia (foothills)

FRENCH (Napoleon)		ALLIES (Wittgenstein)	
NEY			
Victor (I Corps)	13,000		
Ney (III)	30,000		
Lauriston (V)	27,000		
Reynier (VII)	9,500		
Cavalry	4,800	Barcley de Tolly/Tchaplitz	13,000
Total	**84,300**	Tchaplitz	13,000
NAPOLEON		Blücher	22,000
Bertrand (IV)	25,000	Kleist	5,000
Marmont (VI)	22,000	Württemberg	4,000
Guard	19,000	Yorck	5,000
Latour-Maubourg (I Cav.)	8,000	Russian Guard	19,000
Macdonald (XI)	17,000	St Priest	unknown
Oudinot (XII)	24,000	Miloradovich	14,000
Total	**115,000**	Gortchakov	13,000
Grand total	**199,300**	**Approx. total**	**100,000**

preoccupation with the heights of Kreckwitz was in fact fatal for Napoleon's plan.

In the second phase of the battle, Oudinot and Macdonald succeeded in inducing the Allies to concentrate their left, and much of their reserve, against them. When at about noon Oudinot pleaded for reinforcements, Napoleon said to his galloper, 'Tell your marshal that the battle will be won by 3 o'clock, from now till then he must hold on as best he may.'

The Tsar and the King of Prussia sat their horses on the heights near Klein Jenkwitz, south of the main road to Hochkirch, from where at a range of two miles they could make out the Emperor on his grey. Not that Napoleon spent all his time in the saddle: from 9 until 11 o'clock he slept on the ground in the midst of his Guard, shells bursting around him. And while one Emperor slept, the other obliged him by accepting the idea that it was his left that was menaced. 'I will wager my head,' said the more percipient Wittgenstein, 'that this is only a demonstration; Napoleon's idea is to outflank our right and drive us on Bohemia.'

At 11 o'clock Souham's guns of III Corps woke Napoleon, who ordered Marmont forward, and sent Barrois's division (Young Guard) to complete the line between him and Bertrand in the north. Behind Basankwitz the rest of the Guard was drawn up, supported by Latour-Maubourg's cavalry and 80 guns. At about 2.30 pm Franquemont's Württemberg division (IV Corps) made a gallant attack on Kreckwitz. Morand's division advanced simultaneously, and by 3 pm Blücher's hard-pressed troops were back on the line Doberschutz – Kreckwitz.

Before the French reached Preititz, Barclay de Tolly had asked Blücher for reinforcements; these were promptly sent, and when Souham emerged from Preititz he was attacked with vigour and driven out. Ney sent three divisions to retake Preititz, and at about 2 pm Kleist saw them approaching, while Lauriston menaced his right. The French stormed the village, which changed hands twice before the Prussians, their line of retreat threatened, fell back on the heights to the south-west. Enemy cannonades from the heights of Kreckwitz, though well west of his true objective, convinced Ney that he must storm them, despite his Chief-of-Staff's urgings that he should direct his 32,000 men south-east towards the green church spire of Hochkirch. By about 3 pm Blücher, threatened with encirclement, was warned that he must withdraw within a quarter of an hour or the trap would be closed. The Prussians leap-frogged back with great skill. As they withdrew, the French surged on to the Kreckwitz heights, and Ney found to his disgust that his change of direction had only succeeded in bringing him face to face with Bertrand. The two corps (III and IV) became horribly intermingled and it took an hour to disentangle

them. Ney had the mortification of seeing Blücher's troops depart through the gap he had left them, and his orders to Lauriston to cut them off came too late.

Now the Tsar realized that it was the Allied right, not their left, that was threatened. At 4 pm orders were given for a retreat. It was well executed, under the cover of skilful rearguard actions and a providential rainstorm. The Allies had lost 10,850 men of whom 2,790 were from Blücher's corps. Few prisoners were taken: the only trophies were a few disabled cannon.

The young French troops lost double these numbers, probably about 20,000 casualties; these included 3,700 missing, of whom 800 were taken prisoner. The others, stragglers and marauders, may have rejoined their eagles later. After the battle Napoleon, as was his wont, rode over the battlefield amongst the heaps of slain: 'What!' he exclaimed, 'after such a slaughter, no trophies? These people will leave me no claws!'

A hussar reports to Napoleon during the Battle of Bautzen.

Ney has been blamed for the failure to inflict a decisive defeat on the Allies at Bautzen. He undoubtedly allowed himself to be fatally distracted by the struggle on the heights of Kreckwitz, and struck too far west to envelop the Allied right flank as Napoleon had planned; but Blücher was no fool, and was not likely to watch placidly while he was enveloped. Napoleon's scheme for a great combined attack had demanded too much. Staffs were rudimentary and communications bad. Napoleon himself was responsible for developing large armies beyond the control of a commander mounted on his horse. Large bodies of men could not be moved or deployed as though they were single regiments or even divisions. Napoleon himself does not appear to have lost confidence in Ney. He appreciated his difficulties, compounded as they were by the fine fighting performance of the Allied troops.

It was, however, on the heights of Kreckwitz that Napoleon's last chance of saving his German empire vanished. At the time the Allies, retiring disconsolately amid the customary storm of mutual recrimination, had little reason to believe it. Significantly, though, the Prussians did not depart to the north, nor the Russians beyond the Vistula. Their alliance remained outwardly firm, and Napoleon's next move in the face of their opposition was to conclude an armistice, perhaps in the hope that serious peace talks might now begin. His agreement to the Armistice of Poischitz has been hailed as one of his greatest mistakes, and indeed from that time onwards his fortunes began to turn for the worse. He probably had no choice. He had marched and fought his army into the ground, and the Cossacks and Prussian *Freikorps* were constantly raiding his lines of communication which stretched ever further from France. When the Armistice was concluded on 4 June 1813, the Russian General Woronzoff was actually on the point of seizing Leipzig. 'This Armistice will interrupt the course of my victories,' the Emperor wrote on 2 June to General Clarke, his Minister of War. 'Two considerations have made up my mind: my shortage of cavalry, which prevents me from striking great blows, and the hostile attitude of Austria.'

While the war progressed the diplomatists had been at work. Austria had offered her services as an intermediary and Napoleon had tried to treat directly with Tsar Alexander. It had been an exercise in futility. As one side secured a military

see an increase in their strength, which he foresaw might well endanger the security of Austria. He was, however, conscious of the rising tide of nationalism that had begun to sweep across Germany and he detested it. He wished to retain Napoleon but he was not prepared for France to meddle any longer in German affairs. He was convinced that Napoleon's Confederation of the Rhine must cease to exist. But Napoleon was not prepared to dissolve it.

On 26 June 1813, the two men met in the Marcolini Palace in Dresden. Napoleon wore sword and hat. The sword he threatened to draw, the hat he threw at Metternich the better to establish a point. Before the Austrian went in to the nine-hour conference, Berthier buttonholed him and whispered, 'Europe needs peace.' These words, uttered by Napoleon's Chief-of-Staff, showed clearly enough how weary the French had grown of war. At the conference Napoleon tried to threaten and browbeat the Austrian. To Metternich the issues were clear enough. Napoleon could keep the Netherlands and what he could hold of Italy and Spain, but the Confederation of the Rhine had to be dissolved. Napoleon would not give up his foothold in Germany. The wrangle went on interminably. Napoleon at one point confessed, 'Your sovereigns born to the throne may be beaten twenty times and return ... my reign will end when I am no longer strong.' It was a theme to which he kept returning.

Allied cavalry prepare to attack an advancing column of French infantry.

advantage so it raised its bid, only to have it declined by the other, which hoped that the next round of fighting would be to its own advantage. Napoleon could not bring himself to accept terms, and could no longer impose them. Equally, though, the Allies had suffered rough treatment on the battlefield, and they too needed a respite.

Napoleon's desire for an armistice must also be taken as proof of his dissatisfaction with his inconclusive victories at Lützen and Bautzen. But it may be doubted whether the Russo-Prussian alliance would have survived another defeat. A third victory might well have enabled the Emperor to relieve the beleaguered fortresses on the Oder, whose garrisons would have given a welcome stiffening to his conscript army. On the other hand his cavalry was still feeble, his raw troops were unready for another blood-bath, and ammunition and supplies were running low. It is extremely doubtful whether he could have won a third victory at that time.

The diplomatic scene was dominated by the subtle Prince Metternich of Austria, whose suavity concealed a will of steel. He was faced by problems appalling in their complexity. As the spokesman for a multi-national Empire he deeply distrusted nationalism and the ideals of the French Revolution. Napoleon was a bulwark against both. Metternich also with good reason feared the ambitions of Prussia and Russia and had no desire to

With both Royalists and Republicans seeking to unseat him, he could not be tainted by failure. He nevertheless believed there were no issues that could not ultimately be settled on the battlefield, and growled to Metternich that he had beaten the Prussians at Lützen, and the Russians at Bautzen, and soon he would be renewing the argument in Vienna!

The two sides were irreconcilably opposed, and so they were to remain. Napoleon could not believe that his dream of becoming the conquering ruler of a united Europe had vanished; he could not understand how the growth of German nationalism had overtaken him. As the exhausted Austrian finally left the meeting, to the anxious enquiries of bystanders he replied, 'C'est un homme perdu' (He is lost).

Next the Emperor Francis I of Austria pledged himself to go to war if Napoleon did not disband his Confederation of the Rhine and withdraw from Germany. Now Austria had declared against Napoleon the waverers began to follow suit. Bernadotte, the ex-Marshal of the Empire who was now Crown Prince of Sweden, joined the hunt. The old Republican general and opponent of Napoleon, General Moreau, appeared from the United States of America. As both sides prepared for a renewal of the conflict the Allies discussed how best Napoleon might be fought. Moreau told them frankly that they would never beat Napoleon on the field of battle. They prepared a deadly plan. Commanders facing Napoleon should refuse action and withdraw, seeking to exhaust his men by useless marches. Where he did not himself command, his marshals should at once be engaged. Eventually, when Napoleon had been sufficiently worn down and the Allies had a sufficient superiority in numbers, Napoleon himself should be fought. Blücher expostulated angrily against such craven tactics, but had to comply. The plan was quick to bear fruit.

Both sides now exerted the utmost effort to concentrate their forces for 10 August, when hostilities would clearly begin again. Russian reinforcements came wandering westwards from the Steppes. French battalions plodded towards the Elbe, their veteran cadres teaching them the rudiments of drill and weapon training as they went. In June Britain had agreed to subsidize Russia and Prussia to the extent of more than £1.5 million. British munitions poured into Stralsund and Colberg, enabling the Prussian *Landwehr* to exchange their pikes for muskets and to take their place in the line of battle. Before the conference dispersed, the Allies heard good news from Spain. Wellington's great triumph at Vitoria (21 June) had driven the French headlong from the Peninsula. Now France herself was threatened with invasion. The Tsar ordered that a *Te Deum* should be sung, something that had never previously been done for a victory won by other than Russian troops.

On 12 August Austria declared war. By this time Napoleon had nearly as many men in Germany as he had on the Neman in 1812 when he invaded Russia:

Location	Numbers	Commander
Fortresses to the East	50,000	various
Fortresses on the Elbe	25,000	various
Hamburg	40,000 (inc. 12,000 Danes)	Davout
The Rhine	25,000	
	Bavarians	Wrede
Mainz/Würzburg	15,000	
	Cavalry corps	Milhaud
	Infantry corps	Augereau
Grande Armée	400,000	Napoleon
Total	555,000	

With over 12,000 guns Napoleon was very well provided with artillery. His cavalry, some 380 squadrons, now amounted to 70,000 men – though how many of the troopers were expert in wielding their sabres, or in riding their horses, was another matter. The Guard had swollen to a strength of 60,000 men.

The *Grande Armée* was organized into 16 corps, five being cavalry. This great host was by no means all French. It included Poles, Germans, Italians, Dutchmen, Belgians and Swiss, and while some, notably the Poles, were devoted to the Emperor, some were decidedly lukewarm. As early as 22 August two Westphalian hussar regiments, comprising the light cavalry brigade of Victor's II Corps, went over to the Allies, whose field armies had grown to a redoubtable size.

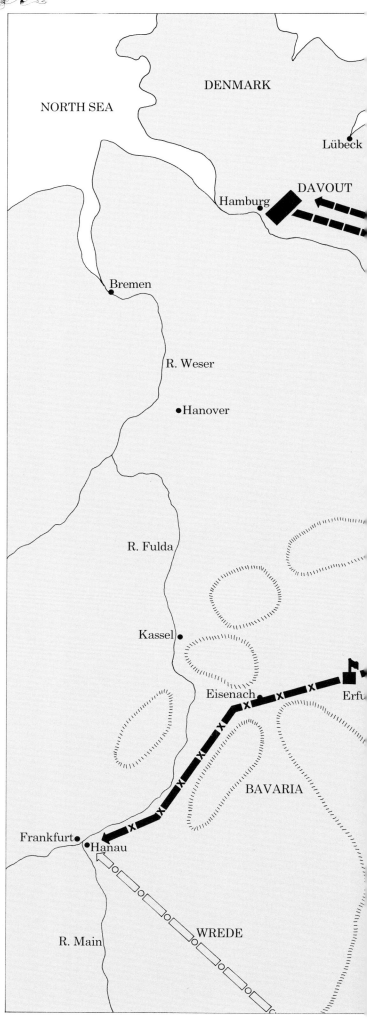

THE LEIPZIG CAMPAIGN AUTUMN 1813

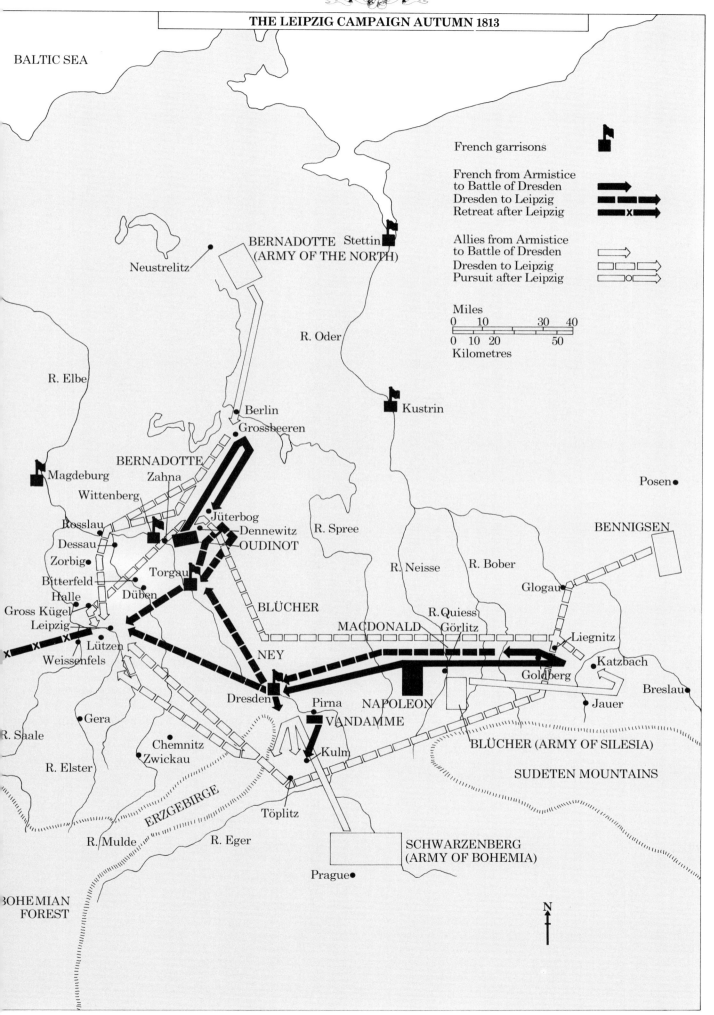

BALTIC SEA

French garrisons

French from Armistice
to Battle of Dresden
Dresden to Leipzig
Retreat after Leipzig

Allies from Armistice
to Battle of Dresden
Dresden to Leipzig
Pursuit after Leipzig

Miles
0   10   30   40
0   10 20   50
Kilometres

BERNADOTTE Stettin
(ARMY OF THE NORTH)

Neustrelitz

R. Oder

Kustrin

Posen

R. Elbe

Berlin
Grossbeeren

BERNADOTTE

Magdeburg
Zahna
Wittenberg
Rosslau
Dessau
Zorbig
Bitterfeld
Halle
Gross Kügel
Leipzig
Lützen
Weissenfels

Jüterbog
Dennewitz
OUDINOT

Torgau
Düben

BLÜCHER

NEY

R. Spree

R. Neisse

R. Bober

BENNIGSEN

Glogau

MACDONALD
Görlitz

R. Quiess

Liegnitz

Katzbach

Goldberg

Breslau

Jauer

Dresden
Pirna
NAPOLEON
VANDAMME

BLÜCHER (ARMY OF SILESIA)

SUDETEN MOUNTAINS

Gera
Chemnitz
Zwickau

Kulm

R. Saale

R. Elster

ERZGEBIRGE

Töplitz

R. Mulde
R. Eger

SCHWARZENBERG
(ARMY OF BOHEMIA)

Prague

BOHEMIAN
FOREST

N

On 26 August, also the first day of the Battle of Dresden,
Blücher's Prussians defeat the French under Macdonald at the Katzbach.
Blücher is shown in the centre of the picture;
on the right a French cuirassier is overwhelmed by Prussian Uhlans (lancers).

The Allies also put a mighty host in the field. It consisted of three armies, as follows:

Army of Bohemia (Schwarzenberg)

	Numbers	Commander
Austrians	125,000	Schwarzenberg
Prussians (II Corps)	37,000	Kleist
Prussian Guard	7,000	
Russians	80,000	Barclay de Tolly
Total	249,000	

Army of the North
(Bernadotte, Crown Prince of Sweden)

Prussians	72,000	Tauentzien/Bülow
Russians	30,000	Winzingerode
Swedes	23,000	Bernadotte
Total	125,000	

Army of Silesia (Blücher)

Prussians	38,000	Yorck
Russians	70,000	Sacken/Langeron
Total	108,000	

The three Allied field armies amounted to more than 480,000 men, as opposed to Napoleon's *Grande Armée* of about 400,000. More than a quarter of Winzingerode's 30,000 men were Cossacks, unfit for the line of battle, and most of Tauentzien's men, being *Landwehr* or reserves, could hardly be classed as first-line troops. But in addition they had a miscellaneous force under Wallmoden opposing Davout's garrison at Hamburg, while other detachments, mainly *Landwehr,* blockaded the French garrisons on the Elbe and to the east. These troops numbered not less than 100,000, bringing the Allied total to nearly 600,000.

When the Armistice ended, Napoleon had most of his army deployed to the east of the Elbe, between Dresden and Liegnitz, able to strike at any one of the three converging Allied armies. From Dresden north to Hamburg the fortresses and passages of the Elbe were in his hands. He decided to strike first at Bernadotte, hoping to loosen the Allies' position in North Germany, and perhaps to relieve Kustrin and Stettin.

The battle-scarred Oudinot took an army of 85,000 to the north. He had some initial success, but on 23 August Bernadotte's Army of the North turned on him at Grossbeeren about 12 miles south of Berlin, and drove him back in confusion. By 2 September he was back at Wittenberg on the Elbe, about 40 miles south-west of Berlin, with his men badly shaken.

Meanwhile Blücher, advancing against Ney, had found the latter reinforced by Napoleon himself; in accordance with the new plan of operations, Blücher beat a hasty retreat eastwards, and despite a vigorous pursuit succeeded in evading the Emperor. Schwarzenberg, seeing Napoleon away in the east, struck northwards. On 23 August Napoleon left Macdonald with four corps to contain Blücher and moved by forced marches from Görlitz to the relief of Dresden. He ordered Macdonald to

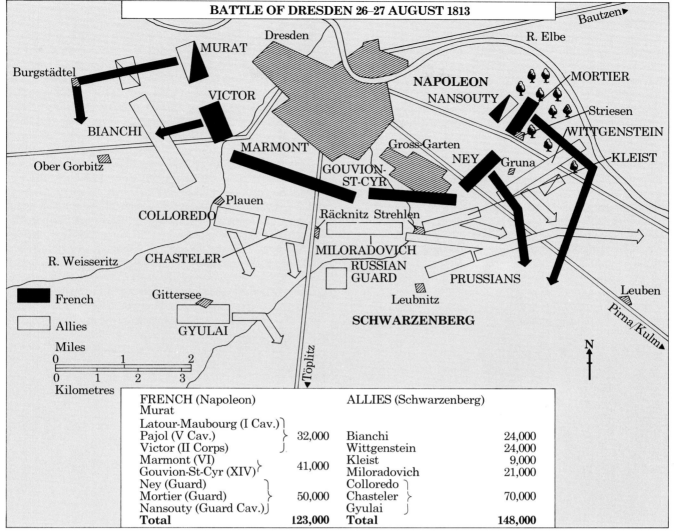

BATTLE OF DRESDEN 26–27 AUGUST 1813

FRENCH (Napoleon)		ALLIES (Schwarzenberg)	
Murat			
Latour-Maubourg (I Cav.) ⎫			
Pajol (V Cav.) ⎬ 32,000		Bianchi	24,000
Victor (II Corps) ⎭		Wittgenstein	24,000
Marmont (VI) ⎫ 41,000		Kleist	9,000
Gouvion-St-Cyr (XIV) ⎭		Miloradovich	21,000
Ney (Guard) ⎫		Colloredo ⎫	
Mortier (Guard) ⎬ 50,000		Chasteler ⎬ 70,000	
Nansouty (Guard Cav.) ⎭		Gyulai ⎭	
Total	**123,000**	**Total**	**148,000**

drive Blücher beyond the river Jauer and then take up a position on the River Bober and so prevent the Army of Silesia from interfering with his operations. Macdonald, however, pressed on to the Katzbach, a tributary of the River Oder about 40 to 50 miles west of Breslau. It was a stream of no great importance but its banks were steep. Macdonald was deceived by Blücher's flight into thinking that the Army of Silesia was tired and demoralized after its long retreat. He then crossed the Katzbach, although he had only 50,000 troops to oppose Blücher's force of 80,000. The Prussian, aware that Napoleon was no longer with the French army, at once turned on his pursuer. Macdonald, taken by surprise at this sudden reversal, was driven back into the river and only extricated himself with the loss of half his force, 100 guns and 18,000 prisoners. He fell back rapidly towards Dresden with his shattered remnants.

In the meantime, on 19 August Schwarzenberg had begun his advance. On the 22nd the Allies crossed the watershed of the mountains oof Bohemia, making for Chemnitz, then decided to turn north-east against Dresden, whose garrison was only 5,000 strong. Napoleon got wind of this move very quickly, for news of it reached him at Görlitz on the evening of 23 August.

The Allied advanced guard appeared before Dresden on the afternoon of 25 August and Gouvion-Saint-Cyr, with 15,000 men, fell back before them. The Marshal had four divisions, one of these being at Königstein, with which to oppose 80,000 Allies. The fortifications at Dresden were not of the best and were also rather too extensive for the troops available. Had the Allies stormed at once they could scarcely have failed to carry the city, but they delayed. This has been blamed on the methodical approach of the Austrians: it seems, however, that Schwarzenberg wished to attack but allowed the Tsar to overrule him. The opportunity for a swift victory was soon gone, for by evening the bivouac fires of Napoleon's Imperial Guard could be seen against the eastern sky.

At 6 am on 26 August the Allies made a general assault which carried the outlying villages and the Gross-Garten, but before they could penetrate the suburbs Napoleon's troops were pouring across the Elbe bridges. Now the Allies put in another general attack. At every point they met with a rude reception. Mortier drove Wittgenstein back past Striesen, while his right-hand division drove Pirch and Ziethen out of the Gross-Garten. Colloredo's Austrians got into a French battery, but the Old Guard threw them out with the bayonet. To the west, between the Weisseritz and the Elbe, Murat, with Latour-Maubourg's cavalry and Victor's II Corps, drove back Gyulai and Bianchi.

Even now the Allies did not retire. This time it was not the Tsar, but the King of Prussia whose counsel prevailed. In view of their numbers, he argued it would be too much of a confession of weakness to withdraw. At the same time, though, the Allies were handicapped by the nature of the ground and the skilful dispositions of the French. Lord Cathcart, who was accompanying them – he

The battle for Dresden. The city can be seen in
the background on the right, and the River Weisseritz
flows across the middleground. Allied guns are pounding
Dresden, while on the far bank Murat has struck back
with the cavalry. The Austrians under Bianchi and
Gyulai have given way and are fleeing to the south-west.
The bridges shown are in fact those over the Elbe,
which here appears to have been confused with the Weisseritz.

General Vandamme,
trapped in the mountains near Kulm,
surrenders to the Allies with 7,000 men and 82 guns.

subsequently died at the Battle of Inkerman in 1854 – described the initial situation thus: 'The concave arc on which the Allied army was formed was nearly six English miles from right to left; and the convex arc on which Napoleon stood was less than three. The Allied line, except at the two extremities, had the advantage of an eminence; but Napoleon's forces stood with their backs to the defences of Dresden, sheltered by regular redoubts, and the loopholed houses of the suburbs were near at hand. This was an attitude in which a much smaller force would have been secure from attack so long as it chose to stand on the defensive; while its concentration placed it in a favourable attitude for assuming the offensive against any weak part of the extended line of the Allies.' He might have added that the River Weisseritz, running through difficult country, would result in the Allied left remaining isolated for a dangerous period of time in the event of a sudden, unexpected attack. Napoleon contemplated just such a move.

On the following day (27 August) the French attacked all along the line. Mortier and Nansouty got round Wittgenstein's right flank, but then Nansouty, outnumbered three-to-one by the Russian Reserve Cavalry, was checked. Starting from the Gross-Garten, Gouvion-Saint-Cyr drove back Kleist towards Leubnitz. The Old Guard and Marmont (VI Corps) held the Austrians in play, Victor (II Corps) stormed the heights to his front, and Latour-Maubourg's cavalry, supported by a single brigade of Vandamme's I Corps, swept round the Austrian left at Burgstädtel.

Around noon the fighting died down, but during the afternoon the French made a decisive stroke west of the Weisseritz. Victor took Ober Gorbitz, cutting off part of Lichtenstein's division and compelling Weissenwolff's to withdraw. French divisions now appeared behind the Austrians' flank. Murat sent in his cavalry, 10 Austrian battalions were cut off and taken, and the rest of the Austrian left wing departed in flagrant rout, Murat's sabres reaping a bloody harvest.

It was fortunate indeed for the Allies that Napoleon, his soldiers tired out by forced marches and hard fighting, did not press them that afternoon. He was waiting for Vandamme's corps, which was approaching from the direction of Pirna, to develop an attack against the Allied flank and rear. During the night the Allies withdrew, toiling back in foul weather across the Erzgebirge. Many Poles in the Austrian service deserted, and some of the Prussian *Landwehr* battalions more or less disintegrated. Still, thanks partly to a chapter of accidents and partly to the gallant resistance of Prince Eugen of Württemberg, Vandamme failed to reach Töplitz before the Allies. Prince Eugen, instead of falling back, then attacked Vandamme. Under cover of this move he slipped Ostermann's division of the Russian Guard across the French front so that it was between Vandamme and Töplitz. Prince Eugen's corps suffered heavily, but he stood at bay next day (29 August), contesting the last pass across the mountains. Ostermann himself lost an arm but eventually he was reinforced. Vandamme came on again on the 30th, but Württemberg was able to keep the French centre in check, while three Austrian divisions assailed Vandamme's left. At this stage Kleist, anxious to retire south beyond the mountains of the Erzgebirge, arrived in Vandamme's rear. Vandamme,

confident he would soon link with the pursuit from Dresden, held his ground and turned upon Kleist furiously. But blocked mountain roads delayed the French pursuers and Vandamme's position was soon desperate. General Mouton, seeing retreat down the highroad through Kulm to be impossible, escaped by making his division take to the hills, but much of Napoleon's I Corps, including its outspoken and stout-hearted commander, was compelled to surrender. Vandamme lost 10,000 killed and wounded, 7,000 prisoners and 82 guns, but not his spirit. Ill-received by the Tsar, who called him a brigand, he had the temerity to remark, 'Nobody has ever reproached me with having assassinated my father', a pointed reference to the death of the despotic Tsar Paul I in 1801.

The last ten days of August 1813 do not show Napoleon at his best. He had lost more men than the Allies. Against his single success at Dresden they could show three clear victories against his lieutenants: the Allied plan was working. If ever Napoleon needed a decisive success it was when at Dresden the Allies challenged his hold on Germany. Had those operations ended in disaster for the Army of Bohemia, the allegiance of the Confederation of the Rhine to the French Empire must have been cemented.

Before the battle ended the French had 120,000 men in and around Dresden. The Allies brought up nearly 220,000. The French had 10,000 casualties, to which must be added those lost at Kulm. Allied casualties in these operations were in the region of 40,000. The French victory was a great achievement, but was nullified by the catastrophe at Kulm. Coignet, the loyal old grenadier who was now the Emperor's baggage-master, was shocked by the criticisms he heard among the staff officers. He wrote, 'This was a memorable victory; but our generals had had enough of it . . . They cursed the Emperor: "He is a ————," they said, "who will have us all killed." I was dumb with astonishment. I said to myself, "We are lost."

Fusilier of the line.

CHAPTER 5
LEIPZIG:
THE BATTLE OF THE NATIONS

Napoleon's great victory at Dresden was made largely valueless by Vandamme's almost inconceivable catastrophe at Kulm. The earlier defeats of his marshals – Macdonald on the Katzbach and Oudinot at Grossbeeren – had shown the effectiveness of the new Allied strategy. Now, as his enemies massed against him, almost every day brought the news of some defection: a lesser man might have accepted defeat, a politically wiser one might have gone to the council chamber to extract what he could from the shambles. Napoleon himself seemed momentarily uncertain, almost unnerved by the extent of his disasters. Such emotions

French troops storm through a village.

never lasted long with the Emperor. He would not admit that his vision of dictating peace on the Vistula or at Vienna was now only an empty dream. One great victory, and all would be retrieved. It was not his destiny to fail.

He must strike at the increasing number of his foes, but at whom? He remained near Dresden and thrust viciously at Schwarzenberg in Bohemia to the south of the great mountain range of the Erzgebirge. Schwarzenberg, safely ensconced behind the mountain passes, shielded by vile roads and even viler weather, thwarted his great opponent while Blücher advanced inexorably in the east. Napoleon might have turned on Blücher but the Prussian would only have run away to Breslau in the east, while Schwarzenberg and Bernadotte joined hands across his communication lines with France. He might have left an army of observation in the south to watch the mountain passes and gone north, but Bernadotte would have refused action and no doubt given ground while Blücher and Schwarzenberg and fresh armies from Russia advanced on his great administrative base at Dresden. He might do nothing and wait for the Allies to blunder, but he was used to creating opportunities, not waiting for them to occur.

He decided that he himself would remain centrally at Dresden where he could deal either with Blücher or Schwarzenberg as might prove necessary. He sent Ney to the north with instructions to take over from Oudinot and then, despite having only 58,000 men as compared with Bernadotte's 125,000, push on for Berlin. Perhaps Ney would drive back the renegade Bernadotte, link with Davout, at present inactive in Hamburg, and trample on Prussia, then rejoin Napoleon for a great offensive in the south.

Ney went to Wittenberg, took command of the Army of Berlin (3 September) and advanced northwards. He was held up by Tauentzien at Zahna (5 September) but, reinforced by Bertrand (IV Corps), pushed the Prussians back to Jüterbog. On the following day he suffered disaster at the hands of Bülow and Tauentzien at the Battle of Dennewitz. He had under him Bertrand's, Reynier's and Oudinot's corps. Bertrand cooperated loyally, Reynier simply disregarded his orders, and Oudinot showed plainly enough that he resented being superseded. Ney lost 10,000 killed and wounded and 13,000 prisoners – mainly Germans – and 83 guns. He wrote to Berthier, 'I can't go on repeating it is almost impossible to make General Reynier obey.' He withdrew on Torgau and was in fact lucky to break clear.

During the rest of September, neither side succeeded in mounting an operation that had any real significance. Schwarzenberg was frustrated from striking a blow towards Leipzig and Napoleon's communications with France, and Blücher pushed Macdonald back towards Dresden. Napoleon's young and hungry infantry, lacking the stamina for frequent forced marches, were insufficiently mobile for him to take full advantage of his central position.

The autumn weeks slipped by and still the Emperor had not been able to achieve the decisive victory that he needed. Clinging to the line of the Elbe, he showed a bold front, but his communications were uncertain, and with the Austrians in Bohemia outflanking the line of the Elbe, his strategic situation was becoming unsound. To retreat to the Saale was to abandon Saxony. The probable effect of such a move on his other German allies, who lay between his army and the Rhine, was all too predictable.

The principal event of the month was diplomatic: The Treaty of Töplitz, signed on 9 September. It was another triumph for the skilled diplomatist Prince Metternich. Under the terms of the Treaty it was agreed that Austria and Prussia should be given back the dominions lost in 1805 and 1806; the House of Brunswick-Lüneberg was to be restored to its former territories, and the Allies, cooperating in friendly fashion, were to decide the fate of the Grand Duchy of Warsaw. Napoleon's Confederation of the Rhine was to be dissolved, but the independence of its member states was guaranteed. Bavaria and Württemberg now knew that the fall of Napoleon need not necessarily spell their own destruction. The first fruit of the Treaty was the defection of Bavaria from the French cause. By the Treaty of Ried (8 October) Bavaria joined the Allies. The immediate military result was that Prince Reuss's Austrian corps, which had been watching the Bavarian General Wrede, was able to cease doing so; instead they joined up, posing a new threat to the French lines of communications. The Bavarians still serving with the Grande Armée now took the homeward road.

Napoleon's strategic position was rapidly deteriorating. He at last accepted that he would have to abandon, temporarily, the east bank of the Elbe. He concentrated the greater part of the Grande Armée at Dresden, a position in which he was still dangerously far to the east. To the north Wallmoden (whose army included the 2nd Battalion of the 73rd Foot, the only British battalion to fight in Germany in 1813) defeated part of Davout's command at Gohrde (19 September); this kept the French from Magdeburg, gave the Allies a foothold on the west bank of Elbe, and encouraged the Hanoverians and the Brunswickers to take up arms with the other Allies. At the end of October, Davout fell back to Hamburg. Every passing day saw recruits replenish the ranks of the Austrians and Prussians. From Russia the Army of Reserve, 60,000 men under Bennigsen, was approaching. No such reinforcement could be expected by the French. Augereau (IX Corps) and Milhaud's cavalry moved up, harassed by the Hetman Platov and Maurice Lichtenstein's division, but they numbered only some 20,000.

On 26 and 27 September the Allies began to close for the kill. The French were clearly ripe for the decisive battle that would drive them out of Germany. Even so, the Allies nearly made a mistake that could have had fatal consequences. As they closed in from the north and south, timing was vital or their armies could be attacked and defeated separately. Napoleon in fact nearly succeeded in doing so, but Blücher, pressing on with his usual immense drive, frustrated him – as he was to do again two years later at Waterloo.

The Allies intended to concentrate behind the River Saale so that by interposing between Napoleon and France they would compel the Emperor to fight. Indifferently served by his cavalry, Napoleon was uncertain of the Allies' movements. By 3 October Blücher had reached the confluence of the Elbe and the Black Elster with 65,000 men. Opposed by Bertrand (IV Corps), Yorck's Prussians forced a passage, though not

The Hetman Platov, who in September 1813 with his Cossacks
harassed Napoleon's movements in Germany.

without loss. Bertrand fell back on Düben and
Bitterfeld, 30 miles to the south, joining hands with
Reynier (VII Corps). The latter had not been able to
prevent Bernadotte from crossing at Rosslau. The
Armies of the North and of Silesia, having gained
the west bank of the Elbe, pushed forward and
linked up between the Mulde and the Saale in order
to menace Leipzig from the north. Meanwhile
Schwarzenberg, who had begun his advance on 26
September, was approaching from the south.

Napoleon remained in Dresden. Every day
from 25 September to 1 October he went out to
review the troops concentrated in the area. Then at
6 am on the 7th he quit Dresden for the last time.
Unwilling to evacuate his base entirely, he left
Gouvion-Saint-Cyr (XIV Corps) and General
Mouton with the remnants of I Corps to hang on to
the city. Now the Emperor made another attempt
to drive back Blücher and Bernadotte. He began by
attacking Tauentzien, but the steady advance of
Schwarzenberg against the 40,000 men left under
Murat to cover Leipzig compelled Napoleon to give
orders (on 12 October) for his main body to return
there. He arrived himself on 14 October. By this
time Schwarzenberg had driven Murat right into
the outskirts of the city. There was fighting around
Wachau and Liebertwolkwitz to the south, and
though the Allies were repulsed the French
counter-attack came to nothing. By the 15th Napoleon's concentration was still incomplete. He had
something like 175,000 men in and around Leipzig,
but one of Ney's divisions had not yet come in, nor
had Reynier.

Schwarzenberg outnumbered the French,
but there was still a chance for Napoleon to snatch
victory before Blücher and Bernadotte threw their
forces into the balance. On the evening of the 15th

Blücher was near Gross Kügel, 12 miles away.
Bernadotte was 20 miles further north. The Emperor, who did not believe that they could intervene next day, spent the evening preparing to
deal with Schwarzenberg on the 16th. He concentrated every available man south of the city.
But he had bargained without the tireless energy of
Blücher.

On the morning of the 16th Marmont (VI
Corps) was about to move from between Breiten-
feld and Möckern to Liebertwolkwitz in order to
support the Emperor's grand attack on the Army of
Bohemia. He found, however, that Blücher was
already pressing in on him. He was compelled to
turn about and face him, with his right flank at
Widderitz and his left at Möckern.

Meanwhile Schwarzenberg was advancing
along both banks of the Elster and the Pleisse. On
his left Gyulai pushed down the line of the Markranstädt – Lindenau road with the object of
joining Blücher and cutting the French line of
retreat through Lützen to Erfurt and Mainz. On
Gyulai's right Merveldt and Lichtenstein were to
cross the Pleisse at Connewitz in order to turn the
French right.

The main front of the Army of Bohemia ran
from the Pleisse on the left to the Kolmberg, an
isolated hill on the French left. The corps of Kleist,
Prince Eugen of Württemberg, Gortchakov and
Klenau were in the first line, with the Prussian and
Russian Guard in reserve. The Army numbered
more than 120,000 men.

The Allies made some progress but Poniatowski, Victor and Lauriston hung on obstinately
to the villages of Connewitz, Wachau and Liebertwolkwitz. By noon the Emperor had prepared his
counterstroke. Macdonald, coming up on the

BATTLE OF LEIPZIG 16 OCTOBER 1813

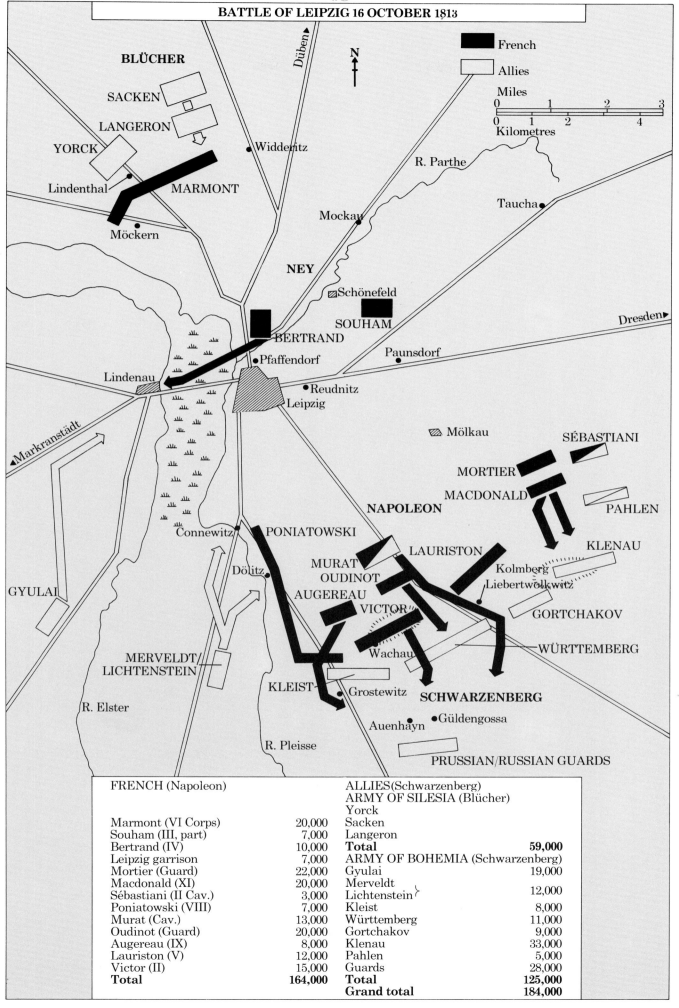

FRENCH (Napoleon)		ALLIES (Schwarzenberg)	
		ARMY OF SILESIA (Blücher)	
		Yorck	
Marmont (VI Corps)	20,000	Sacken	
Souham (III, part)	7,000	Langeron	
Bertrand (IV)	10,000	**Total**	**59,000**
Leipzig garrison	7,000	ARMY OF BOHEMIA (Schwarzenberg)	
Mortier (Guard)	22,000	Gyulai	19,000
Macdonald (XI)	20,000	Merveldt	
Sébastiani (II Cav.)	3,000	Lichtenstein	12,000
Poniatowski (VIII)	7,000	Kleist	8,000
Murat (Cav.)	13,000	Württemberg	11,000
Oudinot (Guard)	20,000	Gortchakov	9,000
Augereau (IX)	8,000	Klenau	33,000
Lauriston (V)	12,000	Pahlen	5,000
Victor (II)	15,000	Guards	28,000
Total	**164,000**	**Total**	**125,000**
		Grand total	**184,000**

French left, released Augereau who moved into line between Poniatowski and Victor. The Young Guard came up to support Lauriston. Drouot, the general of artillery, massed a formidable battery east of Wachau, and Murat concentrated the cavalry for one his great charges, to be directed against the Allied centre.

The counter-attack began well. Macdonald, supported by Mortier, stormed the Swedish redoubt at the Kolmberg with the bayonet, and compelled Klenau to fall back. Augereau drove Kleist out of Grostewitz. The Young Guard stormed Auenhayn. It was only with difficulty that Gortchakov held Lauriston's attack on the Galgenberg, a low feature just west of the village of Liebertwolkwitz.

It was about 3 o'clock when Murat led forward his 12,000 cavalry. He charged through the gap between the corps of Gortchakov and Württemberg, rode over some Russian cavalry, and captured the Allied batteries near Güldengossa. In this crisis Schwarzenberg used his reserves to good purpose. Austrian troops moved up taking the pressure off Kleist and regaining some of the ground taken by Augereau. The cavalry of the Prussian and Russian Guards counter-charged the French cavalry who, their horses blown, and their leader, Latour-Maubourg, severely wounded, fell back. A Russian grenadier division came up to support Württemberg, and drive Victor out of Auenhayn. Klenau, who had succeeded in rallying his men, was able to prevent Macdonald coming round his flank. Evening found the French back on their start lines. It was not only Schwarzenberg's skilful use of his reserves that had saved the Army of Bohemia. Blücher's Army of Silesia had robbed the French on the southern front of the support they had needed and expected from the north of the city.

Napoleon, as we have seen, had not anti-

The picture shows the fighting around Wachau,
on the left,
during the first day.
In the centre a French marshal, possibly Poniatowski,
is receiving a report.
On the right a badly wounded high-ranking officer,
perhaps Latour-Maubourg, is being carried
on an improvised stretcher made from two muskets,
and a surgeon, carrying a box with his instruments,
is running across to him.
(If the officer is indeed Latour-Maubourg,
he is about to have a leg amputated.)

cipated an attack by Blücher on the 16th. He had intended that Marmont should support Macdonald during the counter-attack, but Marmont had not been able to do so; instead he had to cling desperately to Möckern and Widderitz in the north. Ney, commanding in that sector, had sent Bertrand off towards Liebertwolkwitz instead of Marmont, but he too failed to arrive. Gyulai's corps had begun to press on the Lindenau suburb, threatening to cut the French line of retreat, and Bertrand had to be diverted there. Next Souham (III Corps) was sent to support Macdonald, but before he could join him he was summoned to the rescue of Marmont.

Marmont's corps, outnumbered by three to one, fought nobly against Yorck, Sacken and Langeron. Lindenthal fell, Möckern and Widderitz changed hands several times. A division of III Corps, commanded by Delmas, came up and sustained Marmont's right. When night fell the French were holding Möckern, but the corps had

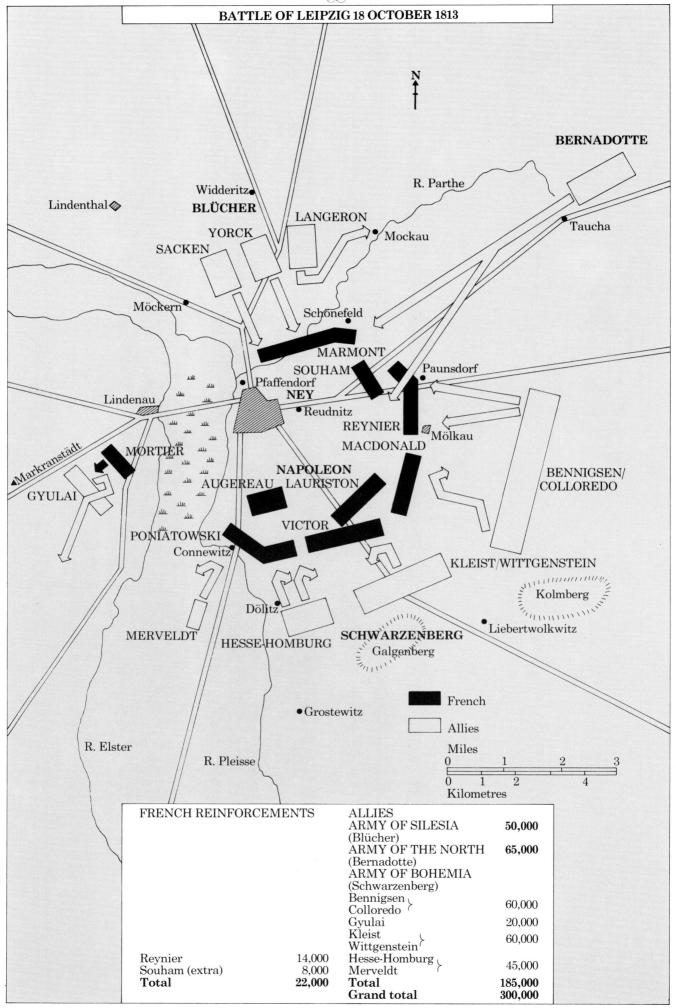

BATTLE OF LEIPZIG 18 OCTOBER 1813

N

BERNADOTTE

R. Parthe

Widderitz

Lindenthal

BLÜCHER

LANGERON

Mockau

Taucha

YORCK

SACKEN

Möckern

Schönefeld

MARMONT

SOUHAM

Paunsdorf

Pfaffendorf

Lindenau

NEY

Reudnitz

REYNIER

Mölkau

MACDONALD

MORTIER

BENNIGSEN/
COLLOREDO

Markranstädt

GYULAI

NAPOLEON

AUGEREAU LAURISTON

VICTOR

PONIATOWSKI

Connewitz

KLEIST/WITTGENSTEIN

Kolmberg

Liebertwolkwitz

MERVELDT

HESSE-HOMBURG

SCHWARZENBERG

Dölitz

Galgenberg

Grostewitz

■ French

□ Allies

Miles

0   1   2   3

0   1   2   4

Kilometres

R. Elster

R. Pleisse

FRENCH REINFORCEMENTS		ALLIES	
		ARMY OF SILESIA (Blücher)	**50,000**
		ARMY OF THE NORTH (Bernadotte)	**65,000**
		ARMY OF BOHEMIA (Schwarzenberg)	
		Bennigsen Colloredo	60,000
		Gyulai	20,000
		Kleist Wittgenstein	60,000
Reynier	14,000	Hesse-Homburg Merveldt	45,000
Souham (extra)	8,000		
Total	**22,000**	**Total**	**185,000**
		Grand total	**300,000**

A contemporary cartoon illustrates how the Saxons
upset the balance of forces by defecting to the Allies.

lost 8,000 men, and in the dark Marmont fell back across the Parthe, abandoning 53 guns. To the south-west of the city, Merveldt and Lichtenstein failed to cross the Pleisse and the former was captured. Bertrand drove Gyulai out of Lindenau, and so kept open Napoleon's line of retreat.

The day's fighting had cost the French more than 25,000 men and the Allies perhaps 37,000. A dozen generals were among the French casualties. They included two of the cavalry corps commanders, Latour-Maubourg, who lost a leg, and Pajol (V Corps) who was severely injured when his horse fell. The 17th was a quiet day. Both sides spent the time reorganizing, but the Allies also brought up reinforcements. Colloredo's Austrians marched in during the evening. Bennigsen was drawing near and the Crown Prince of Sweden had reached Halle – though he was not displaying any excess of zeal.

The battle on the 16th had been indecisive, except to indicate that it was time for the French to go. The Allies now outnumbered them by three to one. The implications of a retreat were, however, fearful; Dresden, Hamburg, the garrisons on the Vistula, the Oder, and in Germany would be left to their fate. If the Emperor retreated, could he stop before the Rhine? Hoping against hope for a miracle, the Emperor decided to fight on. He pulled in his forces so that they formed an irregular semi-circle round the south and east of the city, with the Guard and the cavalry in reserve, and Lauriston in support of Victor and Macdonald. To the north Marmont faced Blücher. To the west Bertrand covered the Lindenau suburb, his outposts facing Gyulai on the Lützen – Weissenfels road. To face the huge Allied concentration in this way, with the city and the River Elster at his back, was an act of desperation.

Schwarzenberg kept his men under his hand. Instead of reinforcing Gyulai, and thereby cutting Napoleon's line of retreat, he called back one of his divisions. It seems he suspected that the French might attempt to break out not to the west but towards the Elbe, through the gap which the cautious Bernadotte was supposed to be closing with the Army of the North.

The battle began at about 7 am on the 18th. The Army of Bohemia put in a general assault along its whole front, made some progress against stout resistance and then was brought to a virtual standstill. Hesse-Homburg took Dölitz and Dösen while, for the French, Poniatowski's Poles hung on to Connewitz. At Probstheida Victor repulsed Kleist and Wittgenstein. Macdonald held General

The bridge over the Elster is prematurely blown,
stranding thousands of retreating Frenchmen
on the wrong side of the river.

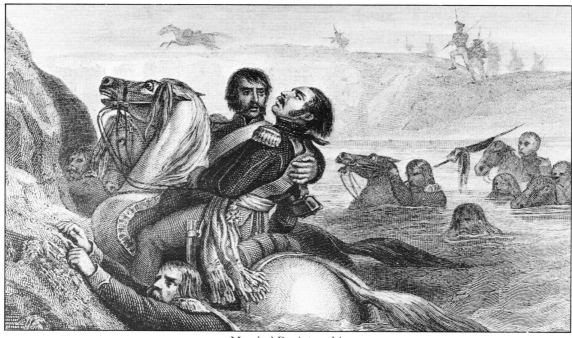

Marshal Poniatowski,
drowned in his vain attempt to cross the Elster.

Klenau until Bennigsen reinforced him and took Holzhausen. Reynier's Saxon division held on to Mölkau and Paunsdorf.

In the north the Army of Silesia, less Langeron's corps, which Blücher had sent to help Bernadotte, drove Marmont's outposts from Gohlis and Pfaffendorf, but made little further progress. Blücher did succeed in getting into Reudnitz, but reinforcements sent in by Napoleon drove him out again. Thus the Army of Silesia, as well as the Army of Bohemia, was held.

It fell to the Army of the North to strike the decisive blow. It was at about noon that Bernadotte's advanced guard reached Taucha, and soon they joined Langeron, who had crossed the Parthe at Mockau. Langeron advanced against Ney's left flank at Schönefeld, and Winzingerode pushed on towards Paunsdorf in order to close the breach between Blücher and Schwarzenberg by linking with Bennigsen. The latter now resumed his attack. Bubna's Austrians, moving forward, were pleasantly surprised to see their opponents throwing down their arms – the Saxons of Reynier's corps were changing sides, and their example was swiftly followed by a Württemberg cavalry brigade of 1,500 sabres. Reynier's remaining division gave way and Bubna took possession of Paunsdorf in the east.

Ney strove to restore the situation, and regained Paunsdorf for a time, but the Army of the

Bellangé's view of a dispirited French soldier:
'J'n'en joue plus!'

North was too strong for him. Still, he managed to withdraw what remained of Reynier's corps. Nansouty brought up the Guard cavalry to Ney's support, but Bülow from the east pushed the French back on Reudnitz, and Langeron, after several attempts, captured Schönefeld. Everywhere the French were being driven back into Leipzig. It was fortunate for them that Mortier with two divisions of the Young Guard had meanwhile got the better of Gyulai and opened the road westwards.

Before noon that day Napoleon realized that the odds against him were too great and that he must go back. Fighting with magnificent courage and determination the French still held Leipzig

when night fell. Napoleon issued his orders for the retreat verbally; no trace of written orders has remained. At about 2 o'clock on the morning of the 19th the retreat began, but after three days of fighting it was understandably hurried and ill-organized. All roads converged on the one causeway across the marshes where the Rivers Elster and Pleisse flowed together in a maze of waterways. As the columns clashed, each exaggerating the peril from the enemy behind, the confusion became indescribable. The art of traffic control over defiles at that time was little understood. Then the bridge over the Elster was blown prematurely, isolating the rearguard under Macdonald, Poniatowski and Reynier in the eastern suburbs on the far side of the

The *Grande Armée* retreats through Saxony.

break. For the rearguard the mishap was fatal. They fought desperately to escape but without avail.

It is easy to censure the bridge commander, but in a retreat closely followed up by the enemy he is placed in an impossible situation. Either he blows the bridge too soon, as at Leipzig, or he leaves it too late, and the bridge is captured intact. The bridge over the Elster was not the first or the last to be blown up at the wrong time.

Poniatowski, already wounded, was drowned in the Elster; Lauriston and Reynier fell into the hands of the Allies, and Macdonald managed to escape by swimming. His men were not so lucky. They called to him, 'Monsieur le Maréchal, save your men! Save your children!' They threw themselves into the water rather than be taken, and many were swept away. Macdonald later said, 'I could do nothing for them'. Overcome by rage, indignation, fury, I wept.' Soaking wet, he walked three leagues to Markranstädt where he caught up with the Emperor and his staff. 'He was seated at a table, a map spread before him, and his head on his hand. With tears I related what had happened . . . I ended by saying that the losses of the army in men and *matériel* were immense, and not a moment should be lost in collecting the remains, and making for the Rhine.' Napoleon did not relish home truths at the best of times. 'Go and get some rest,' he said. It was cold comfort to a man who had recently lost his corps.

Marmont also had a rough time crossing the bridge. Two officers of the 88th of the Line carved him a path across. He recounted, 'My chief-of-staff and his deputy were hit at my side; four aides-de-camp were killed, wounded or captured; seven staff

officers were either killed or wounded. As for myself, I had a bullet wound in the hand, a contusion on my left arm, a bullet through my hat and another in my clothes, and four horses killed or wounded under me. Of the three servants who accompanied me, two were wounded and had their horses killed.'

The French generals, disillusioned though they were, had paid with their persons. Ney was wounded sufficiently severely to be authorized to return to France, which he did on 23 October. Thirteen generals of division were among the casualties on the 18th, and 25 generals of brigade were hit on 18 October and 11 on the 19th. The loss of so many senior officers added to the confusion in the retreating army, which suffered 50,000 men taken prisoner, 20,000 of them wounded, and the capture of 250 guns.

The Allied losses were severe. They have

Allied troops at the Battle of Hanau.

On 12 November 1813 German market traders bring much-needed produce
to a newly liberated town.

been estimated as: Austrians, 15,000, Prussians, 16,000, and Russians, 22,000, making a total of 53,000. More important, however, were the consequences of Leipzig. Napoleon had now to go back to France to consolidate his position. Meanwhile all Western Germany rose against him. In a surge of patriotic enthusiasm Berg, Westphalia and other principalities followed the example of Bavaria. By the Treaty of Fulda (2 November) Metternich guaranteed Württemberg's sovereignty in return for a contingent of 12,000 men. Baden, Hesse-Darmstadt and Nassau lost no time in concluding similar conventions. The dispossessed rulers of Brunswick, Hanover, Electoral Hesse and Oldenburg returned to their thrones.

The somewhat inchoate military machine of the Allies was attempting meanwhile to exploit its strategic advantage. Klenau and Bennigsen were detailed to mop up the French garrisons along the Elbe at Dresden, Torgau, Wittenberg and Magdeburg. Kleist and Winzingerode were directed to take Erfurt. Bernadotte moved north to support Wallmoden against Davout, whose communications with the Emperor were now severed. Early in November Dresden and Torgau surrendered. Before the end of the year Danzig, Stettin and Wittenberg were in Allied hands. In January 1814 Napoleon's Danish allies, pursued into Holstein by Wallmoden, concluded the Treaty of Kiel.

On 23 October Napoleon reached Erfurt where he endeavoured to restore some order to what remained of his *Grande Armée*. Two days later he resumed his retreat. Schwarzenberg and Blücher were following up slowly, but if they were to intercept him he must first be delayed by Wrede's Bavarians and Prince Reuss's Austrians; advanc-

ing from Anspach by Würzburg, the Bavarian and Austrian contingent reached Hanau by 28 October, blocking the main road back to France. Wrede, commanding 40,000 men, held the line of the River Kinzig, with Hanau at his back. The situation looked black for the French, but the resilience of the remnants of the *Grande Armée* was amazing. Drouot massed a great battery, and Nansouty and Sébastiani led all the available cavalry in a massive charge which beat back the Allied left. Wrede retired across the river. On the 31st Napoleon sent in the corps of Bertrand and Marmont, which fought with truly Gallic fervour and gave time for Oudinot (Young Guard) to get around Wrede's flank. On 2 November the wreck of the *Grande Armée* was struggling back across the Rhine at Mainz.

A properly coordinated army under a single chief might well have exploited the victory at Leipzig to more advantage than did the Allies of 1813. While there was no hurry to reduce the French garrisons in Germany, there was good reason to intercept Napoleon east of the Rhine, at least so far as Blücher and the Tsar were concerned (the Austrians at this stage were by no means certain that they wished to unseat Napoleon).

Leipzig, the Battle of the Nations, was the biggest battle of the Napoleonic Wars, bigger than Borodino and bigger than Waterloo. Its very vastness had posed the Allies the same sort of problems over control and the passage of orders which had earlier vexed Napoleon. That they triumphed was due in no small part to the efforts of the brave, modest and tactful Schwarzenberg. On the eve of the battle he wrote to his wife, 'When I look out of my window and see the countless watch-

fires outstretched before me, and when I consider that I face the greatest military commander of our age, and one of the greatest of all time, a veritable emperor of battles, then, my dear Nani, I must admit that I feel my shoulders too weak and will collapse under the gigantic task which weighs upon them. But when I gaze up at the stars, I recall that He who controls them has also marked out my course.' Schwarzenberg, whom we may call the Eisenhower of the coalition forces, proved equal to the task of making them run smoothly. At a banquet a year or two after the battle Blücher proposed a toast to 'the Commander-in-Chief who had three monarchs at his headquarters and still managed to beat the enemy.'

Napoleon, with a courage perhaps never surpassed, refused to capitulate and the Allies swept on towards the Rhine. In the approaching campaign to save France – and himself – he was to touch new heights as a general. He still had not been defeated in the field; this was not to happen to him until the fatal day of Waterloo. In Russia, in his own view, he had been conquered by the weather, at Leipzig by the treachery of the Saxons and the stupidity of an engineer officer. Such rationalizations might strain credulity, but they allowed him to continue to believe in his star.

As he withdrew to France, commanding marshals and generals whose one desire was to enjoy their wealth and estates in peace, the per-

Les Grognards (the Old Sweats).

sonal ascendancy that enabled him to continue the struggle became all the more remarkable. He opened peace negotiations that were to continue for much of the rest of the struggle, but he never seriously contemplated abandoning his conquests while he had cannon and muskets that would be fired at his command. Although the new Allied peace proposals were astonishingly liberal, taking into account his reduced military capacity, he rejected them. He also thought it discreet to throw doubt on the sincerity of the Allies, for he feared their offers of peace might lessen the French will to resist. For Napoleon the truth was always what it suited him to have others believe.

He expected that his garrisons in Germany and along the main approaches to France would cause his enemies to dissipate their forces with lengthy and unnecessary sieges. But by his own example he had trained the Allies too well in the virtues of concentration and speed. They now blockaded the French-held fortresses with second-line troops and continued the war through the depths of winter. In January 1814, as the Allied invasion of France proceeded without a check, Napoleon had once again to take the field, While he might greet this turn of events by boldly raising his glass to toast the advance to the Vistula that he yearned for, his marshals were lukewarm. He, however, was not to be subdued without a struggle worthy of his genius.

Chronology
1813
4 December: Allied Declaration of Frankfurt. Napoleon begins mobilizing National Guard.
1814
1 January: Blücher crosses the Rhine.

4 January: Napoleon rejects Allied peace terms.

25 January: He leaves Paris to join his Army.

27 January: He attacks Russians at St-Dizier.

29 January: He captures Brienne. Murat declares for the Allies.

1 February: Battle of La Rothière.

7 February: Napoleon again rejects Allied peace terms.

10 February: Olsufiev routed at Champaubert.

11 February: Sacken and Yorck defeated at Montmirail.

14 February: Blücher defeated at Vauchamps.

18 February: Battle of Montereau. Schwarzenberg withdraws.

26 February: Augereau advances on Geneva.

27 February: Wellington beats Soult at Orthez. Schwarzenberg defeats Oudinot at Bar-sur-Aube.

1 March: Treaty of Chaumont; Allies pledge no separate peace. Blücher checked at River Ourcq.

3 March: French surrender Soissons.

7 March: Napoleon wins Battle of Craonne.

9 March: He is checked at Laon.

13 March: He captures Reims.

19 March: Peace negotiations at Châtillon finally broken off.

21–22 March: Battle of Arcis-sur-Aube.

25 March: Battles at Fère-Champenoise.

26 March: Augereau abandons Lyon.

27 March: Napoleon routs Winzingerode.

30 March: Battle of Montmartre: Paris capitulates.

4 April: Marmont's corps defects to Allies.

12 April: Napoleon abdicates unconditionally.

13 April: He attempts suicide, but recovers.

4 May: He disembarks at Elba.

PART II

1814

THE FRENCH CAMPAIGN

The Emperor on the march with his staff officers, probably to
Montmirail. The painting, by Jean Meissonier, shows the
appalling state of the roads at that time.

CHAPTER 6
THE ALLIES INVADE FRANCE

O n 25 January 1814 at Châlons-sur-Marne the bleak winter night had closed in on the empty streets. Then towards midnight came the clop-clopping of many hooves. A mud-splashed convoy of five coaches escorted by a handful of Chasseurs of the Guard, reeling in their saddles from fatigue, clattered over the cobbles and drew up at the Prefecture. As the occupants of the coaches prepared to alight the thunder of hooves increased.

A trooper of the Empress's Dragoons inspects the tip of his sabre.

Rank on rank the cavalry of the 1st Division of the Imperial Guard rode by to seek their billets. Out of the second coach stepped a short, square, somewhat corpulent man of 44. A long plain grey overcoat flapped about the ankles of his black riding boots and as usual he wore an unornamented black cocked hat transversely on his head; his large deep-set eyes veiled a fire that few dared brave. As he walked into the house he carried with him an air of effortless, unchallengeable authority. Napoleon, on a purely statistical basis of battles fought and won the greatest soldier of any age, was about to take the field for the last but one of his many campaigns; almost inevitably it was to end in failure, nevertheless it was to be one of his greatest.

He had left Paris early on the 25th, broken his fast at Château-Thierry and driven on to Châlons. Now he listened attentively with no sign of weariness while his senior officers told him their latest news. Their information was contradictory and confused; he learned to his annoyance that Marshal Victor had evacuated St-Dizier and pulled back 20 miles to Vitry-le-François. He dictated a testy letter to his Chief-of-Staff, Marshal Berthier, 'I ordered him to hold it and it is not with a rearguard, every man ready to retire, that a position is held.' However, it was no great matter. He proposed to concentrate most of his army south of Vitry and he thoughtfully instructed Berthier, 'Requisition two or three hundred thousand bottles of wine and *eau-de-vie* so that we can make an issue today and tomorrow. Never mind if it is all champagne; it's better we should drink it rather than the enemy.' Then he dictated the orders for the battle he intended to fight on the morrow.

'Châlons-sur-Marne, 26 January, 9.45 in the morning.

The Emperor orders that the Duke of Belluno [Victor] takes up a position as close as possible to St Dizier across the St Dizier-Vitry road with his right flank resting on the Marne.

The Duke of Ragusa [Marmont] will deploy astride the main road half a league or a league [2,000–4,000 metres] behind the Duke of Belluno and remain ready to move instantly.

The Prince of the Moskva [Ney] with the 1st and 2nd Divisions of the Young Guard will take up a position across the road half a league or a league behind Marmont . . .

General Lefebvre with his cavalry [about 2,500 sabres] will take up a position behind the Prince of the Moskva saddled and ready astride the road.

Imperial Headquarters will open this evening at a village behind the Duke of Belluno.

The Army will be informed that the Emperor intends to attack tomorrow morning.

All baggage not required for the battle will be dumped between Vitry and Châlons.

The artillery is to be deployed ready for action.

Bread and any brandy will be procured and distributed either at Vitry or where obtained.

Localities will be prepared for dealing with casualties.

A reconnaissance will be made of the River Ornain and care will be taken to ensure the good condition of the road bridge and that at Vitry-le-Brûlé; a third will be constructed on a possible line of retreat.'

As couriers departed with the orders Napoleon called for his coach. Before 4 pm he was in Vitry-le-François. The Battle for France was about to begin. After his disastrous withdrawal from Germany he had hoped the Allies would delay until the spring, but he had been granted no respite. However, he was confident that the unlikely alliance would fall apart from the mutual jealousies and suspicions of its leaders. Tsar Alexander thought only of revenging his burnt Moscow and dreamed of dictating terms in a prostrate Paris. Blücher nursed a similar ambition; but his sovereign, Frederick William III of Prussia, remembering the humiliating defeats of Jena and Auerstädt, disliked the prospect of invading France and giving the old magician a chance to perform yet another miracle and win back all he had lost. The guileful Metternich and his Emperor, Francis I of Austria, thought the French Revolution the real enemy. Napoleon had tamed it and was more likely to control the turbulent French than the Bourbons; it remained to persuade him to leave his neighbours in peace. Once France was crippled, Russia would swallow what remained of Poland and Prussia would gobble up Saxony. Francis himself wondered if it was not lacking in family spirit to wage too harsh a war against the husband of his daughter, Marie-Louise, who had already presented Napoleon with a son. Castlereagh for Britain wished to preserve the balance of power in Europe, and like Metternich had no desire to encourage republicanism in France or to see an overmighty Russia.

At Frankfurt in December, largely at the instance of Austria, the Allies had offered Napoleon the 'natural boundaries of France, the Rhine, the Alps and the Pyrenees.' Napoleon rejected the offer and on 4 January wrote to General Caulaincourt, the plenipotentiary he had appointed to negotiate on his behalf, 'I think it is doubtful if the Allies are negotiating in good faith and that England seeks peace. I myself desire it but only on honourable and lasting terms. France without its natural boundaries, without Ostend, without Anvers [Antwerp] could no longer take its place among the other powers of Europe . . . Do they wish to confine France to its ancient borders? They are mistaken if they think the miseries of war can make the nation desire such a peace . . . Italy is intact and the Viceroy [Eugène de Beauharnais] has a fine army. In a little more than a week I shall open a campaign even before my reinforcements from Spain have time to arrive. The depredations of the Cossacks will drive the people to arms and double our numbers. If the nation supports me the enemy marches to his doom. If fortune betrays me my resolution is taken; I will degrade neither the nation nor myself by accepting dishonourable terms. You must find out what Metternich intends. It is not in the interests of Austria to carry things through to a finish.'

As on the afternoon of 26 January his coach rumbled towards Vitry, Napoleon was far from despair. He could still trust to his star. A miracle such as the sudden death of the Tsar, as had saved Frederick the Great, might enable him yet to live like that monarch to an honoured old age. Despite the odds he still felt an inner certainty that he would triumph, that his destiny would bring him through to victory in the end if he would but trust to it.

FRANCE IN JANUARY 1814

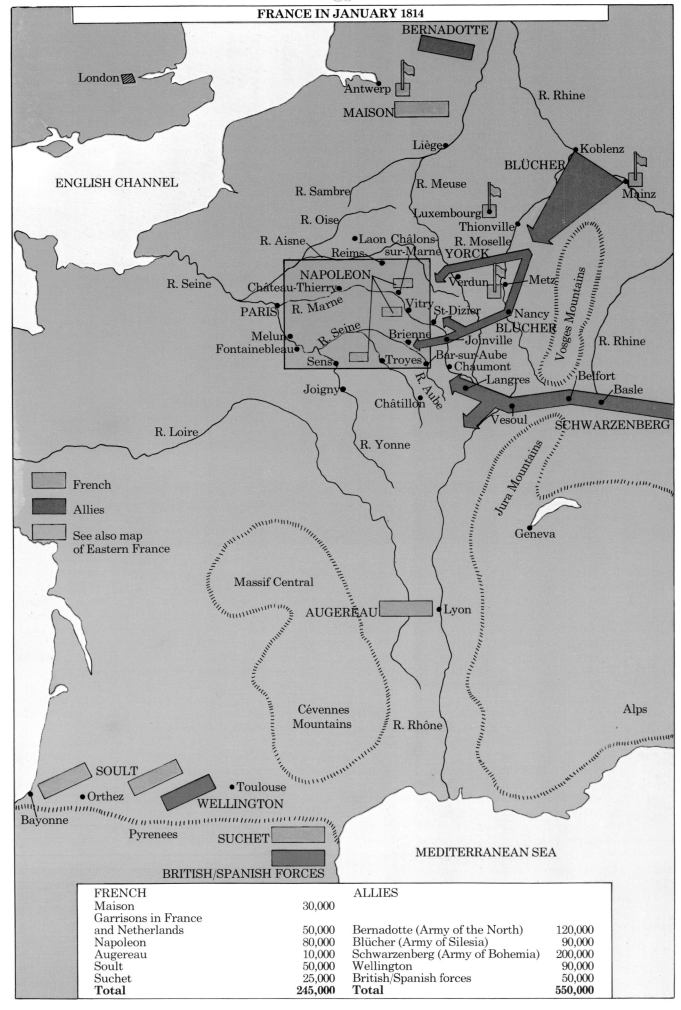

BERNADOTTE

London

Antwerp

MAISON

ENGLISH CHANNEL

R. Rhine

Liège

Koblenz

R. Meuse

BLÜCHER

R. Sambre

Luxembourg

R. Oise

Thionville

Mainz

R. Aisne

Laon Châlons-
sur-Marne

R. Moselle

Reims

YORCK

NAPOLEON

Verdun Metz

R. Seine

Château-Thierry

Vitry

R. Marne

St-Dizier

PARIS

Nancy

BLÜCHER

Melun

R. Seine

Brienne

Vosges Mountains

Fontainebleau

Joinville

Bar-sur-Aube

R. Rhine

Sens

Troyes

Chaumont

Belfort

Joigny

Langres

Basle

Châtillon

Vesoul

SCHWARZENBERG

R. Aube

R. Yonne

Jura Mountains

Geneva

French

Allies

See also map
of Eastern France

Massif Central

AUGEREAU Lyon

Cévennes
Mountains

Alps

R. Rhône

SOULT

Orthez

Toulouse

Bayonne

WELLINGTON

Pyrenees

SUCHET

MEDITERRANEAN SEA

BRITISH/SPANISH FORCES

FRENCH		ALLIES	
Maison	30,000		
Garrisons in France and Netherlands	50,000	Bernadotte (Army of the North)	120,000
Napoleon	80,000	Blücher (Army of Silesia)	90,000
Augereau	10,000	Schwarzenberg (Army of Bohemia)	200,000
Soult	50,000	Wellington	90,000
Suchet	25,000	British/Spanish forces	50,000
Total	**245,000**	**Total**	**550,000**

Allied troops in Leipzig.

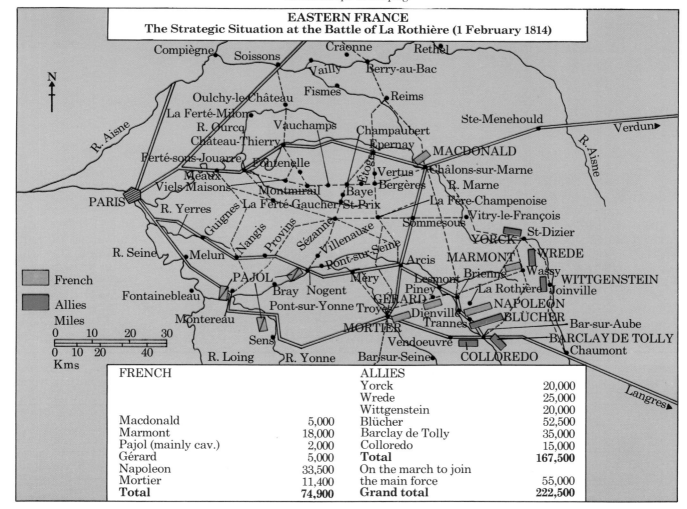

EASTERN FRANCE
The Strategic Situation at the Battle of La Rothière (1 February 1814)

FRENCH		ALLIES	
		Yorck	20,000
		Wrede	25,000
		Wittgenstein	20,000
Macdonald	5,000	Blücher	52,500
Marmont	18,000	Barclay de Tolly	35,000
Pajol (mainly cav.)	2,000	Colloredo	15,000
Gérard	5,000	**Total**	**167,500**
Napoleon	33,500	On the march to join	
Mortier	11,400	the main force	55,000
Total	**74,900**	**Grand total**	**222,500**

Top
Russian grenadiers, infantry of the line and light infantry.
On the left several grenadiers wearing various forms of headdress are singing and being accompanied on a miniature balalaika.
At this time Blücher's army was composed almost exclusively of Russians.

Above
The Battle of Brienne, fought on 29 January 1814.
The French army is advancing along the line of the avenue towards Brienne and the château.
On the right a long column of infantry is deploying from column of route
into column of divisions or companies prior to launching an attack.
On the left another column is advancing with skirmishers guarding its flank.
Some light cavalry are advancing straight down the road towards the château.
One of a series of watercolours by S. Fort.

Besides, unlike Frederick he was not a legitimate monarch. During the peace that had followed the Treaty of Amiens in 1802, France had teemed with intrigues and conspiracies; royalists and republicans alike had schemed to unseat him. Would the nation tolerate a peace that threw away so much that had been gained at so heavy a cost in blood?

There may have been a further, unacknowledged, motive for continuing the struggle. Napoleon himself set little store on courtly pageantry and ceremonial. Perhaps he felt most happy in the ordered simplicity of a military camp – listening to the sounds of the drums and trumpets, the clashing of arms and the shouted words of command – while for the highest stakes in the world he played the strategic game at which he was the acknowledged supreme master.

For him, in January 1814, it was unfortunately true that half a million well-trained troops from all the major states in Europe stood poised on the frontiers of France and indeed had already pierced them, that many of his best soldiers were locked up in fortresses in Germany, in the Netherlands and on the borders of France. But one great victory and the whole ramshackle alliance of Britain and Austria, of Russia, Prussia and Sweden, of Saxony and Bavaria, of Spain and Portugal would fall apart. And even now the Prussian, Blücher, was pressing on impetuously with his Army of Silesia, well ahead of Prince Schwarzenberg and his Army of Bohemia. A quick stroke tomorrow and Paris once again would ring with the news of a new Imperial triumph, its citizens regaled by the sight of long columns of enemy prisoners.

Early on the 27th Victor attacked. A few shots were fired, then General Lanskoi with a handful of Russians disappeared. At 10 o'clock in the morning Napoleon rode into St-Dizier to the plaudits of the inhabitants. But he had used a sledgehammer to crush an egg and now all knew that he himself was once more in the field. However, he heard that Blücher had arrived at Brienne. There might yet be time. He moved swiftly after his quarry.

At Brienne Colonel Müffling, serving on Blücher's staff as Quartermaster-General, was comfortably lodged in the château that overlooked the town. Of his duties he wrote, 'I had to prepare everything relating to the great operations, quarters, encampments, marches, partial and general actions . . . all reports arriving by day or night of the enemies' movements and all depositions of deserters and prisoners or spies were immediately communicated to me. The propositions for movements and the dispositions for combats and battles emanated from me. I laid them before General Gneisenau . . . and when he approved my plans we went to the Field Marshal [Blücher] to whom I again had to state the measures proposed, map in hand . . . The Field Marshal never made any difficulties when the proposals were for an advance or an attack. But at any suggestion of a withdrawal he was apt to become angry.' Müffling possessed an unerring strategical and tactical sense, at least according to his memoirs published some 30 years later, but sometimes he had difficulty in convincing his slower-witted superiors. He had crossed the Rhine on 1 January 1814 with Blücher's Army of Silesia, which with the Army of Bohemia formed the Grand Army of the Allies under the supreme command of the Austrian General Prince Karl Philipp of Schwarzenberg. At Frankfurt, after Napoleon had rejected their terms, the Allied sovereigns drew up their plan of campaign. Initially Schwarzenberg with his army, some 200,000 strong, was to hook through Switzerland skirting the headwaters of the Rhine, thrust west through the Belfort Gap between the Vosges and Jura Mountains and debouch onto the Plateau of Langres. Once his army was concentrated there the sovereigns would discuss the next step. Blücher with his Army of Silesia on the Middle Rhine was to wait until the Army of Bohemia had entered France, then force a crossing and subsequently guard its right flank.

While Schwarzenberg departed on his complicated and circuitous journey, Blücher remained watching the iceflows on the Rhine and chafing at the delay. The rulers of the Allied powers competed to load him with decorations. The old Field-Marshal, now 71 years of age, combined the vitality of a man half his years with the tongue of a bargee. Of his decorations he exclaimed ungratefully, 'I look like an old coach horse with all this stuff and up to date it has brought me nothing.'

On New Year's Day 1814, against negligible opposition he swept over the icy Rhine, crossing simultaneously at Mannheim, Koblenz and Kaub, and scattering some weak French detachments before him. By 12 January he had completed the investment of Mainz and was blockading French garrisons at Metz, Saarlouis, Landau, Thionville and Luxemburg. On that day he wrote to Schwarzenberg, 'I can give battle with 74,000 men or on the 19th in front of Metz with 90,000.' Marmont, watching the Rhine with 10,000 men, fell back. On the 14th Blücher wrote, 'So we are off to Paris. Unless we do something foolish we shall carry all before us.' And again, 'My 50,000 Russians will follow me to the ends of the earth and my own men are unsurpassed in bravery.' The Allied army, with army corps composed of varying nationalities, was an integrated European army such as the world has seldom seen. As often happens in such circumstances, the various allies seemed to dislike each other rather more than they did the French.

Schwarzenberg, after establishing his base at Basle, made his way carefully to the Plateau of Langres, but the impatient Blücher rushed on to Nancy leaving much of his army behind him blockading the frontier fortresses. The Austrian general writing to his wife complained, 'Without placing any considerable force to guard the road from Châlons to Nancy they [Blücher and Gneisenau] rush on like mad bulls to Brienne. Regardless of their rear and flanks they do nothing but plan the fine parties they are going to enjoy in the Palais Royal.' Schwarzenberg had reason to voice his displeasure. He had started a stately and ponderous advance up the valleys of the Aube and the Marne, but the irrepressible Prussian, instead of protecting his right flank, had cut in ahead of him and now spearheaded an advance to which the Austrian had only agreed with extreme reluctance. Now, owing to his impetuosity, Blücher was in danger of becoming isolated.

However, as Blücher, Gneisenau and Müffling enjoyed the delights of the château at Brienne,

A further stage in the Battle of Brienne.
The French are closing in on the town, and some houses have already caught fire.

the disapproval of their supreme commander troubled them not at all. Their troops were almost entirely Russian and consisted of Sacken's corps and Olsufiev's detachment, also 5,000 men and 24 guns from Langeron's large corps that was still blockading fortresses near the Rhine. Blücher placed Sacken at Lesmont, some six miles to the north-west, to guard the bridge over the Aube, and quartered Olsufiev in Brienne itself. He left a small detachment at St-Dizier to safeguard the route to Nancy and the east and put another in Arcis-sur-Aube, 18 miles to the west, to secure its important bridge on the main road to Paris.

On 29 January the Cossacks, who swarmed everywhere practising their peculiar and predatory form of warfare, reported strong French columns marching on Brienne from the direction of St-Dizier. No one doubted that Napoleon led them himself. Müffling recounted, 'General Sacken received instant orders to join the Field-Marshal at Brienne. Immediately after, an officer was brought in prisoner who had been despatched from Vitry the day before with written instructions to Marshal Mortier to join Napoleon from Troyes by way of Arcis. Thus informed we stepped into the castle court and erected our telescopes to observe Napoleon's approach, as from this height we could overlook the whole plain beyond the town of Brienne to Maizières (about four miles to the north-east). Count Pahlen (who commanded the advance guard of Schwarzenberg's army) arrived from Joinville and went to station himself with his cavalry and some Jäger battalions in the plain towards Maizières, so that he covered and concealed the march of Sacken's corps from Lesmont.'

Müffling and Gneisenau estimated that without Mortier Napoleon could only muster 30,000 men and that when Sacken arrived Blücher would have as many. At about 3 o'clock as the chill evening drew on, the French guns opened fire from the direction of Maizières. Olsufiev replied with his own 24. For a while Blücher watched developments from the terrace of the château, but dinner had been announced and he found this engagement the more pressing.

In the course of a cheerful meal cannon-balls began to slam into the château walls. Blücher, who had invited the captured French officer to dine at his table, politely suggested that he should withdraw with his escort. The French officer, not to be outdone in courtesy, replied that he had no desire to leave such excellent company. A citizen of Brienne, who did not appear to share his sentiments, was visibly disconcerted when some of the panelling fell in and plaster dropped down from the ceiling. The Field-Marshal blandly inquired, 'Do you own this castle?' 'No.' 'Then you can rest easy. The castle is solidly built, the cost of repairs will not be great, and in any case you won't have to pay for them.'

Having eaten his fill, Blücher stepped out on to the terrace once more. The light was fast fading. Count Pahlen had fallen back on Brienne and Sacken's men were filing through the town. On the French left he could see some columns of the Young Guard standing in a mass without taking any precaution to cover their open left flank. By now many of the houses in Brienne were well alight and the French beginning to close in, but Blücher decided that such ineptness should not go unpenalized. Müffling galloped off to organize an

attack with some of Pahlen's cavalry. He recalled, 'We rode into the Young Guard and our right wing got as far as the reserve which stood a good way back on the road bordered by trees from Brienne to Maizières. We captured two batteries and the enemy fell into the greatest disorder; but as often happens in a cavalry fight, when all are scattered all command ceased . . . darkness put an end to the combat.'

On returning to Brienne Müffling found the château in the hands of the French. In the darkness a French infantry battalion with great dash had clambered up the ridge and carried it with the bayonet. Blücher had left hurriedly and only just in time. When he learned of the check to the French left he swore 'that fellow' should not sleep in his bed that night and directed Sacken to retake the château. Climbing up the hill in the near-freezing darkness and silhouetted against the burning houses in the town below, Sacken's men could make no impression on the defenders. The château dominated the countryside. At about 10 o'clock that night Blücher broke off the engagement and withdrew to a strong position on the heights above Trannes, about eight miles to the south. The shrewd French thrust on the château had forced him out of Brienne, but his army had suffered no crippling damage and next day the advanced columns of the Grand Army would reach him.

Napoleon had covered the 30-odd miles from St-Dizier to Brienne with remarkable speed. By the morning of 29 January his first troops arrived at Maizières. Their strength built up in the afternoon and at 3 o'clock with 10,000 men he had started to attack. He later reported to General Clarke, his Minister of War in Paris, 'Blücher has been beaten, he has lost five or six hundred prisoners and between three and four thousand men killed or wounded. Generals Forestier and Baste of the Young Guard have been killed and General Lefebvre-Desnouettes suffered a bayonet wound while charging in his usual intrepid fashion. Our loss is reckoned to be 2,000 men (he subsequently raised the estimate to 3,000). If I had veteran troops I might have done more, but with the troops I have, I am happy with what occurred. We have taken up a position two leagues [5 miles] beyond Brienne with our right on the Aube and our left on the wood. The Duke of Treviso [Mortier] is at Troyes and the Duke of Taranto [Macdonald] on the Marne. I approve of your recalling the General who from first to last has shown that he is nothing but an imbecile.' (Possibly the latter was the general who failed to discover Blücher's dispositions at St-Dizier.)

Napoleon had good reason to be pleased with his conscripts of 1813–14, the 'Marie-Louises' as they were known. They had little training, but they made up for that lack in greatness of heart. In one often-quoted incident Marmont came on a 'Marie-Louise' standing steadily in his rank under a hot fire, but with the butt of his musket grounded and making no effort to shoot back. 'Why don't you fire back?' asked the Marshal. 'I would do so gladly,' replied the conscript, 'if someone would show me how to load my musket.' Marmont quietly loaded it for him.

At Brienne Napoleon paused. He had failed in his first attempt to score a dramatic success while his foe was still dispersed. But the strategic situation had begun to crystallize. In the centre, in

Eastern France, Napoleon with about 80,000 men confronted the Allied Grand Army; the latter was about 200,000 strong and its commanders were intent on marching on Paris. In the South of France Wellington, the 'sepoy general' as Napoleon contemptuously dubbed him, must eventually overwhelm Soult, unless by diplomacy Spain could be weaned from the Alliance; but Wellington distrusted his Continental allies and was unlikely to make any damaging stroke: he could be discounted for the present. In the north the situation was radically different. Here Bernadotte, the renegade Marshal of the Empire and present Crown Prince of Sweden, commanded. Although he personally was less than lukewarm about fighting his old chief, large numbers of his troops could undoubtedly soon be free to invade France. At Lyon Augereau was organizing an army but only extremely slowly: the powerfully built former Parisian street urchin showed few signs of recapturing the brilliant qualities that he had displayed long ago at Castiglione.

The elements of the situation stood out with a stark simplicity. With 80,000 men Napoleon had to defeat an Allied army of 200,000 and drive it across the Rhine in some two or three weeks, before fresh armies from the north made his position still more untenable. Perhaps even Napoleon himself did not comprehend the full magnitude of his task. The great commanders of the past on occasion had to face similar odds, but almost invariably their armies in every aspect of training and equipment were vastly superior to those of their enemies. Except for the incomparable Old Guard and some battalions of the New, the well seasoned troops of the Allies were superior to Napoleon's conscripts both in equipment and experience. That in such circumstances he contemplated continuing the war may seem incredible.

However, besides his genius and his ability to inspire his men to accomplish the almost-impossible, Napoleon had certain physical factors in his favour, which he had every intention of exploiting. The large armies he had compelled

Europe to raise were now organized in army corps of all arms. The strength of any army corps could fluctuate widely and its composition was far from standard. A French corps might total about 15,000 men and on the line of march extend for approximately seven miles along a road. In battle, it would normally occupy a front of about a mile and a half or even less. At rest, if there was a danger of attack, it had to be concentrated ready for action. Moving a corps might be likened to uncoiling and pulling an immensely long rope through a system of pulleys to coil it up neatly again at the far end. A rope, of course, would have a constant thickness, whereas the thickness of the corps during a move would vary according to the width and structure of the roads and the number

The Napoleonic triad of horse, foot and guns, as represented by a Garde d'Honneur (here receiving a bullet in the chest), a light infantry grenadier, and two members of the Guard artillery.

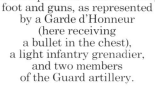

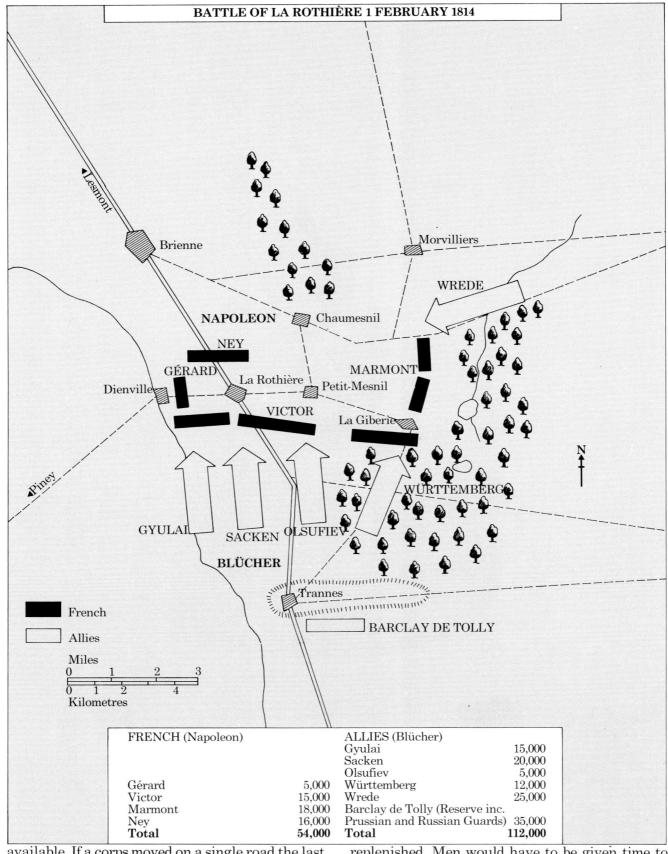

BATTLE OF LA ROTHIÈRE 1 FEBRUARY 1814

Lesmont

Brienne

Morvilliers

NAPOLEON

Chaumesnil

WREDE

NEY

GÉRARD

MARMONT

Dienville

La Rothière

Petit-Mesnil

VICTOR

La Giberie

Piney

WÜRTTEMBERG

N

GYULAI

SACKEN

OLSUFIEV

BLÜCHER

Trannes

■ French

□ Allies

Miles

0   1   2   3

0   1   2   4

Kilometres

□ BARCLAY DE TOLLY

FRENCH (Napoleon)		ALLIES (Blücher)	
		Gyulai	15,000
		Sacken	20,000
		Olsufiev	5,000
Gérard	5,000	Württemberg	12,000
Victor	15,000	Wrede	25,000
Marmont	18,000	Barclay de Tolly (Reserve inc.	
Ney	16,000	Prussian and Russian Guards)	35,000
Total	**54,000**	**Total**	**112,000**

available. If a corps moved on a single road the last unit might get into camp perhaps two and a half hours after the first arrived; this delay would be increased if any defile like a bridge narrowed the width of the column and consequently elongated it.

Near the presence of an enemy it was vital that the last unit should arrive at the camping site well before daylight ended. Regiments had to know where to bivouac for the night, identify their next-door neighbours, detail outposts and alarm posts. Food might have to be issued and ammunition replenished. Men would have to be given time to collect firewood and cook their soup. Failure to meet these requirements over any length of time would mean that the regiments faded away from sickness. The short winter days severely restricted the distances the Allied armies could cover. More-over their generals, looking nervously over their shoulders and wondering what Napoleon had in store for them, trod with great caution. Napoleon, on the other hand, by almost always seizing the initiative, could generally choose where and when

the battle would be fought and was not so bound by the hours of daylight.

The difficulties experienced by a single corps moving down a road were more than doubled if two had to use it. A long column inevitably tended to 'concertina'; while the head moved at a steady sedate pace the tail would be either standing still or running at top speed. In a very long column this characteristic could add enormously to the fatigue of the men marching in the rear. For this reason it was customary to leave an interval of half a day's march, about eight miles, between the head of the second corps and the tail of the first. Winter, therefore, vastly increased the difficulties of the invaders. The wet soggy ground made movement off the roads slow and fatiguing for the infantry and cavalry and virtually impossible for guns and transport.

In the province of Champagne the rivers averaged about 50 yards in width and were deep; in the icy conditions the rare fords were scarcely usable; any marching column of troops would have to cross a river by a bridge which would act as a funnel, compressing and extending it. In addition the Allied sovereigns repeatedly impressed on their generals that they were not fighting the French but only Napoleon, that a national uprising might imperil the whole enterprise and that on no account should the soldiers be allowed to plunder and antagonize the local population. A carefully organized system of supply was essential; but the problems of bringing forward supplies long distances in vehicles that moved little faster than the marching troops were considerable, and the need to protect them *en route* could drain away the strength of field armies.

Napoleon was singularly well qualified to turn these difficulties to his own advantage. He moved and struck so fast that a corps moving apparently within easy reach of its neighbour might be crushed before help could arrive. His phenomenal speed arose not solely from the marching powers of his soldiers, great though these were; it arose in the first place from the rapidity with which he thought and acted. Not for him the lengthy analysis of the situation by some earnest staff officer; he needed no one to tell him what to do. He would take time to deliberate over the form that his campaign might take and what he might be required to do, but, once he had that established in his mind, on the battlefield itself a quick glance or so, a few brief orders given with absolute authority, and matters would be in train. His marshals, inured to the vicissitudes of war, might lack inspiration, but they were superb technicians, master craftsmen of their trade. They translated their Emperor's orders swiftly and undeviatingly into action and the whole army moved into battle with a speed and a smoothness that the Allied armies, seasoned and experienced though they were, could not hope to match; and the sight of the bearskins of the Guard revealing the presence of Napoleon himself generated a feeling of awe almost as of the supernatural.

Now the great conjurer, the great gambler, faced with his accustomed courage and confidence the greatest game of chance of his life. The day after the action at Brienne, while his army took up a position near La Rothière with its right on the Aube and its left on the wooded slopes by La Giberie, he laid out his maps, studied the dispositions of both sides and prepared his plans. Next day his clerks laboured from dawn to dusk; letters poured out from the château while Blücher's patrols skirmished in the plain before La Rothière, and the battalions of the *Grande Armée* came marching up. The blow against Blücher had miscarried; it was time to be gone. However, the bridge at Lesmont had been badly damaged and it would be another 24 hours before it could be used; so, unmindful of the deadly peril developing near Trannes, Napoleon on the 31st laid out the foundations of the coming campaign.

Paris was the key. If it fell, he fell. He had to withdraw so that the advancing enemy armies again became dispersed; then he must aim to keep some columns in play with a light screen of troops while with the main strength of the army he crushed the remainder. River-lines and bridges would offer him the best opportunities. Here the geography of Champagne was well suited to his plans.

The River Aube flowed into the Seine to form with that river a great moat barring the approaches to Paris from the south and south-east, while the River Yonne, flowing from the south into the Seine near Montereau, bounded the area to the west. Three great roads led to Paris. One passed through Brienne, crossed to the south bank of the Aube at Lesmont, followed that bank to Arcis, then turned west to cross the Seine at Méry and again at Nogent; from there it ran to Paris by way of Provins, Nangis and Guignes. Guignes, about 18 miles from Paris, lay just south of the River Yerres, the last river barrier before the capital.

The second principal road ran in the north from Verdun to Châlons-sur-Marne; from that town it followed the south bank of the Marne through Épernay to Château-Thierry; here it changed to the north bank to go to La Ferté-sous-Jouarre where it crossed to the south to cross again at Trilport, going from there to Meaux and Paris. The third, the southern route, started from Troyes, the ancient capital of Champagne, ran westwards to the River Yonne, crossing it at Pont-sur-Yonne, then went over the Seine at Montereau to continue up the east bank through Melun to Paris. In addition to these, a good road ran north from Troyes, cut across the central highway to Paris at Arcis and continued on to Châlons-sur-Marne.

Napoleon planned to concentrate his forces at Troyes then to pivot on Arcis-sur-Aube, using that north-south highway to fall swiftly on the flanks of any enemy column marching westwards towards Paris. He wished to be able to move north or south of the rivers at will, so all the bridges had to be preserved; he ordered the engineers to build redoubts or block-houses at either end, from which small forces of infantry could hold them securely against any attack by cavalry. He directed that his main administrative installations should be sited in the area enclosed by the Marne in the north and the Aube-Seine in the south. His main administrative headquarters he sited at Sézanne, a central position between Vitry and Paris. Depots holding 20 days of biscuited bread – cheaper, Napoleon thriftily noted, than biscuits – together with hospitals were to be formed at La Ferté-sous-Jouarre, Château-Thierry, Meaux and Épernay. The sick and wounded were to be evacuated from them to Picardy. They were not to pass through Paris. It was unfortunate that the central highway between

Arcis and Nogent lay south of the river. To General Clarke in Paris he wrote, 'I require a route to Arcis-sur-Aube from Paris which does not cross the Aube ... I require a route from Arcis to Sézanne and thence to Ferté sous Jouarre. Send sappers and surveyors to reconnoitre the route and improve the roads and bridges as much as possible. No convoy is to move south of the Seine or the Aube, without my special permission.'

He sent a note to his Chief Engineer instructing him that Vitry should be fortified as strongly as possible. Troyes, Arcis and Châlons were to be capable of beating off a sudden assault. 'All the bridges from here to Nogent and from Nogent to Melun and the Pont sur Yonne are to be put in a state of defence.'

During the afternoon of 31 January 1814 he prepared for the move to Troyes. He instructed Berthier at 1 pm, 'Order the Duke of Ragusa [Marmont] to take his corps to Lesmont [from Vassy] and place a rearguard at Maizières. On arrival at Lesmont he will find the bridge established. He will consolidate it ... and push an advance guard to Piney [about six miles west of the

A detachment of Bavarian light cavalry in camp.

river].' But he had left it too late. On the morning of 1 February dense columns of enemy troops began to descend into the plains before La Rothière. He hastily recalled Marmont from Vassy and summoned Gérard from Piney to cross over the Aube by Dienville.

While Napoleon had been perfecting his plans Schwarzenberg had been bringing up his men. Aggressive patrolling by the French on the 31st misled the Allies into expecting an attack. Standing on the heights above Trannes with the Aube on their left and a trackless forest on their right, nothing could have suited them better; they waited patiently for an attack that never came.

By the 31st Schwarzenberg had concentrated about Trannes the corps of Gyulai, that of Prince Eugen of Württemberg and the reserve under Barclay de Tolly, which included the Prussian and Russian Guards. Colloredo with his corps was already west of the Aube and might soon threaten the road to Troyes; Wrede marching up from Joinville was to attack Vassy with Wittgenstein. With about 54,000 men Napoleon confronted perhaps 80,000 in battle array with another 30,000 menacing his flanks. It seemed the war might end that day. Used as he was to making his enemy conform to his wishes, perhaps on occasion he took too little note of what his opponents intended. But it was in part just this arrogant near-contempt for his enemy that made his movements so swift and unpredictable.

Schwarzenberg entrusted the conduct of the Battle of La Rothière to Blücher and put under his orders for the occasion his two corps at Trannes, those of Gyulai and Württemberg. No doubt Schwarzenberg reflected that if Blücher succeeded everyone would be pleased, whereas if he failed the Emperor of Austria might not entirely regret an Allied reverse; in such an event he personally (Schwarzenberg) might find Blücher easier to handle.

On the morning of 1 February the weather grew even more vile; the damp cold bit into the waiting soldiers while a gloomy sky heavy with snow enfolded the scene. At 1 pm the Allied columns came to grips with the French and the snow started to fall, blanketing the whole area in a swirling white fog. The ground, however, was not frostbound and the glutinous blue clay clung to the

Austrian soldiers of the Allied invasion force:
they are, from the left,
a chasseur à cheval, a hussar,
a cuirassier, an Uhlan (lancer) and a grenadier.

boots of the infantry and the hooves of the cavalry while the guns and transports sank axle-deep. Yet despite these appalling conditions a sanguinary struggle developed. Caring nothing for the numbers opposed to them, the French infantry stubbornly stood their ground. On the Allied side Württemberg's corps seized the wooded slopes above La Giberie only to be driven out. Müffling related that Prince Eugen sent messengers asking for reinforcements; Blücher replied that the battle must be decided on the plain of La Rothière where Napoleon stood with his principal forces and reserves. Then, Müffling went on, the Swedish General Toll arrived 'and called out loudly in German "The Crown Prince must have reinforcements". Blücher looked at the General in some surprise then looked away without speaking. General Toll started to scream at him.' Müffling intervened. 'I was so irritated by his behaviour that I called out to him that he who holds the valley holds the heights and he who attempts to decide the battle on a false point deserves to be beaten.' Perhaps not altogether surprisingly, Toll galloped off in a fury to the Tsar, who with Schwarzenberg and the King of Prussia were gazing at the battle in the plain rather as though they were Romans enjoying a gladiatorial show. Even the Tsar was cautious about crossing Blücher and said no more than that the old man could call on the reserve if he needed more troops.

The French line sagged but did not break. Wrede, attacking into a vacuum at Vassy, pushed on towards the sound of the guns. At about 5 o'clock in the evening he drove in on Marmont's left. Marmont gave ground and turned to meet the new threat; then the grey day turned to a blustery night and coordinated operations came to an end.[1] Napoleon had staved off a disaster, but now he had no alternative but to withdraw or be surrounded next day. The withdrawal would be perilous enough in the face of such odds.

Napoleon returned to the château at Brienne and at 9 o'clock that evening dictated his orders for the withdrawal. Marmont was to cover it and remain on the east bank of the Aube, the remainder

to file over the bridge at Lesmont and march on Piney. Any vehicle found on the road after 2 o'clock in the morning was to be burnt. He had to leave some 60 guns and much valuable equipment behind him; there was no hope of extricating them.

At 4 am on 2 February he stood on the terrace of the château looking out over the battlefield. The retreat had progressed remarkably well. Over by La Rothière flickering pinpoints of lights revealed some bivouac fires still alight, but those of the French by now were deserted. All was quiet and his men were beyond the low ridge that separates Lesmont from Brienne. It was time to go. He had broken contact with great skill but had suffered an undeniable reverse. The affair had begun badly. His men tramping over the river and towards Piney through the darkness felt weary and depressed. They had fought like heroes, and now it appeared that it had all been for nothing.

To General Caulaincourt, about to open vital peace negotiations at Châtillon, he wrote on 5 February bidding him to accept any terms he could obtain; then he withdrew his *carte blanche* by insisting that they must neither demean France nor himself. His misfortunes weighed on his spirits, but his inner conviction that his star would reassert itself and triumph in the end, remained unchanged. But meanwhile the Allies made it very clear to Caulaincourt that there could be no question now of conceding the 'natural boundaries of France'.

On the morning of 2 February Müffling rode into Brienne and entered the château once again. The bridge at Lesmont had been destroyed and no immediate pursuit seemed either possible or wise, taking into account the appalling weather and the fatigue suffered by the troops. It did not appear to be necessary anyway. As they exchanged the bitter weather outside for the hospitable atmosphere of the château and the baggage came up, the Tsar optimistically toasted Blücher, 'Today you have set the crown on all your victories; mankind will bless you.' Blücher wrote to his wife, 'For me it is the happiest day of my life ...' The men were as jubilant, and when Blücher went round their bivouacs next morning wild cheering greeted him wherever he went. To General Reynier, about to be released on parole, they boasted that they would be in Paris before him.

---

[1] Some accounts trace attack and counter-attack up until 11 pm. Napoleon left the battlefield at about 8.30 pm and it can be assumed that by that time the serious fighting had ended.

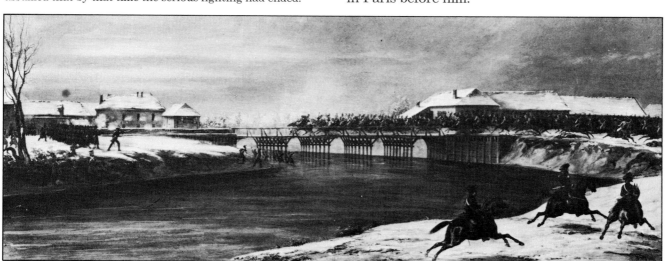

French sappers, covered by some of Ney's infantry,
destroy the bridge at Lesmont as the Allied cavalry are trying to cross.
The wooden bridge is typical of its time.
Watercolour by S. Fort.

CHAPTER 7
BRILLIANT FEBRUARY

As they paused at Brienne the jubilant sovereigns and their generals drew up their plans for what Blücher regarded as little more than a triumphal progress to the capital. They decided that Schwarzenberg should press on towards Paris by the great highway which ran by Bar-sur-Aube to Troyes and on to Paris by Montereau, using the second route by Méry and Nogent to ease his administrative problems and to keep in touch with Blücher. The latter meanwhile would become

French soldiers ease their wounds with brandy.

independent, head to the north, then drive down to Paris along the valley of the Marne. He would pick up Yorck's corps, at that time facing Macdonald near Vitry, and be joined shortly afterwards by Kleist's Prussian corps, and another detachment from Langeron's under General Kapzevich; these last two had been released from blockading frontier fortresses by fresh troops from Germany. Blücher would then have nearly 60,000 men under his command and should be able to look after himself whatever Napoleon might do. The plan had two further advantages; first his supply columns, moving from the Rhine by way of Verdun or Nancy, could keep well clear of the roads to Basle used by Schwarzenberg; secondly French resistance in the Netherlands was collapsing; already General Winzingerode with 30,000 troops from the Army of the North was marching on Laon and could watch his right flank. The old man's eyes must have glistened with delight at the scheme unfolded. Macdonald was now isolated near Châlons-sur-Marne. A swift blow and he could cut him off from the rest of Napoleon's army like a cowboy a steer from the herd.

Yorck, who had commanded a corps under Macdonald during the Russian campaign of 1812, would be unusually well placed to exact a revenge for any slights he had been made to endure, and Yorck was an expert at discerning slights and intrigues. The new deployment took a little time to arrange, for with Wittgenstein's and Wrede's corps to the north-east of Sacken and Olsufiev, the lines of communication had become hopelessly tangled; where the supply convoys of two corps crossed each other the resulting traffic jam was not unlike the chaotic spectacle associated with a 20th-century public holiday.

A short rest was not unwelcome to either side. Napoleon meanwhile had withdrawn unmolested to Troyes. With his great inferiority in numbers he had to wait for his enemy to advance and stretch out his columns before he could develop a strategic plan of his own. For him the time of waiting was testing. His soldiers felt downcast after an apparent defeat, and with the Allied army knocking, as it were, at the outer courts of Paris the nation had begun to panic. In Troyes itself, as the historian Henri Houssaye later observed, 'The only direction in which people exerted themselves was to encourage the desertion of the conscripts . . . a large number, amounting to 6,000 left the ranks.'

Numbers were of the first importance. Napoleon wrote letter after letter to his brother, Joseph, his deputy in Paris, imploring him to raise fresh regiments, and waited with desperate impatience for a corps of two infantry divisions and one cavalry division that he had ordered to join him from Soult's Army of Spain, now defending the south-western borders of France. The news from the Netherlands was black, General Maison being apparently unable to keep the field; but near Lyon Augereau had heavily repulsed an attack by some formations from Schwarzenberg's army under Count Bubna.

Schwarzenberg, worried about a possible French thrust on Geneva, hastily strengthened his forces in the south. Meanwhile he found the sight of the Emperor brooding over the countryside from Troyes bad for his nerves. After his defeat at La Rothière Napoleon should surely be sheltering somewhere north of the Seine. The Austrian Prince feared that if he advanced directly on Troyes he could find himself with a vengeful Emperor in front and an unfordable river behind. The prospect did not please him. He stretched out a tentative hand towards La Guillotière on the Barse, about five miles south-east of Troyes, only to have it smartly slapped by Mortier's Guard. It was enough. He swerved away to the south, and established his headquarters at Bur-sur-Seine, concentrating his army about him. He called down Wittgenstein from Arcis-sur-Aube to a position near Piney. For the next two days (9 and 10 February) he rested his army. Then he began to feel his way westwards well to the south of Troyes, proposing to move carefully to the River Yonne, before turning north towards Paris. He might capture Fontainebleau, but beyond that he was not prepared to plan.

At Troyes Napoleon watched and waited, ready to pounce if the Austrian blundered. As the peril from Blücher in the north became more evident he shifted his main administrative base from Sézanne to Nogent on the Seine. He pulled back Marmont (VI Corps) to defend it and ordered all his reinforcements to concentrate there. Then he fancied he saw a flaw in Schwarzenberg's dispositions; he was about to swoop when he received letters from Joseph in Paris, saying that panic gripped the city and that Blücher was almost hourly expected. On 6 February he left Troyes by way of Fontaine-les-Grés and marched to Nogent, arriving on the 7th. It had been a remarkable strategic performance. Despite the earlier reverse, by pausing at Troyes when a lesser general might well have sought refuge north of the Seine, he had pushed Blücher and Schwarzenberg apart and now stood poised at Nogent with his whole army, except for Macdonald's XI Corps, concentrated between the two and perfectly balanced to attack either. The hand of the great master had lost none of its cunning.

Meanwhile Blücher, under the happy delusion that Schwarzenberg pinned down a Napoleon still reeling from his recent defeat, confidently began his march on Paris. Only Macdonald and perhaps a few semi-trained National Guards without proper weapons stood in his way. It might have been wise to wait for Kleist and Kapzevich, who were marching up from the Rhine, to arrive, but old Marshal 'Forwards' hated to wait for anything or anyone and it was unthinkable to miss the chance to trap Macdonald with his weak corps little more than 5,000 strong.

By 4 February Blücher had already thrust 30 miles north of Brienne to Sommesous. Here everything seemed eminently satisfactory. Yorck had pushed the French out of Châlons and was repairing the bridge there, cavalry patrols had fanned out as far as Sézanne 25 miles to the west, and now came the splendid news from Schwarzenberg that Napoleon had taken refuge in Troyes and was still well south of the Aube-Seine river-line. With Wittgenstein guarding his flank at Arcis-sur-Aube and linking him with Schwarzenberg, Blücher seemed like a matador poised to deliver the fatal blow on Paris.

However, he had to wait three days until the bridge at Châlons, blown by Marshal Macdonald, was again fit to take traffic; despite the fortunate capture of a French ammunition column, his stocks were still dangerously low. By 7 February, however, the wagons were rolling over the bridge and on the 8th the old Field-Marshal, who had been straining impatiently at his administrative leash, plunged forward.

From Châlons, as already mentioned, the great highway to Paris followed the valley of the Marne through Épernay to Château-Thierry; here it crossed to the north bank to avoid the wide loop in the river and ran direct to La Ferté-sous-Jouarre to cross again to the south. Macdonald, retreating down it, was somewhere between Épernay and Château-Thierry. From Châlons, however, another road to Paris described a shallow arc to the south of the main road and the river and followed the valley of the Petit Morin through Bergères, Étoges, Champaubert, Vauchamps, Montmirail and Viels-Maisons to join the main road again at La Ferté-sous-Jouarre.

About eight miles further south a road went westward from Vitry-le-François by Sommesous, La Fère-Champenoise and Sézanne to La Ferté-Gaucher to join the main road at Trilport. It was not a particularly good road. Napoleon himself described the secondary roads as *affreux* and in places covered in mud to a depth of six feet.

Blücher told Yorck to follow Macdonald by the main road along the valley of the Marne, while Sacken, leaving some of his cavalry under General Karpov at Sézanne, raced along the southern road from Châlons to cut the French marshal off north of the river at La Ferté-sous-Jouarre. Blücher himself intended to remain at Étoges with Olsufiev's detachment nearby until Kleist and Kapzevich arrived with their men, probably on about the 10th or 11th. He understood that General Seslawin with 12 regiments of Cossacks would take over responsibility for Sézanne in a couple of days.

By the evening of the 9th Blücher had set up his headquarters in the château at Étoges with Olsufiev holding forward to Champaubert; Sacken was at Montmirail on the southern road, about 12 miles to the west, Yorck on the northern near Dormans, roughly halfway between Épernay and Château-Thierry; Kleist with most of his corps had arrived at Châlons and Kapzevich at Vitry. During the course of the day Karpov reported that the day before (8 February) some French troops had driven in his Cossack outposts at Villenauxe 14 miles south of Sézanne.

That evening a courier brought despatches from Schwarzenberg and the Tsar, dated 6 February. Schwarzenberg stated, 'I will not follow Napoleon who has retreated from Troyes towards Nogent, but prefer marching to the left by Sens to Fontainebleau.' But if Napoleon came northwards after Schwarzenberg had disappeared to the south, the strategic situation would be radically altered and not for the better. The Tsar clearly felt so. He wrote that he was worried by the exposed situation of Wittgenstein at Arcis-sur-Aube and wished Kleist to be sent to join him. To replace him Winzingerode, who was thought to be not far from Laon, would be placed under Blücher's command when he arrived.

At 8 o'clock that evening, as Blücher with his staff officers was sitting in a room of the château pondering the situation, a Russian officer rushed in shouting, 'The enemy is here.' The Russian battalion garrisoning the château stood-to, while Blücher and his staff hurriedly assembled in the courtyard and mounted their chargers. Nothing happened, but Blücher had experienced some uncomfortable moments in châteaux. He took his headquarters to spend an unpleasant night in the fields of Vertus. It transpired that some squadrons of French lancers had charged Olsufiev's headquarters at Baye several times before vanishing in the direction of Sézanne.

This was very strange: Karpov, left in Sézanne by Sacken, must have abandoned that town without bothering to inform anyone. Even though the Cossacks, admirable as light irregular cavalry, were not of much value in large-scale cavalry combat, Müffling felt anxious. Sitting on his horse in the cold dark night he discussed the matter with Gneisenau. 'I represented . . . that squadrons coming from Sézanne announced not only the occupation of Sézanne . . . their resolute attack indicated an offensive power stationed between Sézanne and Baye. The first thing to be done was to recall General Sacken from Montmirail to Champaubert.'

Gneisenau dismissed the first suggestion. Sacken's cavalry had been holding Sézanne and Sacken was best placed to judge the situation. Gneisenau suspected the French had merely stationed a body of troops in Sézanne to block the Vitry-Paris road. He agreed that Müffling should send an ADC to Sacken recalling him from Montmirail to Champaubert, but frustrated Müffling's intentions by adding that if Sacken thought it safe to do so, he could continue the advance to La Ferté-sous-Jouarre.

The next problem was the Tsar's request to send Kleist south to join Wittgenstein, presumably at Arcis-sur-Aube (in fact he had moved farther south). Müffling suggested an ingenious plan. If Kleist and Kapzevich were to move tomorrow to Sézanne it would meet the Tsar's requirements, allow Blücher to retain control over his two commanders and help clear up the mystery of Sézanne. The Field-Marshal assented, and the necessary orders were issued.

During the long, cold and uncomfortable night news came in that Napoleon himself had been seen at Villenauxe. Matters began to look serious. If Yorck crossed to the north bank of the Marne at Château-Thierry he would be separated by the river from Sacken. Blücher despatched orders to him to maintain the closest possible touch with Sacken at Montmirail. Then from some prisoners he learned positively that Napoleon had spent the night at Sézanne. Blücher thought it most probable that the Emperor intended no more than to march west, unite with Macdonald at Meaux and cover the Marne valley route to Paris, but one never knew with Napoleon. At 7 am he wrote to Yorck:[1] 'Vertus 10 February 7 am.

The Emperor Napoleon has moved from Nogent by Villenauxe on Sézanne where according to prisoners he spent the night. This move may be to enable the enemy to join Macdonald and begin an offensive towards the Marne. In that case I must concentrate the army at Vertus. If you have not begun your move on Montmirail do so at once. Send out cavalry patrols from Montmirail towards Sézanne. The bridge at Château-Thierry must be re-established and a bridge of boats thrown across the river, so that if unfortunately the enemy cuts you and Sacken off from my army you can save

---

[1]As quoted in *Montmirail,* by M. R. Mathieu.

yourselves on the right bank of the Marne.'

The morning progressed. About midday Müffling's ADC, Lieutenant Gerlach, rode in from Sacken's headquarters. The General thought the expulsion of his Cossacks from Sézanne of no significance and had gone on to La Ferté-sous-Jouarre. Macdonald, however, had out-distanced him and, destroying the bridges over the Seine at La Ferté-sous-Jouarre and Trilport, had retired to Meaux. Gerlach remarked that he had ridden through Champaubert at 11 o'clock that morning and all seemed quiet. Blücher sent peremptory orders to Yorck to go to Montmirail and himself set out to La Fère-Champenoise where Kleist and Kapzevich were due to meet before going the 11 miles west to Sézanne.

As he went the dull thudding of cannon fire came from the north-west in the general direction of Champaubert and Baye. There was nothing headquarters could do except hope that if Olsufiev was in trouble he would take to the woods. Towards evening some fugitives straggled into La Fère-Champenoise with a story of disaster. Olsufiev had been captured and most of his men killed or taken prisoner. Blücher halted his advance on Sézanne. Kleist's men had already marched a long way and the wild country round La Fère-Champenoise would give some protection against the powerful French cavalry. They bivouacked for the night. Blücher had with him about 13,000 men all told, including about 500 horses; some 4,000 of Kleist's corps including most of his cavalry were still somewhere between Châlons and the Rhine.

In the morning Blücher marched on Bergères and camped; during the day he accumulated about 1,000 stragglers from Olsufiev's unhappy detachment. Some 3,000 must have been either killed or captured. Blücher anticipated that now Napoleon would turn east and attack him. With virtually no cavalry he dared not advance to Montmirail; equally he dared not retreat to Châlons. If the French cavalry caught him in the plains surrounding that town he would be cut to pieces. He stayed in camp and waited for information; none came. For the rest of that day and most of the 12th he remained at Bergères in a hideous state of uncertainty. On the 13th a letter arrived from Yorck saying simply that Sacken had driven Macdonald across the Marne at Trilport, then had marched back to find Napoleon across the road at Viels-Maisons. There the message ended. All remained quiet except that some 800 of Kleist's cavalry rode in and some French were identified at Étoges. Blücher's old impatience began once again to take charge. He advanced, drove the French out of Étoges[2] and stopped at Champaubert, proposing to march to Montmirail next day.

Next morning Blücher had gone about four miles along the Montmirail road and was approaching Vauchamps when his advanced guard ran into a strong enemy post and a dense cloud of cavalry, well supported by artillery, descended on his marching columns. The Prussian cavalry, hope-

---

[2]There is a story that Blücher was misled by a spy planted by the French who told him that Napoleon had retired on Paris. The spy cannot have been deliberately planted as Napoleon at that time had no clear idea who was at Bergères (he suspected the presence of Wittgenstein). Quite probably the odd sequence of events that found Napoleon fighting while facing towards Paris led to some misinterpretation, nothing more.

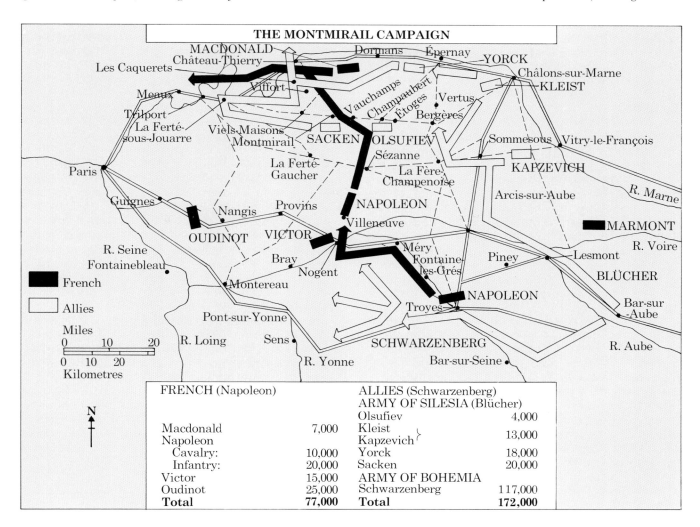

THE MONTMIRAIL CAMPAIGN

FRENCH (Napoleon)		ALLIES (Schwarzenberg)	
		ARMY OF SILESIA (Blücher)	
		Olsufiev	4,000
Macdonald	7,000	Kleist	
Napoleon		Kapzevich	13,000
Cavalry:	10,000	Yorck	18,000
Infantry:	20,000	Sacken	20,000
Victor	15,000	ARMY OF BOHEMIA	
Oudinot	25,000	Schwarzenberg	117,000
Total	**77,000**	**Total**	**172,000**

lessly outnumbered, were soon driven off. A Cossack captured an officer of the French Old Guard. The Frenchman told Blücher that he was in the presence of the Emperor himself. Sacken and Yorck were north of the Marne. Napoleon had just completed a night march from Château-Thierry in order to destroy him.

Blücher and his army were in mortal peril. His one chance was to retreat before the French infantry could catch him up. He put Kapzevich on the right of the road and Kleist on the left while the guns travelled down it, dropping in and out of action as they went. During the bleak, cold afternoon the two columns slowly progressed eastwards while the French cavalry with their shouts of 'Vive l'Empereur!' came roaring down in charge after charge. Müffling, marching with Kleist and checking progress with his habitual thoroughness, became alarmed. The French cavalry might head the columns by a wooded defile near Étoges and the survivors be compelled to surrender. Blücher, fearlessly riding about and encouraging his men, was moving with too measured a tread. Müffling sent a message suggesting it would be wise to hurry. The old man replied with his accustomed bluntness. 'If Kleist did not run so immoderately fast all would remain compact.' Müffling noted that a regiment of French cuirassiers had cut in ahead of the advanced guard, composed of three raw Russian infantry battalions, and was preparing to charge. The Russian infantry halted quite steadily and allowed the cuirassiers to close in. Then on the word 'Fire', every man blasted off his musket in one stupendous volley. It was poorly aimed and few Frenchmen fell; fortunately the cuirassiers turned and trotted off for, with their muskets empty, the Russian infantry lay at their mercy. Müffling thought 'this was the time to make these inexperienced soldiers believe they had done something heroic. I hurrahed them loudly. They moved briskly on, their drums struck up a march and all the drums of the other corps followed in their beat.'

The light began to fade from the heavy skies and the muddy ground either side of the road prevented the French from bringing up their guns. This probably saved Blücher from complete destruction; but passing through Étoges, the French cavalry under Grouchy moved in ahead of the Allied rearguard and charging down the narrow streets virtually annihilated them. Beyond Étoges Napoleon called off the pursuit and the weary, ravaged columns halted at their old camp at Bergères to restore some form of order. After a few hours' rest they continued on to Châlons. Blücher had lost some 6,000 men.

When he arrived at Nogent on 7 February Napoleon discovered that Macdonald, heavily outnumbered by Yorck with some 18,000 men, had kept his own troops concentrated and left the roads to Paris by Montmirail and Sézanne completely unprotected. There was nothing to stop Blücher hammering at the gates of Paris. But Schwarzenberg had swung away to the south, and a sudden and sharp blow might be dealt to the impetuous Prussian. He ordered Marmont with 2,000 cavalry, 1,000 infantry and six guns to march that evening to Sézanne 20 miles away to the northeast. While probing Blücher's dispositions on the Montmirail road, Marmont was to ensure the enemy knew nothing of what passed between Nogent and Sézanne.

At about 4 pm, while he was meditating over his next move, despatches arrived from the peace negotiators at Châtillon. Napoleon read them and blenched. With their armies less than 100 miles from Paris and no signs of a mass rising by the French people, the Allies were now prepared to offer nothing more than the borders to France as they had been in 1792; in the north these would exclude Antwerp and the Rhine. Berthier and his Foreign Minister, Maret, begged him to accept. He retired to his own room to ponder. At last he reappeared and passionately rejected the terms. 'Never,' he cried. 'Never will I leave France smaller than I found it.' Baron Fain, his secretary, remarked that he again withdrew and threw himself on his bed. If he did, it was not to repine. Already he was organizing his next move. He himself declared that he had a mind like a desk full of drawers; when he wanted to examine one he pulled it out, then when he had finished with it he shut it away and pulled out another. When he wanted to sleep, which was seldom, he shut all the drawers.

That night he worked late. He constituted a VII Corps made up of the 7th and 9th Divisions from Soult's Army of Spain. He gave the command to Marshal Oudinot, recently recovered from typhus contracted in Germany, instructing him to watch the more westerly approaches to Paris. Pajol's cavalry division at Sens and Allix's infantry at Pont-sur-Yonne were to come under him. He was to place troops at Nangis and Provins and be responsible for Montereau with a total of nearly 25,000 men (Napoleon always overestimated the number of troops he placed under the command of any of his generals). Victor with 15,000 men including Gérard's troops, now only a division strong, was to remain at Nogent and guard the crossings over the Seine to the east. The two marshals were to liaise closely over their plans. With 40,000 men between them they should be able to keep Schwarzenberg in check.

This left Napoleon a field force of 30,000 men and 120 guns, comprising all the best regiments in his army. His infantry would consist of the two divisions of conscripts in Marmont's VI Corps, two divisions of the Old Guard and three of the Young numbering in all about 20,000; for cavalry he had the Cavalry of the Guard, totalling 6,000, which with Defrance's Garde d'Honneur[3] and I Cavalry Corps, each of 2,000, gave him 10,000 troopers in all.

He estimated Blücher could muster 45,000 men. With help from Macdonald's XI Corps, now increased to about 7,000 men, he concluded he should be strong enough to defeat him. Writing to his brother in the midst of his other preoccupations, he found time to include a postscript about Josephine: 'Keep the Empress happy, she is dying of consumption.' Then with his small but choice army he set out to demolish Blücher, little knowing he now commanded nearly 60,000 men.

The rain fell steadily and the road to Sézanne became a sea of mud; movement was hideously difficult and the misery of the soldiers acute. Marmont (VI Corps), after herculean efforts, had

---

[3] Defrance's Garde d'Honneur was composed of young sprigs of the aristocracy and the upper middle classes, put there to keep them out of mischief. Napoleon cordially disliked it and starved its members of decorations.

arrived on the 8th and during the 9th patrolled forward, identifying Olsufiev at Champaubert and Sacken 10 miles to the west at Montmirail. Yorck, Napoleon knew, was chasing Macdonald somewhere near Château-Thierry. Although much of his army was still well short of Sézanne, teams of cavalry horses were needed to drag the guns out of the mud and, as he informed his administrative chief, the army was dying of hunger. The Emperor ordered an advance to Montmirail via Champaubert on the 10th.

Marmont led. Olsufiev left the bridge over the Petit Morin undefended. He made no attempt to hold the difficult country near the river, here little more than a stream. Then he suddenly elected to make a stand and fight in the flat open country round Champaubert, country excellently suited to Napoleon's powerful force of cavalry. It must be supposed that the French advance was unexpected and that Olsufiev was unable to oppose it any earlier. Perhaps some rather unpleasant comments about the conduct of his corps at Brienne, suggesting that he and his troops left unnecessarily abruptly, may have weighed with him. His decision to stand and fight was disastrous. During a wet, overcast afternoon Marmont's conscripts drove fiercely forward, while Napoleon directed his cavalry to cut the Montmirail road on both flanks of the unfortunate Russians. After a stubborn resistance they were overwhelmed. Characteristically Napoleon claimed to have captured 40 of their 24 cannon and 6,000 out of the detachment of 4,000. It sounded better for the *Bulletins*.

Now he did not waste a moment. He told Marmont to clear up the battlefield with a single division and gave him I Cavalry Corps with which to mask Blücher. He ordered the remainder to press on through the night to Montmirail, 10 miles to the west. But it was not until 1 o'clock next morning that the inhabitants of Montmirail awoke to the clop-clopping of many hooves and threw open their windows to see the leading squadrons of the Cavalry of the Guard ride by, their splendid uniforms drenched and plastered with mud.

On the evening of the 10th Sacken's advanced guard reached La Ferté-sous-Jouarre, 20 miles west of Montmirail, to find Macdonald gone and the bridges there and at Trilport destroyed. Late that evening orders came from Blücher summarily recalling him to Montmirail to join Yorck who was to come down the Château-Thierry road from the north to meet him. No doubt much of his corps was strung down the road to the east, but taking into account the appalling condition of the roads the head of his infantry column could scarcely hope to arrive at Montmirail before the early afternoon of the 11th.

Château-Thierry surrendered to the cantankerous Yorck at about 9 o'clock on the morning of the 10th. He received his orders to abandon his excellent highway and march southwards to Montmirail with the loud-voiced derision with which he was wont to greet any orders from a superior authority. He knew that Sacken was some distance to the west and unable to arrive at Montmirail for some time: he shrewdly suspected that Napoleon was already either near or on the Montmirail road. In accordance with his instructions, therefore, he intended to avoid action and take refuge north of the Marne.[4] If he occupied Montmirail he might find himself alone and opposed to Napoleon, a situation few generals contemplated with equanimity. On the other hand, if he could persuade Sacken to swing north by the minor roads from Viels-Maisons, six miles west of Montmirail, he would shorten Sacken's march by six miles and add the same distance to Napoleon's.

It cannot be said with certainty how far these considerations influenced Yorck, but he left 5,000 men to hold Château-Thierry and the crossing over the Marne, pushed an advanced guard into Viels-Maisons, and bivouacked with the remainder of his corps, about 11,000 strong, in the area of Viffort, eight miles north of the junction between the Château-Thierry and Paris roads. Paradoxically, for his army of the three took least part in the battle next day, on that chill winter evening he was closer to Montmirail than either of the other two.

Sacken, an able, thrusting general, arrived at Viels-Maisons probably about midday on the 11th. At this time a considerable portion of his army must still have been marching up. Rain fell steadily out of the dark, heavy sky and the fields were mere bogs in which guns and wagons sank up to their axles. At this time he must have received a message from Yorck advising him of his plans. The Prussian advanced guard in Viels-Maisons, having contacted Sacken, withdrew to the friendly shelter of Château Rozoy-Bellevalle three and a half miles to the north. Pirch II, with a brigade from Yorck's corps, occupied Fontenelle on the high ground overlooking the road from the north and about a mile and a half from the road junction. Pirch expelled some *voltigeurs* from the village and could confirm that Montmirail was held in strength. The rest of Yorck's troops were well to the north. If both corps were going to pass through Château-Thierry, roads were likely to become congested.[5]

Now Sacken faced a problem. He had to move with his baggage and heavy guns to the north knowing the French would attack his right flank as he did so. He had to protect the road while the transport and heavy guns filed by. The ground, if unfit for wheeled transport, was very open particularly to the north towards the gently sloping hills behind which Fontenelle nestled. South of the road lay the villages of Marchais and Le Tremblay, and south of them a steeply sloping ravine down to the Petit-Morin that nearly ran up to the road itself by Montmirail. The country south of the road was therefore more suitable for infantry while the flat open country north of it was ideal for cavalry. The muddy ground would slow down a charge, but, since it could not take heavy artillery, on balance it

---

[4] Yorck has been heavily criticized for his actions; it is difficult to understand why. But for Napoleon's phenomenal speed of movement he could probably have effected his junction with Sacken and the two moved north of the Marne unharmed. It could, of course, be argued that the two with their superiority in numbers should have crushed Napoleon, but at that time it was still the Allied policy to avoid fighting Napoleon himself.

[5] Timings vary in the most extraordinary fashion and seem to bear little relation to distances covered. Napoleon himself wrote, 'it is probable that Yorck and Sacken joined forces on the evening of the 10th . . . What will he [Sacken] do today? Go to Montmirail or else throw himself into Château-Thierry?' Napoleon wrote these words in a letter to Marmont dated Champaubert 11 February, morning. These timings agree with those of Müffling. It follows that, whatever may have been written, it was not physically possible for the battle to start much before the early afternoon of a short winter's day.

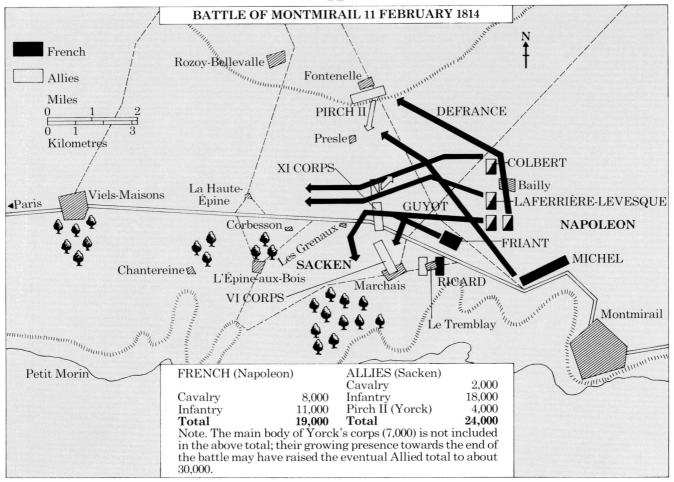

BATTLE OF MONTMIRAIL 11 FEBRUARY 1814

French

Allies

Miles
0   1   2

0   1   3
Kilometres

Rozoy-Bellevalle

Fontenelle

PIRCH II   DEFRANCE

Presle

COLBERT

XI CORPS

Bailly

La Haute-
Épine

LAFERRIÈRE-LEVESQUE

Paris   Viels-Maisons

GUYOT   NAPOLEON

Corbesson

FRIANT

Les Grenaux

MICHEL

Chantereine

SACKEN

L'Épine-aux-Bois

Marchais   RICARD

Montmirail

VI CORPS

Le Tremblay

Petit Morin

FRENCH (Napoleon)		ALLIES (Sacken)	
		Cavalry	2,000
Cavalry	8,000	Infantry	18,000
Infantry	11,000	Pirch II (Yorck)	4,000
Total	**19,000**	**Total**	**24,000**

Note. The main body of Yorck's corps (7,000) is not included in the above total; their growing presence towards the end of the battle may have raised the eventual Allied total to about 30,000.

A panorama of the Battle of Montmirail.
The left-hand road goes to Paris and that in the centre curves to the right on its way to Fontenelle
and Château-Thierry. On the far left is Marchais; to the left of the Paris road Ricard's men are
contesting Le Tremblay; in the centre Ney is leading an attack on Les Grenaux,
while on the right the cavalry of the Guard are beginning to attack the Allies along the Château-Thierry road.
In the background, far right, Michel is coming to grips with Pirch II.
Watercolour by S. Fort.

was probably best suited to cavalry action.

Sacken commanded the Allied VI and XI Infantry Corps–VI Corps having three, and XI two weak divisions – and a cavalry corps under General Wassilshikov; his army numbered about 20,000 men with 90 guns. He directed his VI Corps to hold Marchais about 1,000 yards south of the road and XI to hold the road and the farmhouse of Les Grenaux about 300 yards north of it. Wassilshikov with his cavalry was to be deployed to the north of the farmhouse and to keep touch with Pirch in Fontenelle.

Some time after midday Sacken put his plan into effect. On his right VI Corps without much difficulty drove Ricard's division of weary conscripts, who had been fighting and marching almost continuously for the last 24 hours, out of Marchais. On the left his XI Corps against neglig-

ible opposition took up a position astride the Paris road with its left established in Les Grenaux Farm. Having firmly blocked the Paris road and with Pirch across the Château-Thierry road at Fontenelle, Sacken felt comfortable enough. He started moving his transport and heavy guns to the north towards Montfaucon and the main Château-Thierry road.

Napoleon was in a quandary. Although most of his cavalry was present, only two infantry divisions had come up, Ricard's men and Friant's division of the Old Guard. He dared not commit many of Friant's men as this would leave him without a reserve. Any advance north of the road would be risky while the Prussians could threaten his flank. For a time the cannon boomed on amid heavy showers of rain which must have added to the hazards facing the gunners. Ricard's outnumbered division, which had retired to Le Tremblay, made an unenthusiastic attack on Marchais and was repelled. Then the Russians counterattacked and secured a foothold in Le Tremblay. Now the battle languished. Ricard still held part of Le Tremblay to the south of the road, while Friant with his division of the Old Guard watched the Russians in Les Grenaux. Napoleon lined up Guyot's, Laferrière-Levesque's and Colbert's divisions of the cavalry of the Guard and Defrance's Garde d'Honneur east of Château-Thierry and north of the Paris roads ready to launch them against the Russian cavalry, but while the Russians held Les Grenaux and an undisclosed number of Prussians the heights by Fontenelle, such an attack could not be contemplated. The terrible state of the roads appeared to have ruined all Napoleon's plans.

Then in the distance a long line of bearskins came into view. Michel with his division of the Old Guard was approaching. Napoleon, watching the battle on horseback with his customary indifference to fire, at once ordered Friant to storm Les Grenaux while Michel guarded against any enemy reaction from the direction of Fontenelle. Friant's Old Guard went into action with an irresistible *élan*. Ney, his divisions of the Young Guard still on the road marching up, led the Old Guard forward on foot. The serried ranks of bearskins plunged into the farm. Pirch over at Fontenelle came forward to help his stricken ally. Michel swung his division round to face him and a bloody struggle ensued.

Ney and his veterans speedily overwhelmed the Russians in Les Grenaux. The way forward was open. Napoleon gave the word and his massed squadrons crashed down on the Russian horse and broke them. Now the French cavalry erupted all over the plain. Sacken had begun his withdrawal towards Château-Thierry when the thunderbolt struck. In the gathering darkness the Russian infantry formed their squares and moved slowly northwards harried by Colbert's and Laferrière's troopers. Guyot plunged southwards to attack Marchais from behind while Ricard, aided by a couple of battalions of Friant's Old Guard, attacked from in front. The Russians withdrew, taking cover from the relentless cavalry charges in the woods south of the Paris road. The fighting reached its greatest fury near Fontenelle where the Château-Thierry road switch-backed to the north over the low range of hills. Michel's division, led by Marshal Mortier in person and aided by Defrance's cavalry, strove desperately to break through along the Château-Thierry road. A break here might have isolated most of Sacken's army. But Pirch's division, fighting with magnificent determination, gave ground but refused to break. Yorck, now himself on the battlefield, fed forward some of his cavalry under Jurgas. Pirch was severely wounded; his brigade lost 1,000 men, a quarter of its strength, but it kept the road barred. Then the night and the weather closed in on a scene of wild confusion and the fighting perforce had to stop. Most of the isolated Russian right wing found its way in the darkness to Viels-Maisons and thence northwards, but 1,000 men were captured and eight guns. In addition the action cost the Russians 1,500 casualties. The Prussians lost 1,200 men – relatively speaking far more than either of the other two contestants – and the French 2,000.

Next morning the Allies began their retreat to Château-Thierry with the Prussians furnishing the rearguard. Napoleon launched a brilliant pursuit. While one column of cavalry followed up the main road to Château-Thierry, another made a detour to Viels-Maisons and then pushed north, well placed to outflank any rearguard position. Hampered by the guns and transports of two corps, all crammed onto a single road, the Prussians withdrew only slowly. With the scent of victory in their nostrils the French cavalry raced after them. At Les Caquerets, five miles south of Château-Thierry, they drove the Allied cavalry from the field and broke the rearguard. They then rampaged over the flat valley of the Marne to Château-Thierry itself. Some 3,000 prisoners, 30 guns and innumerable baggage wagons fell into their hands, before the last Prussians crossed to the north bank of the Marne and burnt down the bridge behind them.

For Napoleon it had been a remarkable victory. The two Allied armies totalled 30,000 seasoned fighting men under able and tough commanders. Napoleon probably never had more than 20,000 men at his disposal and at times far less. Seldom can an army so inferior in numbers have harried so unmercifully an enemy not only superior in strength but by no means deficient in courage or skill. Well might Napoleon write lyrically of the achievements of his Guards. The battle was curiously paradoxical. The battlefield was reported to be a bog, but cavalry have rarely been used to greater effect. The armies of Yorck and Sacken suffered their worst losses retreating before an enemy greatly inferior to them, after fighting a battle that had by no means been an irretrievable disaster. Magnificently as his soldiers fought, it would almost seem that Napoleon defeated his opponents as much by imposing his will on the two Allied generals as by actually beating them in the field. He later suggested that had Macdonald advanced to Château-Thierry, not an enemy would have escaped. This is merely an Imperial flight of fancy. He gave no instructions to Macdonald to advance to Château-Thierry. The Marshal would have had two broken bridges to cross, and if by some magic he had arrived, Yorck had taken due precautions against an attack and had ample resources with which to beat it off. The Allied generals did not pay Napoleon's marshals the reverence they paid to the great master himself. As an interesting possibility, had there been no escape open to them, Sacken and Yorck might have exploited their numbers to more advantage. It does no justice to the extraordinary speed and certainty exhibited by Napoleon to suggest that his opponents were inferior; they were only inferior to him.

On the 13th as Napoleon rested his weary men, he heard that Marmont had been forced out of Étoges by some strange enemy. Conscious that he had defeated all the formations of the Army of Silesia which he had previously identified, he suspected that the newcomer must be Wittgenstein, placed under Blücher; the old Field-Marshal by now must be somewhat short of troops. Napoleon left Mortier to pursue to the north, telling him to keep a watchful eye on Soissons, and marched himself by night to Vauchamps. He personally left Château-Thierry at 3 am on the 14th to meet Blücher blundering along towards Mont-

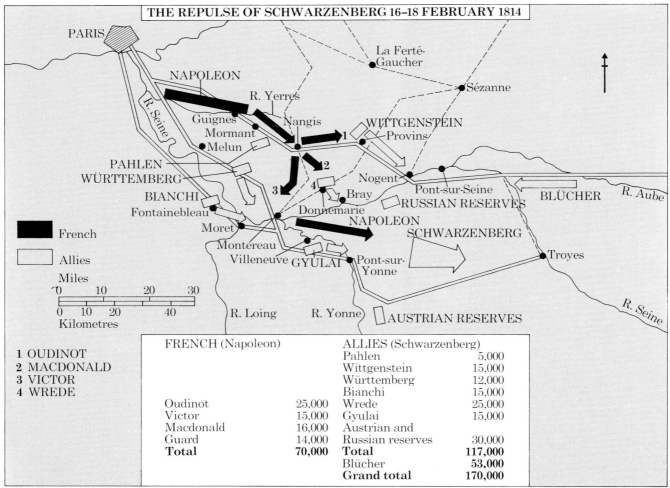

THE REPULSE OF SCHWARZENBERG 16–18 FEBRUARY 1814

1 OUDINOT
2 MACDONALD
3 VICTOR
4 WREDE

FRENCH (Napoleon)		ALLIES (Schwarzenberg)	
		Pahlen	5,000
		Wittgenstein	15,000
		Württemberg	12,000
		Bianchi	15,000
Oudinot	25,000	Wrede	25,000
Victor	15,000	Gyulai	15,000
Macdonald	16,000	Austrian and	
Guard	14,000	Russian reserves	30,000
Total	**70,000**	**Total**	**117,000**
		Blücher	**53,000**
		Grand total	**170,000**

At Montereau, a column of the Guard has moved up ready to consolidate the capture of the bridge, taken by Pajol's cavalry. On the left are the heights of Surville. Watercolour by S. Fort.

mirail, and tore his army apart (see page 84). However, in the west Schwarzenberg, grateful for Napoleon's absence, was approaching dangerously close to Paris. That morning before leaving Château-Thierry Napoleon had arranged for Macdonald with 16,000 men to march from Meaux to the aid of Oudinot and Victor. At 3 o'clock on the morning of the 15th he followed with his Guards.

After he had rested his troops Schwarzenberg began on 10 February a well organized advance towards Paris. He moved on a broad front to ease his administrative difficulties; this also enabled him, with his advantage in numbers, to penetrate between the positions taken up by Victor and Oudinot and force them to retire. After a sharp combat his I Corps (now commanded by Bianchi, Colloredo having been wounded) forced their way across the Yonne, at Pont-sur-Yonne, carried on over the Loing via Moret and occupied Fontaine-

bleau. Prince Eugen of Württemberg crossed the Seine at Montereau, Wrede at Bray and Wittgenstein at Pont-sur-Seine. Bands of Cossacks roamed the countryside down to Orléans terrifying the local inhabitants and making any form of guerrilla warfare difficult to organize. By the 14th Schwarzenberg in places had advanced some 60 miles and Oudinot and Victor, with fewer than 40,000 men with which to oppose his 90,000, had been forced to concentrate their forces behind the River Yerres, centring them on Guignes, only about 18 miles from Paris.

By 15 February Schwarzenberg had some four corps forward on approximately a 30-mile front. On the left, west of the Seine, Bianchi was in Fontainebleau. Ten miles to his right Württemberg bestrode the Melun – Montereau road with Gyulai in support south of the river at Villeneuve-la-Guyard. About 10 miles to the east or right of Württemberg, Wrede was in Donnemarie with

Schwarzenberg himself behind him at Bray; 10 miles further to the east Wittgenstein held Provins on the main road to Paris, supported by the Russian reserves south of the river between Nogent and Bray. The Austrian reserves under Prince Maurice of Lichtenstein were positioned well to the south between Sens and Joigny. Count Pahlen with an advanced guard of about 5,000 men held Mormant, five miles from Guignes. The leading corps each had a separate road for their communications and were well placed for an advance, but they were too dispersed to fight a battle. The roads, however, converged as they approached Paris. In the next two or three days it seemed that, whatever he might wish, Schwarzenberg would find himself compelled to capture Paris. He paused to consider so momentous a possibility. Since his reserves were situated south of the Seine, he might find it difficult to meet a sudden threat should he himself be attacked. Hearing that Blücher was in trouble he meditated swinging his army to the east, but left it too late. He halted, wondering apprehensively what Napoleon would do next.

Macdonald was already near Guignes by 16 February. After an incredible march in which he requisitioned country carts to carry his infantry, Napoleon arrived that evening. He had been forced to join his main army rather than operate on his adversaries' rear, his favourite ploy, since after leaving Mortier to watch Sacken and Yorck north of the river and Marmont to watch Blücher, he was too weak to indulge in independent activity (he was to do so later with unfortunate results). As soon as Schwarzenberg heard that Napoleon was present, although the Emperor had only about 70,000 men, he had no doubt what he should do. He ordered a general retreat. Unfortunately Napoleon was too quick for him.

As Count Pahlen was rubbing the sleep out of his eyes on the morning of the 17th Victor with his corps descended upon him. Pahlen's cavalry disappeared at a gallop with the French in hot pursuit while most of the infantry prudently threw down their arms. The French cavalry drove on down the main road towards Nangis oversetting one of Wrede's cavalry divisions *en route*. Wrede, by now fully aware what was happening, rapidly withdrew south of the Seine at Bray leaving a bridgehead behind him. At the same time Wittgenstein hastily backed away from Provins and, as the bridge at Nogent had been broken, marched to Pont-sur-Seine.

Napoleon had directed all his forces initially on Nangis, thereby ensuring a breakthrough. Now he sent Victor to capture Montereau, hoping to trap Württemberg north of the river. Victor, however, ran into a retreating division of Wrede's Bavarians and to Napoleon's fury was late. Unmolested, Württemberg pulled back to the heights of Surville above the bridge at Montereau and there prepared a rearguard position partly to cover Bianchi moving eastwards from Fontainebleau towards Troyes, and partly to enable his own corps to retire in good order.

On the bitterly cold morning of 18 February Victor hurled his corps against the heights of Montereau. He made little impression. The town of Montereau was built on the far side of the river. The bridge not only spanned the Seine but the Yonne as well. The heights of Surville drop steeply down to the river then flatten out into a narrow tongue of land that runs beside the river bank. Napoleon led the next attack himself; his presence, as ever, electrified his soldiers. The defence began to crumble and the Württembergers to scramble down the slopes and hasten to the bridge. Napoleon loosed Pajol with his division of cuirassiers round the western edge of the heights and along the narrow tongue of land that led to the bridge. Many of Pajol's men had been but recently enlisted and were fully occupied with staying on their mounts without worrying unduly about much else. As they crashed into the Württembergers in a wild, uncontrollable gallop, they scattered them in every direction and were over the bridge before there could be any question of destroying it. The bridge was now in French hands and intact.

Meanwhile Napoleon himself had established his guns on the heights of Surville and directed them at the retreating Württembergers. His secretary Baron Faim remarked, 'The enemy made vain attempts to dismount our batteries. His balls hissed like the wind over the heights of Surville. When his gunners objected to their Emperor exposing himself in this fashion he replied, "Come on my brave fellows, fear nothing, the ball that is to kill me is not yet cast." '

Pajol's tremendous charge had opened the way to the south bank of the Seine, but the Allies held the other bridges; Macdonald at Bray and Oudinot at Nogent hesitated to try and force them. Napoleon called them back to cross at Montereau. The resulting congestion caused a delay that allowed the Austrians to slip away towards Troyes.

Then the winter took a hand: the temperature dropped well below zero, the ground froze solid and it was possible to march across country. Napoleon commented bitterly on the luck of the Austrians as Schwarzenberg managed to concentrate his army successfully at Troyes. Blücher meanwhile had reorganized and with 53,000 Prussians was at Méry menacing Napoleon's left flank. The Emperor seemed to be trapped. The Austrian Prince nerved himself to fight the decisive battle that would settle the war.

However, the situation was altered when two French divisions, following up Schwarzenberg, to their vast surprise ran into the Prussians at Méry. In the ensuing combat they succeeded in burning down the bridge and so confining Blücher, at least for the time being, to the east bank of the Seine. Then Augereau in the south showed signs of moving on Geneva. Schwarzenberg at once detached large numbers of troops to check him, thankfully gave up the idea of fighting the decisive battle and withdrew to Bar-sur-Aube.

And so the second round came to its conclusion. Napoleon had accomplished the unbelievable and with 70,000 men had driven back an invading army of more than 150,000. But there were signs that the strain of his prodigious activity was beginning to tell.

Unfortunately for Napoleon his very military success was fatal. He could not believe he could be defeated, and again refused the offers of the Allies as inadequate. It was to be his last chance. In the South of France Wellington on 27 February had heavily defeated Soult at the Battle of Orthez. In the North little remained. The writing was clear enough for all to see; only Napoleon, the great gambler, would not give up.

CHAPTER 8
FATAL MARCH

At noon on 15 February a chastened Blücher watched his army march gratefully into Châlons to find very welcome stocks of food and forage awaiting them. Over the next two days Yorck and Sacken came in; from the Rhine Kleist's last units rejoined and Langeron arrived with the balance of his corps. By the 19th most of the recent losses had been replaced. Blücher wrote to Schwarzenberg, 'I will be at Méry ready for battle with 53,000 men and

French dragoon on outpost duty;
painting by Meissonier.

300 guns on the 21st.' And into battle once again sallied the redoubtable Prussian. So remarkably rapid a recovery suggests that, roughly as they had been handled, except for Olsufiev's unfortunate detachment none of his army had been routed or badly disorganized.

At Bar-sur-Aube the Allied sovereigns and plenipotentiaries conferred. They agreed that Schwarzenberg should detach troops sufficient to form an Army of the South to deter Augereau in Lyon and protect the lines of communication to Switzerland. The two main armies comprising the Allied Grand Army, the Army of Bohemia and the Army of Silesia, were to act independently, but to operate on a sort of see-saw principle. The army opposed to Napoleon would give way under his weight, as it were, while the other swung up against Paris. When Napoleon changed ends, the army menaced would withdraw, while the other advanced. By this means it was hoped gradually to approach the capital without running into hopeless administrative difficulties. Once they were sufficiently near Paris, the two armies could unite and there fight the decisive battle.

To begin with, Schwarzenberg was to remain on the defensive, prepared to retreat to Langres if Napoleon pressed him, while Blücher with his Army of Silesia was to cross north of the Aube-Seine river-line and menace Paris. Now began a most astonishing game of blind-man's-buff, in which neither opponent knew the strength nor the intentions of the other. On 24 February Blücher crossed the Seine at Anglure and prepared to thrust on Paris. Winzingerode with 30,000 men was at Reims, Count St Priest with 16,000 at Vitry, and Bülow with 20,000 was expected at Soissons on 26 or 27 February. It seemed that the war must soon be ended.

Blücher, initially opposed by Marmont who was subsequently joined by Mortier, pressed on towards Meaux, 28 miles from Paris. The two Marshals, their total force numbering only about 10,000, fell back with great skill, husbanding their men; they crossed the Marne at Trilport and retreated to Meaux. Blücher had with him some 50 canvas pontoons. He turned back towards La Ferté-sous-Jouarre, threw a bridge of boats across the river near that town and hooked back towards Meaux. As he went he learnt that Napoleon was on the march north.

Blücher had summoned Winzingerode to Meaux. The Russian has assented to the move with his usual courtesy, but Blücher looked for him in vain. He had yet to learn that Winzingerode's impressive courtesy was only surpassed by an even more impressive incompetence. Confident that the Russian would appear, he decided on a stroke that was truly Napoleonic. He was occupying the central position beloved by the Emperor; he resolved first to destroy Marmont and Mortier and then turn on Napoleon with, as he expected, some 80,000 men. The plan was worthy of the great master; the execution was not.

On 28 February and 1 March he attacked the two French Marshals who had taken refuge behind the River Ourcq; their command had now swollen to 16,000 men, but they were still vastly inferior to their opponent. However, Mortier at Lizy, seven miles north-east of Meaux, and Marmont at May and Crouy administered stinging repulses; Blücher drew back towards La Ferté-Milon, the French on his heels. Müffling said of the action that 'this enterprise of the hostile generals is one of their finest in the whole campaign'.

Now Blücher began to feel apprehensive. Napoleon's vanguard was reported at La Ferté-sous-Jouarre, only about 12 miles to the south. On 2 March he moved eastwards some 10 miles to Oulchy-le-Château, hoping to meet Winzingerode, but of that worthy there was no sign. From Oulchy-le-Château the main road ran to Soissons about 13 miles to the north: here there was a good bridge leading to the far bank of the Aisne, a bank that was beginning to look decidedly attractive. Unfortunately a small French garrison consisting of a Polish battalion 700 strong and a few gunners held the town of Soissons which, it turned out, even now Bülow and Winzingerode with about 45,000 men were engaged in besieging, though so far they had made little progress.

By the morning of 3 March it was clear that Blücher had either to fight where he stood, or else cross the Aisne before Napoleon could catch him. To give battle to Napoleon on, as he thought, level terms did not accord with the strategic plan, nor for that matter with his wishes. His army was weary and footsore and somewhat downhearted after the repulse on the Ourcq. He ordered his baggage to leave early in the morning and go by Fismes and Berry-au-Bac to the north bank of the river. The rest of the army would rest until 4 o'clock that afternoon, then cross the river either on pontoon bridges near Vailly, where Bülow had already erected one such, or continue towards the fine stone bridge at Berry-au-Bac 30 miles farther east.

After the baggage had gone beyond recall, the news came in that Soissons had surrendered. Blücher at once switched his line of march to that town and by evening was united with Bülow and Winzingerode. By all accounts the meeting was not notably harmonious.[1] Winzingerode and Bülow had viewed their transfer from the Army of the North without marked pleasure. Bülow, watching the Army of Silesia filing into Soissons, remarked to the effect that that Army certainly led the field in shabbiness, and wondered audibly why the troopers thought it unnecessary to feed their horses. Tattered and weather-beaten after nights spent frozen under the stars or thrashed by the rain, the Army of Silesia ground their teeth as they passed the sleek, well-fed troops from the north, who had moved from one sheltered billet to the next.

Now with about 90,000 men under his com-

---

[1] It has been asserted that the surrender of Soissons saved Blücher, and a stream of abuse has since been directed at the unfortunate garrison commander, General Moreau, for sparing the town from a storm. Winzingerode and Bülow, having exhausted the efforts of their 45,000 men besieging a garrison of about 1,000, had every reason to exaggerate the importance of their capture. Napoleon's fury – he wrote, though without effect, that Moreau should be shot – stemmed in the first place from the belief that the defence was not as stubborn as it might have been, and secondly from his intention to use the bridge for an advance on Laon. As for Blücher's predicament, Bülow had already constructed a pontoon bridge at Vailly nine miles to the east of Soissons and had the material to build more, while Blücher had with him his 50 canvas pontoons. Napoleon was still about 12 miles away. Had he got closer, the Prussian might have lost some tail-feathers, but that would have been all; and had Blücher persuaded Bülow and Winzingerode to come south of the river, Napoleon might have found himself gravely outnumbered. When Winzingerode, having put him in peril in the first place, explained to Blücher how grateful he should be that Bülow and he had saved him, Blücher nearly exploded.

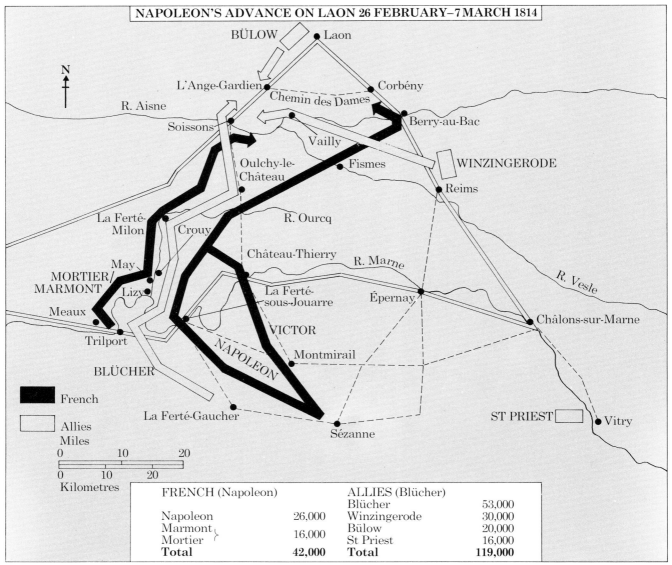

NAPOLEON'S ADVANCE ON LAON 26 FEBRUARY–7 MARCH 1814

N

BÜLOW   Laon

L'Ange-Gardien   Corbény

R. Aisne

Chemin des Dames

Soissons   Berry-au-Bac

Vailly   WINZINGERODE

Oulchy-le-Château   Fismes

Reims

La Ferté-Milon

Crouy   R. Ourcq

May   Château-Thierry

MORTIER/MARMONT   Lizy   La Ferté-sous-Jouarre

Meaux   Épernay   R. Marne   R. Vesle

Trilport   VICTOR   Châlons-sur-Marne

BLÜCHER   Montmirail

NAPOLEON

French

Allies

La Ferté-Gaucher   ST PRIEST   Vitry

Sézanne

Miles

0	10	20

0	10	20

Kilometres

FRENCH (Napoleon)		ALLIES (Blücher)	
		Blücher	53,000
Napoleon	26,000	Winzingerode	30,000
Marmont Mortier	16,000	Bülow	20,000
		St Priest	16,000
Total	**42,000**	**Total**	**119,000**

mand (it is difficult to estimate wastage rates from sickness and battle casualties, for adequate records were not kept) Blücher prepared to fight the 80,000 or so troops he thought accompanied Napoleon. He spread his troops along the north bank of the Aisne from Soissons to Berry-au-Bac and waited. On 5 March some French troops attacked Soissons, penetrated a suburb and were then thrown out; they marched off eastwards. At noon on the 6th Blücher, to his stupefaction, heard that a strong French column had been seen near Corbény on the Reims-Laon road, and French cavalry patrols were reported to have reached Laon itself; this last report proved to be exaggerated. The incompetent Winzingerode had been responsible for guarding the bridge at Berry-au-Bac and in consequence Napoleon had crossed the Aisne without difficulty (but then, as Müffling had tartly observed, Winzingerode was an excellent swordsman). By the time Blücher arrived at Craonne he found the French in full possession of Corbény and preparing to advance on Craonne. This could be troublesome, for Winzingerode had omitted to garrison it properly. The old Field-Marshal deduced that the French troops which had attacked Soissons must still be some way away and that therefore Napoleon would not have all his army with him next day, the 7th. It seemed a good day to give battle.

The road from Soissons to Laon met the Reims – Laon road to form the obtuse apex angle of a triangle whose base was the 16-mile Chemin des Dames running parallel to the Aisne. The Chemin des Dames, famous in two world wars, ran from Corbény on the Reims road up onto a plateau at Craonne and thence along the plateau to drop down to L'Ange-Gardien on the Soissons road. The plateau had steep, forested sides, falling sharply to the valley of the Aisne in the south and equally sharply to the valley of the Ailette in the north. It varied considerably in width, sometimes being up to 1,000 yards wide; its narrowest part, a neck only about 150 yards wide, occurred by the farm of Heurtebise about two and a half miles west of Craonne. It would be dangerous to advance down the Reims road to Laon without first establishing a firm grip on the plateau.

Blücher deduced that Napoleon from the foothold he had already secured in Craonne would strike westwards next day to L'Ange-Gardien. He accepted that he had lost Craonne. He ordered Winzingerode's infantry under General Woronzoff onto the plateau to hold the ground from the neck at Heurtebise westwards, and put Sacken behind him in support. He judged it useless to deploy any more men on the constricted area of the plateau. Instead he concentrated 10,000 horsemen out of the cavalry of his various corps, assembled them at Chévrigny in the valley of the Ailette north of the plateau and put them under the noted swordsman. It was one way of disposing of Winzingerode but

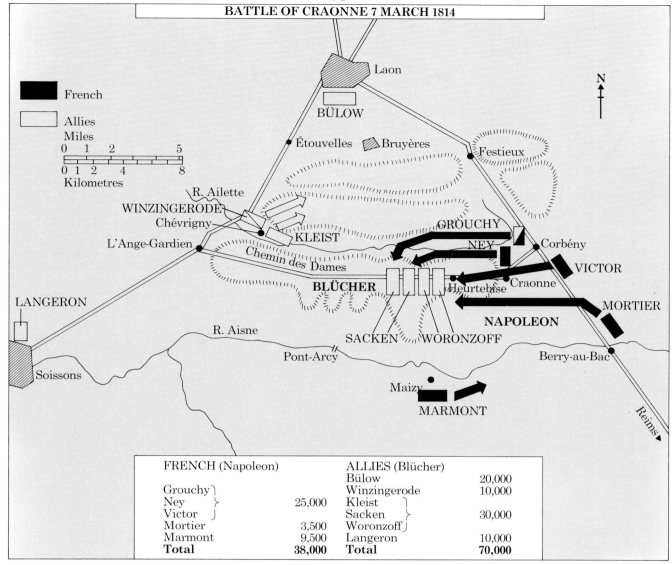

BATTLE OF CRAONNE 7 MARCH 1814

Laon

BÜLOW

French

Allies

Miles
0 1 2 5
0 1 2 4 8
Kilometres

Étouvelles   Bruyères   Festieux

R. Ailette

WINZINGERODE

Chévrigny

GROUCHY

L'Ange-Gardien   KLEIST   NEY   Corbény

Chemin des Dames   VICTOR

BLÜCHER   Heurtebise   Craonne

LANGERON   MORTIER

NAPOLEON

R. Aisne   SACKEN   WORONZOFF

Pont-Arcy   Berry-au-Bac

Soissons

Maizy

MARMONT   Reims

N

FRENCH (Napoleon)		ALLIES (Blücher)	
		Bülow	20,000
Grouchy ⎫		Winzingerode	10,000
Ney ⎬	25,000	Kleist ⎫	
Victor ⎭		Sacken ⎬	30,000
Mortier	3,500	Woronzoff ⎭	
Marmont	9,500	Langeron	10,000
Total	**38,000**	**Total**	**70,000**

not possibly the best, as Blücher was to discover. Winzingerode with his cavalry and with Kleist's corps in support was to go to Festieux on the Reims road and sweep down it to Corbény, taking Napoleon's expected attack in flank and rear. It was a shrewd piece of anticipation. Blücher placed Bülow to hold Laon itself and left most of Langeron's corps to hold Soissons. His guess was partially confirmed that evening when the French launched a vain attack to capture Heurtebise and cross the narrow neck of land before dark. Firing ceased at nightfall and the soldiers bivouacked. It began to freeze.

Victor had yet to come up from the direction of Berry-au-Bac when at 10 o'clock on a raw, damp morning Ney, impatient for battle, led forward his divisions of the Young Guard to the attack. The neck by Heurtebise, in the face of concentrated Russian gunfire, was a death-trap. Ney tried to climb onto the plateau to the west of it. The slopes were steep and slippery and the guns skidded and stuck. Time and again the French penetrated to the edge of the plateau only to be hurled off it. Victor came up and joined in the fearful struggle. Colbert and Exelmans with their divisions of the Guard cavalry threaded their way up precipitous tracks onto the plateau, taking the defence in the flank and rear. The Russians drew back, then counter-attacked and nearly thrust the French off the plateau. The battle raged on with mounting in-

tensity. Blücher listened intently for the sound of gunfire from the east. None came. He rode off to Chévrigny to find his missing cavalry divisions. He had not far to go. Winzingerode having courteously agreed to carry out his task had apparently been too courteous to order his men to move beyond Bruyères.

The aged Field-Marshal, feeling desperately unwell, tried to lead them forward himself. The going was difficult, the roads atrocious. It became evident that he would never arrive in time. He gave up the attempt and discarded his original plan; instead he resolved to concentrate every soldier under his command around Laon and fight there a battle to the finish. He called in the 10,000 men from Langeron's corps, at that time garrisoning Soissons, and ordered Sacken and Woronzoff to withdraw from the Chemin des Dames towards Laon.

On the plateau the ferocious struggle continued. The Russians were enraged by the order to withdraw. One Russian general exclaimed, so the historian Henri Houssaye records, 'I will die where I stand, I will not retreat an inch.' His senior calmly replied, 'If your excellency wishes to die here, I have no objection, but I must insist that your brigade retires at once.' Mortier after a long march came up and the artillery of the Guard deployed 72 guns on the plateau. The Russians sullenly gave back, pressed all the way by the French. Darkness

At the Battle of Craonne, the Chemin des Dames is shown viewed from the direction of Craonne.
A French attack is going in on Heurtebise, and the gunsmoke on the far right indicates an attempt to outflank the farm;
the steep, forested sides of the plateau are clearly delineated by the artist, S. Fort.

fell as the last Russians reached L'Ange-Gardien on the Soissons road and the savage combat came to an end. Initially the French had been heavily outnumbered. Towards the end the numbers were about equal, 25,000 taking an active part on each side, losses for each totalling about a fifth.

Both armies reorganized for the battle they knew would inevitably come next day. Blücher commanded an unhappy army. The Russians questioned why they had fought on the Chemin des Dames at all and noted sourly that the Prussians apparently had not thought it necessary to join in. The old Field-Marshal himself was feeling seriously ill. Perhaps for this reason he gave up all attempt at frills and resolved to fight a simple, straightforward defensive action. He centred his defence about the town of Laon which stands on a solitary hill in the middle of a plain. Bülow remained garrisoning the town and the two suburbs of Semilly and Ardon down in the plain to the south of it; Winzingerode deployed his corps to the west of the town, and Kleist and Yorck ranged theirs to the east; Sacken and Langeron in reserve took post behind the town to the north, concealed by the hill. Blücher awaited battle with about 80,000 men. During the day the French closed up to Etouvelles on the Soissons road, which Winzingerode was holding as an outpost.

As night fell it began to snow. At 3 am French infantry materialized out of a blizzard and stormed into Etouvelles. As the darkness receded a thick fog rolled down, blanketing the scene in a white mantle pierced by the sudden flames of the guns. A fearful struggle developed for the suburb of Semilly while the French broke into Ardon and established a firm position there.

Blücher with his staff stood on a wall of the ruined castle of Laon, peering helplessly into the noisy whiteness below. Then towards noon the fog thinned and cleared; they rushed to level their telescopes. But where were the French? Some had established themselves in Ardon and were disputing fiercely the possession of Semilly. But this relative handful of men could not be all the French; not even Napoleon surely would be so rash. Then a large column was reported coming up the road from Berry-au-Bac. Perhaps this was the main French attack. The column captured Festieux, driving out

some Prussian cavalry, and ploughed its way forward towards Athies. About 3 o'clock in the afternoon a great pall of smoke mushroomed in the east. The Prussians had fired Athies and withdrawn. The guns thundered on, but still Blücher gazed on the scene in bewilderment. This could not be all the French. He instructed Bülow to probe forward in the centre. Probably Napoleon had a powerful force concealed here waiting for Blücher to reinforce his flanks before smashing through the Allied centre and capturing Laon. Bülow pushed aside the French in Ardon and advanced towards Leuilly, severing the two wings of the French attack and preventing them having any knowledge about the fate of the other. Bülow found no trace of a powerful, uncommitted reserve. Reassured, Blücher now planned a counter-stroke. The country on his left was open and very suitable for such a move. First he ordered a demonstration to be made on his right towards Clacy to fix the French attention in that direction. They reacted strongly and took Clacy, but it was becoming plain that on this flank the French attacks were losing their bite.

Now the Prussian gave orders to his two reserve corps, those of Sacken and Langeron, to move out from their cover and take over from Kleist and Yorck. When they had been relieved the two Prussian corps were to assault Athies and drive forward down the Reims road. Night had fallen before the Prussians could form up for the attack, and the flickering bivouac fires had begun to pierce the darkness. They moved quietly forward; there was to be no firing; only the bayonet.

When on 25 February Napoleon heard that Blücher with, he estimated, about 8,000 men had crossed to the north bank of the Aube, presumably to join Winzingerode who was reported to be near Soissons with about 16,000 men, he determined to follow the rump of the Army of Silesia and finally liquidate it. He then proposed to march on the eastern frontier, pick up his blockaded garrisons, tear apart the lines of communication of the Allied Grand Army and compel it to retreat, when he would surely find an opportunity to catch it at a disadvantage. Macdonald as the senior of his marshals he left with his own, Oudinot's and Gérard's corps, in all about 40,000

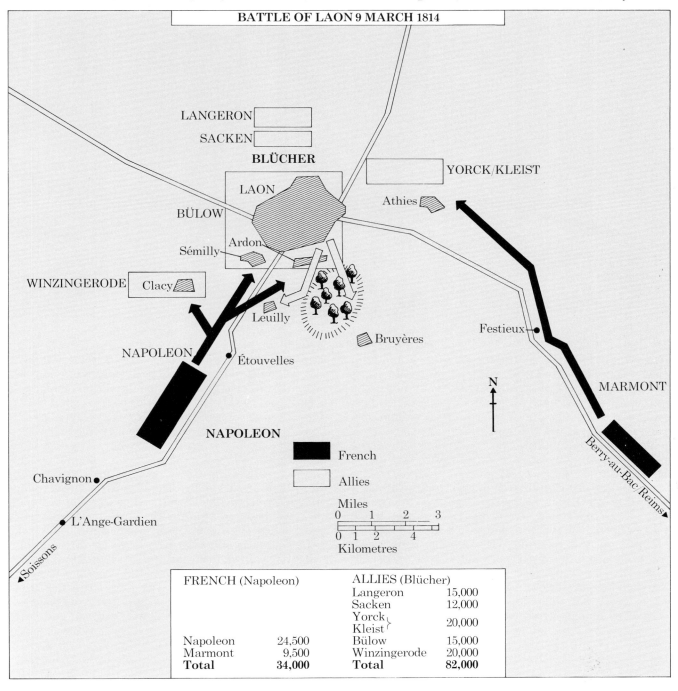

men, to watch Schwarzenberg at Bar-sur-Aube. He told him that he expected to be gone only three days; then with Victor, recently given a new corps of the Young Guard, Ney with his men, and Grouchy with the cavalry of the Guard under Nansouty and a corps of cavalry, he went off to deal with Blücher.

On 2 March he reached La Ferté-sous-Jouarre with Ney while Victor with his corps approached Château-Thierry. Both bridges were down, there were no pontoons and it was not until early on 3 March that they could get across the river. The infuriating surrender of Soissons delayed his advance on Laon which he intended as a bastion in the north. He ordered Marmont and Mortier to retake it but they were repulsed; then Nansouty, discovering the bridge at Berry-au-Bac to be lightly held, at once forced his way over. Napoleon now directed his whole army on Berry-au-Bac and advancing on Laon encountered a strong Allied force west of Craonne astride the Chemin des Dames. The ferocity of the battle for the plateau surprised him; partly it was due, he thought, to a premature attack by Ney who had not waited for Victor. However, the Russians had been driven off the plateau and he anticipated that Laon would not be strongly held. He had no idea of the numbers Blücher now had at his disposal.

On the 8th he massed the three corps of Ney, Mortier and Victor on the Soissons road for the decisive thrust on Laon. Victor had been wounded the day before and Charpentier had temporarily replaced him. Marmont was at Berry-au-Bac just north of the river, having completed his crossing that evening. Napoleon ordered him to advance next morning on Laon by the Reims road. If he came across to the west he would never be in time for the battle. There was a certain amount of risk in the order. Marmont would be operating widely separated from the rest of the army, but Marmont was an extremely able general and if the main attack pinned the enemy down his thrust might prove decisive. The chances were that Laon was only held by a rearguard.

Early on the morning of 9 March, despite the astonishing odds, the fire and sheer audacity of the

BATTLE OF LAON 9 MARCH 1814

FRENCH (Napoleon)		ALLIES (Blücher)	
		Langeron	15,000
		Sacken	12,000
		Yorck/Kleist	20,000
Napoleon	24,500	Bülow	15,000
Marmont	9,500	Winzingerode	20,000
Total	**34,000**	**Total**	**82,000**

French carried them almost onto the lip of Laon. On the right Marmont was late in arriving. Coming up from near Berry-au-Bac he ran into the fog and waited for it to clear. However, he pressed on at midday and forced his way into Athies. Beyond it the Prussian resistance stiffened. Marmont with his 9,500 men saw in front of him Kleist's and Yorck's men. Behind them in the distance he could see further masses – Sacken's and Langeron's corps – while a large body of cavalry under General Ziethen threatened his flank if he made a move forward. Marmont realized such a move would be decidedly unwise, and welcomed the onset of darkness which concealed the poverty of his resources. Deeply embroiled in battle, he did not at once inform Napoleon of the totally unexpected situation that he had encountered. Later he found all communications with the left wing had been blocked. He himself had no idea of what had happened in the west.

Weary and ill-fed after days of marching and fighting, Marmont's young conscripts failed to post proper guards. They were scattered gathering

little progress. That night, certain that but for Marmont's unfortunate affair Blücher would have abandoned Laon, Napoleon marched back to Soissons. He was still unaware of the appalling dangers he had escaped.

On the evening of the 9th, after hearing about the rout of Marmont, and the readiness of the Prussians to fight having been clearly demonstrated to the Russians, Blücher issued his orders for the next day. Yorck and Kleist were to pursue the fugitives towards Berry-au-Bac, Bülow and Winzingerode to continue holding their present positions, Sacken and Yorck to push through the empty centre to Bruyères and from there turn right-handed towards L'Ange-Gardien, cutting off all the French on the Soissons road. It could mean the end of the French army.

On the morning of the 10th Müffling, himself recovering from fever, 'repaired to the Field Marshal whose large ante-room was quite filled up with officers. Among them I observed many Russian generals . . . and those croakers who are to be found at all headquarters when great events fright-

At Berry-au-Bac, Nansouty has led the cavalry of the Guard across the bridge
and is driving off a party of Cossacks.

firewood or cooking their evening meal when long lines of bayonets that glittered in the firelight came at them out of the frosty darkness. They panicked and fled. A few were bayoneted, some 2,000 surrendered to Kleist and Yorck and the remainder ran away towards Festieux and Berry-au-Bac, leaving 50 guns, 120 wagons and all their baggage behind them. Napoleon's right flank had evaporated.

Napoleon, convinced that Blücher was about to pull out of Laon, spent the night at Chavignon five miles from that town on the Soissons road. He had risen and was pulling on his boots at about 4 o'clock on the morning of the 10th when two agitated dragoons appeared out of the darkness and craved an audience; they told him that utter disaster had overtaken Marmont. He received the news with his accustomed equanimity. Unconscious of his extreme peril, he remained outside Laon during the whole of the 10th. A counter-attack by Winzingerode to recapture Clacy failed, but efforts by the French to penetrate into the suburbs of Laon not surprisingly made equally

en them.' Wondering about this curious conclave he learned to his horrified amazement that all forward moves had been cancelled. Blücher's health had finally collapsed. His eyes were swollen and he could scarcely see. Convinced he was dying, he refused to consider any military matters or give decisions, considering such matters irrelevant for one about to enter a new and better world. Gneisenau, his Chief-of-Staff, was distraught. Langeron, the next senior, knew himself to be incapable of exercising the authority of a commander-in-chief. When he saw the ailing Blücher he cried with more force than tact, 'For God's sake, whatever happens let us take that corpse along with us.' The Chief-of-Staff on his own initiative dared take no positive action. For the next few days the Army of Silesia lay paralysed. Yorck, convinced that Blücher had died and that Gneisenau was concealing his death to mount some sinister intrigue against him, sent in his resignation, changed into civilian dress, stepped into his coach and started driving away to Brussels. Blücher, by then partially restored to this world, scrawled a few almost indecipherable lines imploring him to return. Certain now that Blücher still lived, he consented to come back.

Although he had been forced to withdraw from Laon, Blücher's Army of Silesia seemed overcome by a curious lassitude and Napoleon thought once more of going east to collect his troops immured in the frontier fortresses. But the news from Macdonald at Bar-sur-Aube was bad. He had tried to conceal his Emperor's absence. Schwarzenberg, however, soon heard of Napoleon's departure and struck at once. In a series of actions between 27 February and 2 March, although the Austrian Prince himself was slightly wounded, he drove the outnumbered French away from Bar-sur-Aube. Now, to Napoleon's indignation – he did not see why his marshals should not triumph over superior numbers in the same way as he did – Macdonald proved completely incapable of stopping the Austrian. While Macdonald fell back towards Paris, Napoleon learned that the renegade Frenchman, Count St Priest, had taken Reims.

of me." "Push the whole lot in the ditch, I must be in Reims by midnight."

'This was done in a minute and the battery passed under the Emperor's eyes as he stood watching with his back to the fire . . . he gave the signal, the cuirassiers dashed into line . . . the charge was so terrible that they carried everything before them. The people shut up in their houses put lights in their windows. Every place was lighted. One could have picked up a needle. The Emperor was in Reims by midnight.'

St Priest fell, mortally wounded by a cannonball, and his corps was dispersed. It was a welcome success. Napoleon had lost 11,000 men in the three days near Laon and Blücher had only been checked. His situation had begun to look extremely gloomy. Now he was astride Blücher's communication lines with his bases at Châlons and Vitry and the way to the French garrisons on the border lay open. He sent order after order to General Durutte to break out of the frontier fortresses, unite with the other blockaded garrisons and join him with, he optimistically estimated, 12,000 men. Meanwhile it had

French infantry march up to the outer suburbs of Laon.

St Priest had come up from Vitry to Reims to re-establish communication with Blücher in Laon. He never thought to encounter Napoleon. When out of a grey afternoon on 13 March French soldiers appeared advancing on Reims, he went out to meet them. By evening he had sought shelter behind its none too solid walls. Captain Coignet, the Emperor's baggage-master, has left a description of the scene.

'Near the gate which faces the road to Paris there was an elevated piece of ground surmounted by a windmill. Here the Emperor established his headquarters in the open. We made him a good fire. We could not see two steps before us . . . He called for his bearskin and stretched himself out by the fire while we all watched. The Russians began to advance at about ten o'clock at night. They made a sortie with a tremendous discharge of musketry.' Hearing the noise Napoleon thought the hour ripe for a counter-attack into Reims itself. He called up a captain commanding a siege battery. "Where are your guns?" "On the road." "Bring them here." "I can't get through, the artillery of the line is ahead

become urgent to check the Austrian advance on Paris. Once again the heads of Schwarzenberg's columns were north of the Seine.

Napoleon called for a secretary and paper. Three possible courses of action he set out and analysed. First, he could go to Sézanne, thence to Provins and on to Meaux. The roads were bad, but he might well cut off that part of the Allied Grand Army that was north of the Seine. Second, he could go straight to Meaux by the main highway and join Macdonald. Such a move would forfeit surprise and give him no strategical advantage at the outset of a battle. Third, he could cross the Aube at Arcis; by the 20th he calculated he could be at Méry and moving on Schwarzenberg's headquarters at Troyes. He could, however, be adventuring into the heart of the Grand Army with only about 25,000 men. The risks were enormous, the possible results incalculable. He might deprive the Grand Army of its commander and lock it up west of the Seine in fearful confusion. Macdonald with 30,000 men could press it from the north, Augereau could come up from the south and he could disrupt its supplies.

The peasants, antagonized by the Cossacks and soldiers desperate for warmth and shelter, had begun to rise and attack Allied convoys. Cut off from its base and harassed by partisans, the Grand Army might disintegrate. Napoleon knew that he had only bought himself a few days before Blücher's Army of Silesia recommenced operations. In that time he had to score a major victory over the Allies, something more than merely mauling a single corps. He selected his third alternative.

But already Schwarzenberg had begun to withdraw. It was enough for him that the Emperor was on the move towards him. The news of the loss of Reims made him anxious about his line of communications. Once more the roads were carpeted with retreating Allied soldiers, while the peasants watched with silent rage as the unending columns filed through their villages for hour after hour.

By the evening of 19 March Rayefski with VI Corps – he had taken it over from Wittgenstein who had been invalided home – Württemberg with his IV Corps and Gyulai with III Corps were all in the area of Troyes. Wrede with his Bavarian V Corps was at Chaudrey about six miles east of Arcis. Macdonald, surprised by the sudden withdrawal, had lost contact with the retreating columns. The same day Napoleon, determined not to lose an hour and at last in possession of bridging equipment, flung pontoon bridges across the Aube at Boulages and Plancy while Ney crossed at Arcis. His advanced troops reached Méry, but from Troyes the birds had flown. He wrote defiantly that he had achieved all he had set out to do. But he knew that time was now running out for him and that he must land a damaging blow on his slippery adversary.

He ordered his whole army, except for Mortier and Marmont, to concentrate next day at Arcis-sur-Aube. The main road ran south of the river. He arranged for Sébastiani to take the three cavalry divisions of the Guard along the main road, while the infantry of the Old Guard followed minor roads along the north bank. He assumed Schwarzenberg would resume his retreat in his customary manner towards Bar-sur-Aube. Indeed Schwarzenberg had already issued orders for such a move, when the ubiquitous Cossacks told him that Napoleon with about 25,000 men was south of the Aube between Plancy and Arcis. For Napoleon with so small an army to take such a position within striking distance of the Allied Grand Army and with his back to an unfordable river was an unpardonable liberty, even for the Emperor. Schwarzenberg cancelled his original instructions and directed his corps commanders to drive forward towards Plancy and Arcis-sur-Aube.

The three corps from Troyes, advancing on Plancy, missed the main body of Napoleon's army but roughly handled a cavalry division doing rearguard duty, forcing it back on Méry. Wrede marching westwards along the south bank of the Aube ran into Ney at Torcy, one and a half miles from Arcis, while nearly the whole of the Allied cavalry, riding directly on Arcis, cannoned into Colbert's and Exelmans's divisions. In great strength the Allied horsemen thundered down. The French broke under the impact. The troopers turned their horses and galloped off towards the river in a wild mass, racing each other to be first across the bridge.

It was a moment of supreme crisis. The cavalry of the Guard might be routed and Ney isolated and forced to surrender. Napoleon himself rode to the bridge. The familiar square, grey-clad figure barked out, 'Who will cross the bridge before me?' The shame-faced troopers reined in. They turned their mounts once more to face the foe and reformed their ranks, but the lines were ragged and shaky. Then there came a sight that had turned many a battle. On the far bank appeared the bearskins of the Guard. Steadily the veterans filed over the bridge. The strain of the disasters of the the last two years and of the last few weeks, when fate seemed determined to frustrate his finest designs, had weighed down the spirits of the Emperor. He later confessed to Caulaincourt that on the field of Arcis he deliberately sought a bullet to end all his perplexities. Now he spurred his horse into the hottest fire and personally deployed each battalion of the Old Guard. A howitzer shell burst underneath his horse. Horse and rider disappeared in a cloud of dust. When it cleared Napoleon could be seen stepping from his dying charger, escaping by some miracle without a scratch. The situation stabilized. Ney beat off all attacks by Wrede's Bavarians, while the rock-like squares of the Old Guard stood immovable against the charges of the Allied cavalry. As night fell, the Allies withdrew.

Napoleon had little idea with whom he had been fighting. His enemy seemed to be a strong force of cavalry supported by Wrede's corps. Mac-

donald was coming up the north bank and should arrive by the evening of the next day. Beyond Arcis the rising ground obscured the view and in the dusk all he could see was a ring of solitary Cossack sentries on their horses surveying his movements. It was not fitting that Napoleon should withdraw before a mere corps of the Allies.

Early next morning he sent out his cavalry, 9,000 strong, to reconnoitre forward of the high ground in front of him. As the splendid lines of horsemen approached, the Cossacks wheeled their horses about and galloped away. Then the French topped the rise. A horrifying sight greeted their eyes. Ranged in a great arc about them were endless columns and squares of infantry checkered with guns and horsemen. The whole Grand Army, with 100,000 men, lay spread out before their gaze. Before such a multitude a battle was hopeless. The cavalry turned about. Now nothing remained to Napoleon but to escape across to the north bank of the river – if he could.

Schwarzenberg held his ground waiting for the Emperor to attack. So the morning passed. Then the Austrians saw Frenchmen climbing up the north bank of the Aube. Schwarzenberg ordered a general attack. It was too late. Leval's division from Soult's Army of Spain fought a desperate rearguard action in the town of Arcis, then skilfully extricated itself destroying the bridge behind it. Once again Napoleon's aura had saved his army from destruction.

For Napoleon however, the end was in sight. He was now too weak to fight either Blücher or Schwarzenberg; he himself was becoming weary of the struggle and his marshals only remained with him because their loyalty overbore their sense of reality. Bordeaux under the impact of Wellington's victories in the south had declared for Louis XVIII. Augereau had abandoned Lyon without a fight. Napoleon plunged desperately towards the border fortresses hoping to draw the Allies after him. Briefly they hesitated, then they marched on Paris with only Marmont and Mortier to oppose them, sending Winzingerode with 10,000 cavalry and some infantry to observe Napoleon.

Despite a magnificent stand at Fère-Champenoise by Pacthod and a division of National Guardsmen, Marmont and Mortier fell back before impossible odds towards Paris. Learning that his capital was menaced Napoleon returned by forced marches, taking the road by Fontainebleau. In a fever of impatience he left the marching columns, climbed into his coach and rushed on towards Paris, leaving his army strung out over the roads to the east. At the Cour de France, a posting inn at Juvisy about 10 miles south of Paris, he was waiting while the horses were changed when in the dusk he saw a column of cavalry coming down the road from the direction of Paris. He recognized General Belliard of Mortier's corps at the head. After a few rapid questions he learned the fatal news: Paris had capitulated early that evening (30 March). The Emperor turned his coach round and drove back to Fontainebleau. Still he refused to abandon hope.

By 3 April Napoleon was in the process of concentrating 60,000 troops about him. Early that afternoon he reviewed Friant's division of the Old Guard and a division of the Young. Then he addressed all officers and NCOs. 'Soldiers, by stealing three marches on us the enemy has made himself master of Paris . . . in a few days I will attack Paris. I count on you.' There was no response. Napoleon looked around him then cried, 'Am I right?' The old magic reasserted itself; there was a tornado of sound: 'Vive L'Empereur, à Paris, à Paris.' But the marshals and the generals stood in a group apart, stony-faced and silent. The parade dismissed but they moved away deep in discussion. Then Ney, Lefebvre and Moncey went off to speak to their Emperor.

They burst into his room where he was discussing future plans with Berthier. Ney roughly pointed out the futility of further resistance. Napoleon outlined his plans for the future and spoke of the drive he was about to launch on Paris. By then Macdonald and Oudinot had come in to report the arrival of their corps. All listened to his proposals in a deadly silence of dissent. Then Macdonald exclaimed, 'We do not intend to expose Paris to the fate of Moscow.' Napoleon replied firmly that he was going to march on Paris. Ney interjected, 'The army will not march on Paris.' Napoleon looked sternly at his marshal, raising his voice. 'The Army will obey me.' 'Sire,' returned Ney. 'The army will obey its generals.' For a few moments no one spoke while the assembly waited for the thunderbolt to strike. Then Napoleon quietly asked his marshals to withdraw and leave him with Caulaincourt, who had been conducting negotiations with the Allies; it seemed a tacit

This panoramic view by Heydeck shows Schwarzenberg's attack on the outnumbered Oudinot at Bar-sur-Aube on 28 February.

admission of defeat. Yet he could not, would not, accept this. A march on Paris might not at present be possible, but he was certain that his soldiers and junior officers remained loyal. He must bring over the marshals and the generals. A restoration of the Bourbons would jeopardize their titles and estates. He decided to offer the Allies a conditional abdication, perhaps hoping that when they rejected it, as they almost certainly would, he might induce his marshals and generals to fight on.

During most of the day he discussed the drafting of his abdication in favour of his son, first with Caulaincourt and then with Ney and Macdonald. Its sentiments had to be suitably noble and altruistic so that if the Allies rejected it no one should doubt that he had to continue the struggle. Finally he wrote, 'The Emperor Napoleon, faithful to his word, declares he is ready to descend from the throne, to leave France and even this life for the good of the country, inseparable from which are the rights of his son and the Empress . . .' It might work. He could not believe that his star had suffered a final eclipse. The great gambler was not prepared to leave the table when he had the price of a stake in his pocket, however small that might be, and however impossible the odds.

Caulaincourt, Ney and Macdonald departed in two coaches to take the conditional abdication to the Allies. They reached Essones, the headquarters of Marmont, at about 4 pm. They dined with him while permission was sought for them to continue their journey. Marmont admitted with some embarrassment that he had told Schwarzenberg that he was prepared to acknowledge the authority of the provisional government that the Allies had constituted in Paris. However, since official negotiations had overtaken his personal one, he proposed to ask Schwarzenberg to release him from his undertaking.

Permission to proceed was received at about 6 pm and the three negotiators set out for Schwarzenberg's headquarters accompanied by Marmont. The Austrian Prince on their arrival sent out ADCs to arrange for them to interview the Tsar and other Allied dignitaries. While they awaited authority to enter Paris Schwarzenberg seemed disinclined to talk with them, although he consented, in view of the changed circumstances, to release Marmont from his undertaking.

It was at about 3 o'clock on the morning of 5 April that the three envoys and Marmont were ushered into the presence of the Tsar who awaited them with representatives from the newly constituted provisional government and other plenipotentiaries. For two hours Caulaincourt and Ney argued Napoleon's case for a conditional abdication, while everyone else present opposed them. Then at 5 am there came appalling news. Marmont's corps, 11,000 strong, the biggest in Napoleon's attenuated army, had marched into the Allied lines and in effect had deserted. It appeared that General Souham, officiating as corps commander in Marmont's absence, had been summoned to Fontainebleau for orders. Instead of

A troop of Allied cavalry exacts bloody revenge on partisan villagers who had risen against them.

Napoleon at Juvisy, 10 miles from Paris, learns that his capital has fallen. Defeat, and exile, are near.

obeying, he had followed what he thought to be the wishes of Marmont, and had marched the corps inside the Austrian lines.

Horrified at the news, Caulaincourt and Ney abandoned the unequal struggle and accepted unconditional abdication on their Emperor's behalf. The rest of the day Caulaincourt spent soliciting what crumbs he could for his master. Meanwhile Napoleon, apparently putting no great faith in the activities of his envoys, had issued detailed instructions for a move towards Orléans.

On his return to Fontainebleau Caulaincourt, who in his distress seemed not to need sleep, woke his master up at 2 o'clock in the morning to inform him that Marmont had gone over to the Allies and that his envoys had been compelled to accept an unconditional abdication. Napoleon was thunderstruck. The defection of so substantial a part of his army ruined all his plans. He declared he could still find a few brave fellows to die with him; but the marshals were not among their number. For Napoleon it was the end.

For a terrible week Caulaincourt shuttled to and fro between Fontainebleau and Paris trying, as he put it, 'to save the merest plank out of this colossal wreck'. It was decided that Napoleon should rule Elba despite Allied misgivings that the island was uncomfortably close to Europe. The marshals left to make their peace with the provisional government. On 12 April the Emperor signed the agreement relinquishing all claims on France. At 3 am on 13 April the Emperor sent for Caulaincourt. Caulaincourt found him lying ashen-faced in bed.

He had taken poison that evening. Since 1812 he had carried a poison sachet round his neck or in his medicine chest. But with the passage of time it had deteriorated. He was violently sick and it became evident that he was likely to recover. He begged his attendants, for by this time Caulaincourt had summoned help, to give him some more, for life had become nothing but a torment to him. They could not bring themselves to do it.

In February, Napoleon had fought a brilliant campaign. In March his actions at Craonne and Laon were astonishing in their boldness and in the extraordinary enthusiasm with which he inspired his army. However, years of success, sometimes against all probability, had dulled his sense of military reality; he was the victim of the myth he himself had propagated: he believed himself invincible.

Schwarzenberg, the much-maligned Austrian supreme commander, knew that he was fighting a genius and adapted his strategy accordingly – as the Roman Fabius had done before him and with a similar lack of acclaim. His initial slowness may have owed something to politics, but his habit of withdrawing before his great adversary, of swaying with the punch, thwarted Napoleon and led him to treat the Austrian with a contempt that finally proved fatal.

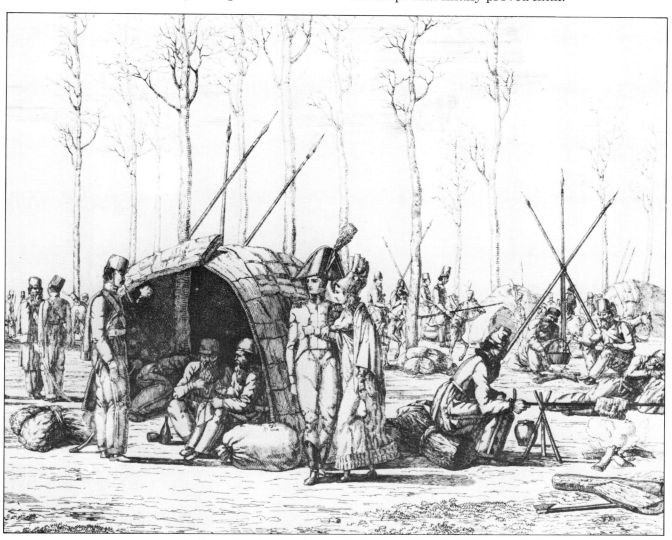

The Cossacks take over, bivouacking in the Champs Elysées.

CHRONOLOGY
1814
September: Congress of Vienna convened.
1815
25 February: Napoleon embarks for France.
1 March: He lands near Cannes.
19 March: Louis XVIII departs for Ghent.
20 March: Napoleon enters the Tuileries. He is outlawed by the European Allies.
3 May: Murat routed at Battle of Tolentino.
12 June: Napoleon leaves Paris.
14 June: French Army of the North concentrates near Charleroi.
15 June: Napoleon crosses the Sambre.
16 June: Battles of Ligny and Quatre-Bras.
18 June: Battles of Waterloo and Wavre.
22 June: Napoleon proclaims his abdication.
24 June: Blücher refuses to end hostilities.
25 June: Napoleon goes to Malmaison.
4 July: Allies enter Paris.
15 July: Napoleon surrenders to HMS *Bellerophon.*
December: He takes up residence at Longwood, on St Helena.
1821
5 May: Death of Napoleon.

PART III
1815

THE HUNDRED DAYS

The moment of collapse.
Napoleon, surrounded by his marshals, retires from the field of Waterloo.

CHAPTER 9
THE RETURN

On 4 May 1814 the frigate HMS *Undaunted* dropped anchor at the little port of Ferrajo on the island of Elba. Napoleon, his Empire wrenched from his grasp by the Allies, had come to govern his new realm. The man who was arguably the greatest soldier of the age now commanded an army about 1,500 strong including 400 of the Old Guard who had volunteered to accompany him. Journeying through the South of France he had met with real hatred from his former subjects. The boldest of men, he always feared and detested the rancour of the mob: going through Provence he had even disguised himself in the uniform of an Austrian

The house on Elba where Napoleon lived during his brief stay.

dragoon and sported an Allied white cockade. He knew, however, that an army of occupation rarely endeared itself to the country it occupied and that the mob which threatened at one minute to tear him in pieces, at the next would carry him shoulder-high. Meanwhile he turned his restless energies to organizing his island, reforming its defences and reshaping its roads. But here was no real outlet for a man such as Napoleon, happy only when working 18 hours a day.

In France the fat, stupid, amiable Louis XVIII ascended the throne, and the blue-blooded *emigrés,* who had, as it was trenchantly observed, 'forgotten nothing and learnt nothing', came swarming in after him. Although Louis XVIII lacked political address, he had sufficient wisdom to give Napoleon's marshals important military posts; but the old nobility, who had lost none of their wounding wit, ridiculed these jumped-up soldiers with their absurd high-sounding titles,

Allied statesmen at the Congress of Vienna, which opened in September 1814.
It was still in session on 6 March the following year,
when news arrived of Napoleon's escape from Elba.

Duke of this battlefield or Prince of that.

The garrisons in Germany returned to find an army reduced in size that had no use for their services. After only a few months France became heartily sick of the Bourbons. It was widely resented that they owed their restoration to a foreign army, and in a cartoon Louis XVIII was depicted riding behind a Cossack galloping over the prostrate bodies of French soldiers.

In September 1814, wracked by dissension from the beginning, the Congress designed to solve all Europe's problems opened in Vienna. Russia claimed Poland, Prussia wanted Saxony. Austria disliked intensely the prospect of either country substantially increasing its territory. Britain, wedded to the concept of a balance of power in Europe, and deeply suspicious of Russia, was equally hostile. So bitter grew the dispute that Austria, France and Britain signed a secret treaty directed against the other two. It seemed that the quarrels of the council chamber might spill over on to the battlefield.

From Elba the eagle watched, ready to fly as soon as the moment was opportune. In France the Royalists complained that Napoleon was too close to Europe, and they asked Britain to blockade Elba; but Britain declined to blockade an independent sovereign power in time of peace. Talleyrand, the King's Foreign Minister, planned to abduct the ex-Emperor, almost certainly to assassinate him; but his plans came to nothing. Nap-

oleon bided his time. He had early resolved to return; he wished to wait until the ministers had dispersed from Vienna so that a combined European reaction to his escape would be difficult to accomplish. On the other hand, the sea voyage would be easier and less perilous when the nights were long.

Impatience overcame him. On 26 February 1815 he embarked for France while the Congress was still in session. On 1 March he landed with about 600 troops under Cambronne at St Juan, between Cannes and Antibes. His first test came at La Mure, near Grenoble. Here a battalion of the 5th of the Line deployed across the road in a threatening manner. They withdrew to the village of Laffrey but here stood firm. Then came the order, 'Fire'. Not a musket spoke. Napoleon strode forward, opened his greatcoat and revealed the famous green uniform jacket beneath. 'Which of you will fire on his Emporer' he asked. In response the soldiers hoisted their shakoes on their bayonets amid wild shouts of 'Vive l'Empereur'. Napoleon entered Grenoble in triumph, the men of the 5th hurling away their white cockades and finding tricolours with surprising ease.

He advanced to Lyon while his army grew daily in strength. Ney took a force forward to destroy him. The red-haired Marshal rashly promised Louis XVIII to bring back his old master in an iron cage. It was an unfortunate phrase. When Napoleon wrote to him from Lyon, it was evident the Emperor could not be overthrown without a battle. Ney pondered. He hated the members of the *ancien régime* who mocked him and reduced his wife to tears. Should he risk a civil war? Would his soldiers fight against their old master? Could he? He ordered his soldiers to go over to the Emperor, an order they obeyed with tremendous enthusiasm; one or two of his senior officers who demurred had to spur away for their lives. He joined Napoleon at Auxerre, salving his conscience by presenting the Emperor with a long and windy document about how he should govern. The Emperor thoughtfully tore it up. Their first meeting was far from cordial. Napoleon did not forget that Ney had forced his abdication at Fontainebleau and the mention of an iron cage still rankled. Except for one or two ceremonial appearances, Ney took himself off to his house in the country, away from the limelight.

Meanwhile Napoleon continued his advance. The wits of Paris suggested that there was no point in Louis XVIII sending troops towards him as he had soldiers enough. On 18 March the fat King published a manifesto reminding his soldiers of their oath to remain loyal. Next day, gauging its probable effect accurately enough, he bolted for the northern border and Ghent. On 20 March Napoleon entered the Tuileries. He was cheered to the echo by small bands of Bonapartists but many of those present seemed curiously apathetic. In gen-

The return: Napoleon sails for the south coast of France. Painting by Louis Garneray.

eral the populace might loathe the Bourbons, but all, except a few of the soldiers, were sick of war and the women dreaded losing their sons on the battlefield. The Emperor paid lip service to peace and democracy, but in the troublesome Vendée already there were signs of insurrection. To placate the left and the radicals he made Fouché chief of police; he later confessed he would have done better to guillotine him.

On 6 March the news of Napoleon's escape reached Vienna. The Allies had managed to compromise; Prussia was to content itself with half Saxony, Russia to allow a fragment of Poland to endure. The news of Napoleon's escape further cemented unity. The Emperor had shown he could be bound neither by treaties nor the most solemn declarations. Any form of negotiation therefore was clearly a waste of time. The Allies declared him an outlaw and proclaimed that their war was with Napoleon not France; they withdrew their diplomats from Paris. Arrangements were put in hand for nearly a million men to converge on France. Marie-Louise, who had steadfastly refused to visit her husband in Elba, put herself under the protection of her father, Francis I of Austria.

Napoleon himself after so many disasters had lost the old inner certainty, his belief in his star, that had so often enabled him to contemplate catastrophe unmoved. He began to doubt the wisdom of his return. But the die was cast and with his usual immense energy he set about reorganizing his army. Of his active marshals Soult, Davout and Suchet rallied to their Emperor. Victor, pilloried after Montereau and wounded at Craonne, remained with Louis XVIII at Ghent. Mortier initially joined Napoleon, but found himself to be crippled with sciatica and deftly sold his horses to Ney. Oudinot with his 20 wounds thought, not unreasonably, that he had fought long enough and retired into private life, as did Macdonald. Berthier mysteriously died falling from a window in Bav-

aria. Marmont and Augereau, the so-called traitors, were proscribed. In Italy Murat began a war in favour of his Emperor – which infuriated Napoleon, who thought it precipitated Allied action against France; Murat was defeated by the Austrians and came to France as a fugitive. As for Ney, Napoleon was not certain what he thought about Ney. It was noticeable that the marshals who had fought under him in Eastern France were reluctant to fight again.

His first concern, however, was with men. He took over an army of 200,000, woefully inadequate to face the coming storm. He hesitated, then reluctantly decreed conscription, conscious that it was universally disliked. By the end of May he had formed 10 army corps and a corps of reserve cavalry under Grouchy, newly promoted a marshal. In addition there was the incomparable Imperial Guard.

In 1814 he had planned to hold the border

Napoleon lands in the Gulf of St Juan
on 1 March 1815.

fortresses and fight inland near Paris. He had hoped that the Allies would be attenuated by a long advance that compelled them to leave behind large bodies of men to mask the border fortresses, man key points on the lines of communication, set up and protect ordnance and supply depots and so on; in this way they would be reduced to a strength that he could match. He had concentrated his armies close to Paris. The plan, which had in part been forced on him by circumstances, had not worked. Valuable troops had been locked up in the frontier fortresses; the Allies had bypassed them and blockaded them with third-rate troops while keeping their field forces intact. In the South of France Soult had successfully kept Wellington in play, but in the North French resistance had collapsed; when Napoleon had defeated one Allied army, hydra-like, two more sprang up in its place. Now he planned to strike first, while the Allies were still at a distance.

The Allied armies necessarily took time to form. In the north Wellington with about 104,000 men and Blücher with 124,000 lay along the French border. Schwarzenberg in Austria was still assembling his troops, while Barclay de Tolly with the Russians had far to come. After separating detachments to watch the borders and restrain the dissidents in the Vendée, Napoleon could muster an army of about 120,000 men. This he thought would be sufficient for him to deliver a lightning blow in the north, drive Blücher and Wellington apart and capture Brussels. Many in Belgium looked on Napoleon with affection, and were deeply angry with the Allies at Vienna for proposing that they should come under Holland. Belgium might therefore declare for the French and a disaster in the north might also incline the Allies to retreat. It would certainly dislocate the Allied plan for the invasion of France, give an enormous fillip to the faint-hearted in France and provide time for more regiments to be organized and trained.

Napoleon formed an Army of the North consisting of five corps, the Imperial Guard and the Reserve Cavalry. Of his old marshals he made Davout Minister of War and Soult Chief-of-Staff to the Army. He detached Suchet to command the Army of the Alps, which was to watch the exits from those mountains. Ney he invited to join him as an observer. Both Soult and Davout were fine commanders in the field. Posting the iron Davout to watch over Paris and organize the new armies was understandable: Joseph and Clarke between them had failed notably in both tasks. Throughout the Campaign of 1814 Paris had been a potent source of weakness; many of its citizens had shown themselves liable to panic while others were actively disaffected. Under Davout disaffection would in future be sternly repressed.

The campaign in the north, Napoleon considered, would most probably prove to be no more than a curtain-raiser to a long-drawn-out struggle. It might also be that Soult, used to the wider perspectives of command, would be a little at a loss at first as Chief-of-Staff. However, he had done similar work before and could soon adapt to the role; he was an intelligent and extremely experienced officer, one whose authority few would wish to query (nevertheless, in retrospect the wisdom of the appointment might be questioned). There was one further consideration: Napoleon had felt in 1814 that on occasion his old marshals had been lacking in drive. He suspected that having obtained honours and wealth, and with no further prospects of promotion, they may have decided that in a battle they had everything to lose and nothing to win. In 1815 Napoleon wished to have young, ambitious corps commanders who had yet to clinch their careers by becoming marshals of the Empire.

By 14 June Napoleon had concentrated his army near the northern border of France with such secrecy and skill that neither Blücher, dozing in Namur, nor Wellington, dancing in Brussels, was aware of its presence. The brief campaign that followed is one of the most dramatic in history. Napoleon, the irresistible force, met Wellington, the immovable object. The Emperor's speed and boldness dazzled Wellington; equally the Briton's tactical skill in defence and the musketry of his infantry were something the Emperor had never encountered. His generals knew these qualities only too well, but by that time it was impossible to tell Napoleon anything about soldiering; he listened to no one, took no one's advice.

Accounts of the campaign and criticism of all taking part cover enough paper to sink a ship of some size. To most of these criticisms the criteria proclaimed by Prince Hohenlohe-Ingelfingen might well be applied, namely that 'strategy is not so easy in practice as it may seem', and that 'all make mistakes and . . . the best is he that makes fewest' (see also page 5). The generals, particularly Wellington and Napoleon, were probably as able as the world has known; to suggest that either made blunders through ignorance or stupidity is inherently unlikely. To take an analogy from the boxing ring: if a champion boxer confronts a novice his skill and speed will be evident to all beholders, until his bemused and helpless adversary is carried from the ring, from which he himself will step unmarked. But if he meets an opponent comparable in skill to himself the spectacle will be very different. Each will surprise the other; blows which would demolish a more mediocre opponent will hit air, others penetrate a guard impenetrable to lesser mortals. At the end, although one may win by a knock-out, both will have been severely mauled.

So it was to be in the short campaign that culminated at Waterloo. It was fought with a speed and ferocity that has probably never been surpassed and seldom been equalled.

A horseman of the Hundred Days campaign: a French dragoon of the Garde Royale.

CHAPTER 10
NAPOLEON STRIKES

In distant Silesia, Blücher, recovered from his illness, viewed the world morosely. He was extremely and vociferously angry. Wellington and Wrede had been included in the Congress that had assembled in Vienna, while he rusted at home. What he heard about the Congress provoked him into fresh paroxysms of rage. The confounded politicians seemed to be giving away all that had been gained by the toil and blood of his men.

The news that Napoleon was once again in France delighted him. 'What a piece of luck,' he exclaimed. 'Now the war will begin again and the armies make good all that has been lost at Vienna.'

A French cavalry outpost.

He shouted for his uniform to be unpacked. Then a letter came, appointing him Commander-in-Chief and directing him to take command of the Prussian army that Kleist was assembling in the Netherlands. But if Blücher was delighted, Gneisenau was not. He was once again appointed Chief-of-Staff and in common with many chiefs-of-staff he was certain that he did all the work while his commander took all the credit. He had hoped for an independent command. His wishes, however, were to be partially fulfilled. Blücher was old, his health uncertain, and many doubted his ability to understand a plan of campaign. Yet his courage, his determination and his hold over his men were unrivalled. When he said, 'Forward', his favourite word of command, forward his men would go. Gneisenau therefore was virtually authorized to plan the strategy of the campaign, a subject that the old man found both boring and incomprehensible, while Blücher was to command on the

The 'Old Hussar', Field-Marshal Blücher, drawn in 1814 by Denis Dighton.

field of battle. If anything happened to Blücher, Gneisenau was to succeed him. To avoid complications over seniority, Blücher's corps commanders except for Bülow were selected from generals junior to his Chief-of-Staff. Bülow with his IV Corps was not expected to join in the invasion of France; he was to maintain order in Prussia's new Rhineland possessions.

In the methodical Prussian fashion, Blücher's army consisted of four identical corps each of four infantry brigades and one cavalry. These brigades were stronger than French infantry divisions and for the sake of clarity will be called divisions, although, as already mentioned, the divisional organization did not exist in the Prussian Army at that time. The corps and their brigades were numbered consecutively: Ziethen commanded I Corps, Brigades 1–4; Pirch I commanded II Corps, Brigades 5–8; Thielmann, III Corps, Brigades 9–12; Bülow, IV Corps, Brigades 13–16. Earlier, General Borstell had commanded II Corps, but he was relieved of his command in rather unusual circumstances.

The quality of the four German corps was somewhat impaired by the inclusion in each of a Westphalian *Landwehr* division, the latter being a form of militia. Worse still, Blücher had a strong contingent of Saxons and they were furious over the treatment meted out to their country. Blücher quartered them in Liège and to show his confidence in their fidelity established his headquarters among them. They responded by mutinying. First the Saxon Guards made an unarmed protest; they were despatched to Borstell's II Corps at Namur. Then the Saxon line regiments mutinied and, armed with sabres, attacked Blücher's house, compelling the aged and infuriated Field-Marshal to escape by a back door.

Blücher had the mutineers surrounded by Prussian units and disarmed. He wanted to decimate the regiments, but more merciful arguments prevailed. The Saxons were ordered to produce seven ringleaders. Müffling, who had been Chief-of-Staff to Kleist before Blücher arrived, noted that six out of the seven names had already been identified as the leaders by other informants, so that in his opinion there was no miscarriage of justice. The seven were shot. In Namur, Blücher directed Borstell to burn the colour of the Saxon Guards. Borstell had been talking with the Guards and thought that he could now depend on them. To burn their colour would be to forfeit all he had achieved. He queried the instructions. Blücher sent him a direct order. Borstell refused to comply. Blücher relieved him of his command and had the colour burnt. Borstell himself was court-martialled, found guilty of insubordination and imprisoned, an unusual fate for a corps commander. The Prussian generals after that incident must have thought hard before they queried an order. Pirch I took over II Corps. The Saxons remained unreliable and were sent away.

Wellington contemplated with considerable distaste the army that he had been sent to the Netherlands to command. It was an amalgam of hastily raised British, Dutch, Belgian, Hanoverian, Brunswick and Nassau regiments. Although most of them were to show a good spirit on the battlefield, many were poorly trained, and the mixture of races and languages made the task of an inexperienced staff far from easy. The Duke sighed for the magnificent Anglo-Portuguese army he had commanded in 1814. A suggestion that he might be sent some of his old Portuguese regiments fell on deaf ears. To ease the problems of command and communication, he incorporated his Hanoverian brigades into his British divisions; but the Brunswickers, not unnaturally since they were commanded by their Duke, had to be kept together, and the Prince of Orange steadfastly refused to have the Belgo-Dutch-Nassau divisions broken up.

Largely for administrative reasons, for he was not fond of the French device of the army corps, he organized his army into two corps consisting basically of infantry, a cavalry corps, and a reserve that was equivalent to another corps. In battle he fully intended to work directly with his divisional commanders. He placed his II Corps,

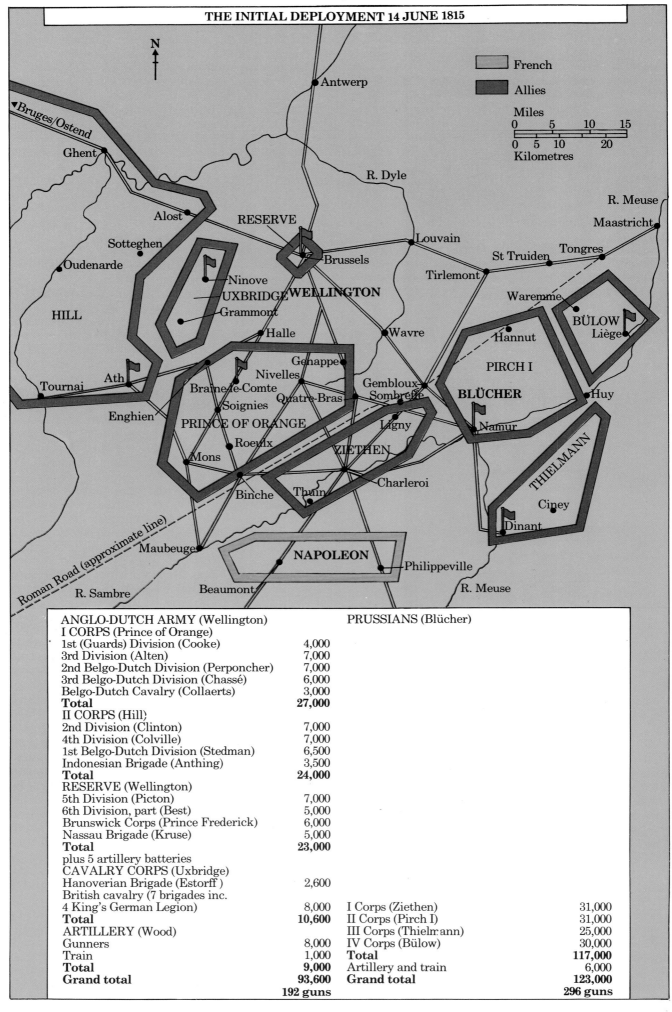

THE INITIAL DEPLOYMENT 14 JUNE 1815

N

French

Allies

Miles

0 5 10 15

0 5 10 20

Kilometres

Antwerp

Bruges/Ostend

Ghent

R. Dyle

Alost

RESERVE

Louvain

R. Meuse

Maastricht

Sotteghen

Brussels

Tirlemont

St Truiden

Tongres

Oudenarde

Ninove

UXBRIDGE

WELLINGTON

Waremme

BÜLOW

HILL

Grammont

Wavre

Hannut

Liège

Halle

Genappe

PIRCH I

Ath

Nivelles

Tournai

Braine-le-Comte

Gembloux

BLÜCHER

Huy

Enghien

Soignies

Quatre-Bras

Sombreffe

PRINCE OF ORANGE

Lagny

Namur

Roeulx

ZIETHEN

THIELMANN

Mons

Charleroi

Ciney

Binche

Thuin

Dinant

Roman Road (approximate line)

Maubeuge

NAPOLEON

Philippeville

R. Sambre

Beaumont

R. Meuse

ANGLO-DUTCH ARMY (Wellington)		PRUSSIANS (Blücher)	
I CORPS (Prince of Orange)			
1st (Guards) Division (Cooke)	4,000		
3rd Division (Alten)	7,000		
2nd Belgo-Dutch Division (Perponcher)	7,000		
3rd Belgo-Dutch Division (Chassé)	6,000		
Belgo-Dutch Cavalry (Collaerts)	3,000		
Total	**27,000**		
II CORPS (Hill)			
2nd Division (Clinton)	7,000		
4th Division (Colville)	7,000		
1st Belgo-Dutch Division (Stedman)	6,500		
Indonesian Brigade (Anthing)	3,500		
Total	**24,000**		
RESERVE (Wellington)			
5th Division (Picton)	7,000		
6th Division, part (Best)	5,000		
Brunswick Corps (Prince Frederick)	6,000		
Nassau Brigade (Kruse)	5,000		
Total	**23,000**		
plus 5 artillery batteries			
CAVALRY CORPS (Uxbridge)			
Hanoverian Brigade (Estorff)	2,600		
British cavalry (7 brigades inc.			
4 King's German Legion)	8,000	I Corps (Ziethen)	31,000
Total	**10,600**	II Corps (Pirch I)	31,000
ARTILLERY (Wood)		III Corps (Thielmann)	25,000
Gunners	8,000	IV Corps (Bülow)	30,000
Train	1,000	**Total**	**117,000**
Total	**9,000**	Artillery and train	6,000
Grand total	**93,600**	**Grand total**	**123,000**
	192 guns		**296 guns**

A Prussian hussar officer of 1815.

which comprised the 4th and 2nd British Divisions and included Prince Frederick's of the Netherlands corps of the 1st Belgo-Dutch Division and General Anthing's Indonesian brigade, under his old trusted comrade of Peninsular days, General 'Daddy' Hill, and positioned it in the west around Ath and towards Oudenarde. I Corps, largely for reasons of protocol, he put under the Prince of Orange, a courageous but inexperienced youth of 22. It contained the 1st and 3rd British Divisions, 2nd and 3rd Belgo-Dutch Divisions, and Collaerts's Belgo-Dutch cavalry division, and was cantoned about Nivelles and Enghien. Lord Uxbridge commanded the Cavalry Corps, which had eight brigades and was stationed between Brammont and Ninove. Around Brussels itself, strategically placed to deal with any unrest in the city, he billeted the Reserve consisting of the 5th British Division, Best's Hanoverian brigade of the 6th Division and the Duke of Brunswick's corps. It remained directly under his command.

Wellington's field army totalled about 90,000, of whom 32,000 were British or of the King's German Legion. The men of the King's German Legion were largely drawn from the old Hanoverian Regular Army and were excellent troops. The other Hanoverian brigades were, however, inexperienced and composed of hastily raised units of militia. The Belgo-Dutch troops had mostly served under Napoleon, and fought against their old comrades with some reluctance. Moreover the Belgians deeply resented being placed under Holland, and although they did not emulate the Saxons at Leipzig and change sides, Wellington was fully aware that they might prefer fighting for the French. He thought it essential therefore to wage a defensive battle where he could keep a tight control of his men. He distrusted the ability of his army to manoeuvre, and while he had some experienced generals under him, he suspected that anything but the simplest offensive would almost certainly end in calamity.

As his Anglo-Dutch Army built up its

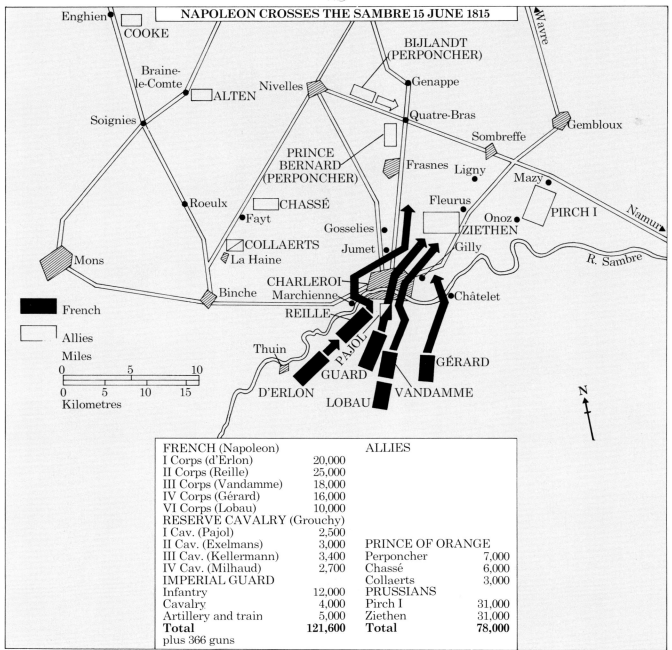

FRENCH (Napoleon)		ALLIES	
I Corps (d'Erlon)	20,000		
II Corps (Reille)	25,000		
III Corps (Vandamme)	18,000		
IV Corps (Gérard)	16,000		
VI Corps (Lobau)	10,000		
RESERVE CAVALRY (Grouchy)			
I Cav. (Pajol)	2,500		
II Cav. (Exelmans)	3,000	PRINCE OF ORANGE	
III Cav. (Kellermann)	3,400	Perponcher	7,000
IV Cav. (Milhaud)	2,700	Chassé	6,000
IMPERIAL GUARD		Collaerts	3,000
Infantry	12,000	PRUSSIANS	
Cavalry	4,000	Pirch I	31,000
Artillery and train	5,000	Ziethen	31,000
Total	**121,600**	**Total**	**78,000**
plus 366 guns			

strength, there were the usual scares and alarms. In particular, on 30 April a French attack was reported to be so imminent that Wellington made specific preparations to meet it. He carefully analysed Napoleon's possible courses of action. Brussels would be his most likely objective. An approach round the eastern flank by the Meuse valley and Namur seemed extremely unlikely. The difficult hilly country of the Ardennes with its poor roads was peculiarly unsuitable for Napoleon's lightning type of fighting. A strike in the centre, aimed at separating the British from the Prussians, was possible but should create no problems; it would be rather as though a nut were courteously to insert itself between the jaws of a nutcracker. At a meeting with Blücher at Tirlemont it was agreed that, were Napoleon to attack in the centre, Blücher should concentrate at Sombreffe and Wellington at Nivelles. They would crush the intruder between them. An attack in the west round Wellington's right flank, either down the excellent road from Mons or from even further west, could be much more dangerous. Napoleon could cut the Anglo-Dutch Army off from its base at Ostend and head towards Brussels along the British line of communication. Such a move would force Wellington to deploy with the Prussians well to the east and behind him. If Wellington's army was slow and clumsy in its movements, and it gave every indication that it would be, the powerful French cavalry might catch it off-balance. Even if Napoleon only captured Brussels and the Anglo-Dutch Army managed to extricate itself successfully and join the Prussians, the Belgians might well declare for France. The Prussians already suffered difficulties over supplies. If they were joined by Wellington's army without any means of sustenance, the resulting administrative chaos in the middle of a hostile countryside could cripple both armies. Wellington could recall unhappy memories of once retreating from the Netherlands to Hamburg to embark for England. He had no wish to repeat the experience.

Since the western approach seemed the most dangerous it was wise to expect Napoleon to take it. Wellington considered that Napoleon's most likely plan would be to feint to the east to distract the Prussians, then to slam home a hammer-blow in the west, most probably along the road from Mons. He would not be caught by such a stratagem.

The scare came to nothing. Others equally baseless succeeded it. Accurate information was almost impossible to obtain. The Allied Governments, anxious to impress on the French that the war was with Napoleon not France, forbade any attempt to patrol across the border until they gave the word and the great invasion began. This prohibition acted like a bandage tied over the eyes of the two Allied commanders. The best they could do was to arrange a British cell in the Prussian headquarters and a Prussian cell in Wellington's. Müffling found himself posted to the British. He had a long interview with Gneisenau before he went. The secret treaty between Britain, France and Austria had been revealed when Louis XVIII had decamped to Ghent. To Gneisenau the news that Britain was prepared to make an alliance with France, and that the alliance should be directed partly against Prussia, was evidence of the blackest treachery. And the Duke of Wellington had been a party to the intrigue. Müffling afterwards related that Gneisenau 'warned me to be on my guard with the Duke of Wellington for his relations with India and his transactions with the deceitful nabobs . . . had so accustomed him to duplicity that he . . . could outwit the Nabobs themselves.'

Blücher ignored such pettifogging matters as a possible treaty between Britain and France. He liked Wellington and that was enough. He did not understand politics and loathed politicians. Müffling fortunately kept an open mind. The general he relieved made no secret of his delight at leaving. He said the British officers kept their hats on in his presence and appeared quite incapable of understanding his impeccable French. He wished Müffling joy. Müffling discovered, however, that his revered chief, Blücher, was greatly admired by the British, and he liked what he saw of the British army. He was soon on excellent terms with Wellington, and made what arrangements he could for the passage of information between the British and Prussian headquarters, then some 38 miles apart.

In addition Wellington arranged for General Dornberg, commanding the 3rd Cavalry Brigade in the Reserve, to go to Mons and set up a form of intelligence centre to keep him posted about what was happening inside France. No reliable information came back, however. The original date for invading France was 1 June. By the middle of May the Allied armies in Belgium, including garrisons, amounted to about 250,000 men. Both Wellington and Gneisenau judged that they were now too strong for Napoleon to attack.

When, owing to the absence of the Austrians, Bavarians and Russians, the invasion date had to be put back first to 15 June and then to 1 July, Blücher suggested that he and Wellington should invade France on their own, an offer that was firmly turned down by the Allies. As was to happen 130 years later, a slower attack on a broad front was deemed the safer. All thought of an attack by the French was abandoned and Wellington turned his talents to the organizing of balls in Brussels. The Duchess of Richmond was holding a big one on 15 June and he had begun to plan one on the 21st to celebrate his victory at Vitoria.

During June the usual crop of unsubstantiated reports arrived. On 6 June Dornberg reported that Napoleon was going to attack on 7 or 8 June. He intended to feint at Maubeuge and then thrust down the Mons road. On the 10th Napoleon was reported with 80,000 men at Laon and planning to go to Lille. Murat was said to be in Avesnes. It all seemed rather improbable.

Then on 13 June the reports of French activity suddenly grew in volume. Dornberg had a report that the whole French army was assembled about Maubeuge. A French drum major had deserted and told General Steinmetz, commanding the 1st Division in Ziethen's I Corps, that Napoleon with the Imperial Guard was at Maubeuge and intended to attack on the 13th or 14th. Then Ziethen himself found out that half the 60,000 troops about Maubeuge were National Guardsmen and had no artillery. The whole thing seemed utterly confused.

But the reports became more insistent. Dornberg said that he had been told that there were 80,000 French near Beaumont and 100,000 at Maubeuge – the excessive numbers made the proposition suspect. Gneisenau, however, suddenly felt uneasy. At midday he ordered all corps to concentrate their outlying brigades and be ready to move to concentration areas. Then at 11.30 that night he received some information that he considered could not be ignored. Probably it was from General Bourmont, commanding the 14th Division in Gérard's IV Corps, who deserted that night. Gneisenau ordered Thielmann to march at once with III Corps from Dinant to Namur – a most important decision. Pirch I with his II Corps was to concentrate by morning between Mazy and Onoz, and Ziethen, if attacked, was to withdraw to Fleurus. Curiously, he did not wake Blücher to tell him what he was doing, nor did he inform Wellington. To Bülow at Liège he sent orders for IV Corps to move to Hannut, about 19 miles west of Liège; but he couched his instructions to his senior in such vague terms that Bülow thought there was no urgency in the matter. Gneisenau and the somewhat cranky Bülow were by no means friends, and possibly Gneisenau feared being ridiculed for an unnecessary alarm.

At 4 o'clock on the morning of 15 June the storm broke. Events now succeeded each other with the speed of a hurricane. By 8.15 am Ziethen reported to Blücher that Thuin was lost and that his 1st and 2nd Divisions were withdrawing to the line Gosselies – Gilly. Napoleon had been identified with his Guards. Blücher received the report at 8.45 am and reiterated his orders to his corps commanders to concentrate their corps. At 11.30 a second report came in. There had been heavy fighting on the Gosselies – Gilly line. Blücher sent a copy of the report straight to Brussels remarking that the Prussian army would concentrate at Sombreffe by next morning. His headquarters would move there in about two hours' time. All communications should be channelled through Genappe.

At 5 o'clock that morning the Prince of Orange disappeared, ostensibly to inspect his outpost line near Mons. He was not seen again until he rode into Brussels to attend the Duchess of Richmond's Ball as Wellington's guest. In his absence his Chief-of-Staff, Constant de Rebeque, had to take all necessary decisions, particularly as he thought it indiscreet to reveal that the Prince had disappeared.

At midday news arrived from General Behr

in Mons that Steinmetz's 1st Division had been attacked that morning and that alarm guns had been fired all along the line of the Sambre. Prince Bernard of Saxe-Weimar with his brigade from Perponcher's division was in the area of Frasnes, just to the south of the important cross-roads of Quatre-Bras. De Rebeque reinforced him with the other brigade of Perponcher's division (Bijlandt's), sent Chassé with his infantry division to Fayt, about eight miles south of Nivelles, and Collaerts with the cavalry division to La Haine, about two miles further south. A little before nightfall French cavalry attacked a leading battalion in Prince Bernard's brigade. He withdrew with it to the woods about Quatre-Bras and there opened up on them with the 16 guns of the division. The cavalry were supported neither by infantry nor artillery, and after a time disappeared in the direction of Frasnes to the south.

In Brussels information was slow in arriving. At 3 o'clock in the afternoon there was a rumour that the French had attacked Ziethen's outposts and been beaten off. Then about 4 o'clock Ziethen's report of 8.15 am came in, and finally at about 7 o'clock a fat, slow-moving officer arrived carrying Blücher's letter; it stated that Blücher would concentrate at Sombreffe and wanted to know what Wellington proposed to do.

Wellington weighed up the situation. He found the information too vague to merit a firm decision. The attack on Ziethen's two divisions might well be just the diversion he expected Napoleon to make, and the main strength of the French might even now be poised to strike at Brussels down the Mons road. He ordered all his divisions to concentrate and be at instant readiness to move, but told Müffling it was too early to decide on the point of concentration for the whole Army.

By 10 o'clock that night no further news had arrived. Nothing had been heard either from Dornberg at Mons or from Rebeque at Nivelles. He decided to wait no longer but to start concentrating towards his left. He ordered the Reserve consisting of the 5th and 6th Divisions and the Brunswick Corps (it had only the strength of an ordinary division and about 900 cavalry) to march to Mont-St-Jean. That would cover the Charleroi road to

Brussels. The 3rd Division was to go from Braine-le-Comte to Nivelles, the 1st Division to Braine-le-Comte and the cavalry to move to Enghien, as were the 2nd and 4th Divisions. All troops were to move as soon as possible. Then he took the Prince of Orange to the Ball. As he was sitting down enjoying his supper, a dusty ADC strode in with an urgent despatch. Rebeque reported that Prince Bernard had been attacked at Quatre-Bras. The situation had begun to crystallize.

On the night of the 14th Napoleon made ready for his masterstroke. The lines of communication of the Allies ran parallel to their fronts and in opposite directions, Wellington's to Ostend, Blücher's through Liège to the Rhine. If either army were beaten it might be expected to retire down its line of communication and therefore away from its ally. He proposed to thrust from Charleroi towards Brussels, split the Prussian army from the British by the speed of his advance, beat them separately and capture Brussels. Then he hoped the Belgians would rise. It was an incredibly bold plan, typical of the Emperor at his greatest. To achieve success he would have to beat each army in turn.

He had his army organized in five army corps each consisting of three or four infantry divisions, a light cavalry division and five or six batteries of guns. The guns were distributed on a scale of one eight-gun battery per infantry division and one in reserve, and one six-gun horse artillery battery with the light cavalry divisions. The latter were about equal to a strong Allied cavalry brigade, and the infantry divisions in general were only two-thirds the strength of an Allied one (Napoleon believed in making his armies sound as imposing as possible). In addition to his five army corps he had the Reserve Cavalry under Marshal Grouchy; each of its corps was only slightly stronger than an Allied cavalry division of two or three brigades. Finally he had the Imperial Guard of three infantry divisions, one light cavalry division, one heavy cavalry division and the artillery of the Guard totalling 118 guns.

He arranged that the advance should be made in three columns. On the left Reille with II Corps was to cross the Sambre at Marchienne

Model of a 12-pounder Gribeauval cannon, one of the standard field-pieces in Napoleon's army.

followed by d'Erlon with I Corps. In the centre Pajol with I Cavalry Corps would lead, followed by Vandamme with III Corps, Lobau with VI Corps and the Imperial Guard. These would cross by the bridge into Charleroi itself. On the right Gérard with IV Corps would cross by Châtelet, a little more than two miles further east. He planned therefore to cross the Sambre on three bridges over a front of about five miles. He was making a pencil-thin stab between the two Allied armies. There would inevitably be congestion and confusion while crossing on so narrow a front with 120,000 men and 366 guns; he expected that the surprise and the impetus gained by so concentrated a thrust would compensate for the disadvantages. At this time he had yet to formulate his detailed plan. That would have to depend on the reaction of the Allies and how well the crossing was performed.

That there would be confusion was already apparent. Soult found the detailed staff work more taxing than he expected. Already on the way to the concentration areas he had forgotten to issue orders to Grouchy, who had been forced to make his cavalry ride hard to pick up lost time. Then the ADC he sent with orders to Vandamme fell off his horse, broke his leg and failed to deliver the orders for the advance. Berthier would have double-checked; but Soult rode off unconcernedly and the move was well under way before Napoleon began to wonder where Vandamme had got to. He was discovered still in his concentration area awaiting orders. Gérard with IV Corps was late in starting because General Bourmont, commanding the 14th Division, had mysteriously disappeared and could not be found; eventually the command arrangements had to be reshuffled.

Nevertheless, with remarkable skill and celerity the Sambre was forced. Pajol with his cavalry was opposite Charleroi at 10 o'clock in the morning, but in the absence of Vandamme's infantry dared not become embroiled in the narrow streets of the city. Napoleon fed forward Duhesme's division of the Guard to replace the errant Vandamme. Pirch II, commanding the 2nd Division in Ziethen's I Corps and now fully recovered from the wound he had suffered at Montmirail, fell back to Gilly. From Marchienne, Reille moved on Steinmetz's powerful division, 9,000 strong at Gosselies. The two Prussian divisions fought stoutly in their respective positions, but were driven back. By nightfall Ziethen's corps, having suffered about 1,200 casualties, had collected around Fleurus, eight miles north of the Sambre, as Gneisenau had ordered. Pirch I with II Corps was in the area of Mazy, and Thielmann's III Corps was at Namur; both were in easy distance of Sombreffe. Bülow, moving towards Hannut, was still 20 miles away.

Ney, in his curious capacity as an observer, rode into Imperial headquarters at Charleroi about 3 o'clock that afternoon. Napoleon welcomed him warmly and told him to take command of the Left Wing consisting of Reille's I Corps, d'Erlon's II Corps, and Lefebvre-Desnouette's light cavalry division of the Guard which would remain attached at least for the 16th. The whole was to operate down the Charleroi – Brussels road. Ney rode on to meet Reille at Gosselies, where he was re-organizing his men after their stiff fight with Steinmetz. As the Prussians withdrew towards Fleurus, Lefebvre-Desnouettes prospected along the Brussels road northwards. At Frasnes he ran into what he thought was a Belgo-Dutch battalion and chased it over the hill towards Quatre-Bras a couple of miles away. As he approached that hamlet, something like 16 guns opened up on him from a wood. He had no infantry or guns himself and so withdrew to Frasnes. With the Prussians at Fleurus, any advance beyond Frasnes might open a very vulnerable right flank. Reille's men settled down for the night on the ground they had won.

Napoleon climbed wearily down from his horse and entered his residence for the night at about 9 o'clock. He had been close on 15 hours continuously in the saddle. His army was undoubtedly across the Sambre in strength. That was about all that he knew. There had been a traffic jam of bewildering size in Charleroi. What should be his next move? How had the Allies reacted? How many of his divisions were over the Sambre? He could make no decisions until some of these questions had been answered. He resolved to snatch a few hours' sleep. He gave instructions that he should be woken at midnight, by which time some of the reports should have come in.

A pig volunteers for the stewpot.

CHAPTER 11
A BLOODY PRELUDE

Now events gathered momentum. In a matter of minutes commanders had to take vital decisions on imperfect if not positively misleading information, often when they were bone-weary and in considerable personal danger. There was no time for deep patrolling and deliberate reconnaissance, for the careful sifting of information, for logical and painstaking 'appreciations of the situation'. Possibly only generals of the proven capacity of Napoleon or Blücher or Wellington could have withstood these appalling pressures and delivered their decisions clearly and confidently and with that certainty that restores calm when those beneath

Napoleon issues orders on the battlefield at Ligny.

them have begun to panic. But the strains were immense and strange things occurred.

On the evening of 15 June, Napoleon felt reasonably satisfied. He had begun to drive a wedge between the Duke and the old Field-Marshal. No doubt Wellington was assembling his army in his usual slow, methodical fashion somewhere to the west. Blücher had one corps quartered at Dinant, 18 miles to the south, and another at Liège, 35 miles to the north-east. The Prussian might be able to muster two corps on the morrow and bar the way with 50–60,000 men. (For the consumption of the *Armée du Nord* a figure of 40,000 might be more encouraging; it could be suitably increased for the *Bulletins* in due course.) It could all wait to the early hours next morning. He was asleep by 9.30, so Coignet, his baggage-master, recorded.

By midnight he was up, studying the reports as they came in. The troops must have fallen in at about midnight the previous night. Then the dreary stop-go advance, with long waits to cross the bridges and in Reille's case a stiff fight at Gosselies, must have all combined to tire the troops out. Equipment vehicles would have probably gone astray, and staff officers would be uncertain where the various headquarters of their subordinate units had reached. Reille had most of his corps about Gosselies, and Vandamme his a little to the north of Gilly; d'Erlon's corps stretched from Jumet to Marchienne, on the far side of the river. The Guard was over and bivouacked a little to the south of Fleurus, and most of the cavalry were over as well. Only part of Gérard's corps was on the north bank, and Lobau's corps had not even begun to cross.

While Napoleon was studying the situation, Ney came riding in through the darkness. He had a large command, but no staff of any description and he wished to know what the Emperor intended. Napoleon told him that he had decided to operate in two wings with the Guard as a central reserve immediately under his orders. He would move with one or the other wings. He would send detailed orders out next morning. Ney left to go back to his headquarters at about 2 am.

In Charleroi the congestion and confusion inevitable in such a move continued. The situation was still very obscure. It was not until well into the morning that Napoleon was able to despatch to Ney his written orders.

'Charleroi 16 June

Mon Cousin,

I am sending to you my aide de camp General Flahault who will bring you this letter. The Chief of Staff ought to give out the orders but you will receive mine quicker because my officers go faster than him.

I am sending Marshal Grouchy with III and IV Corps to Sombreffe. I will send my Guard to Sombreffe and be there myself about midday. I will attack any enemy I meet and patrol forward to Gembloux. I expect to be there at three in the afternoon or by the evening. My intention is that immediately I arrive there you should be ready to march on Brussels. I will support you with the Guard . . . and I wish to arrive in Brussels tomorrow morning. You should start marching there this evening. You should dispose your troops as follows. Your leading division two leagues [about 5 miles] beyond Quatre-Bras if it is reasonable to do so, six infantry divisions about Quatre-Bras, one division at Marbais, so that I can call it to Sombreffe if I want to, Kellermann's cuirassiers should be at the intersection of the Brussels and the Roman road, so that I can call on him if I want to. I wish to have with me Lefebvre-Desnouette's division of the cavalry of the Guard and am sending Kellermann's two divisions to replace it.

I have decided as a general principle in this campaign to divide my army into two wings and a reserve. Your wing will be composed of the four divisions of I Corps (Reille) the four divisions of II Corps (d'Erlon) two divisions of light cavalry and the two cavalry divisions of Kellermann giving you about 45–50,000 men. Marshal Grouchy commanding the right wing will have nearly the equivalent.

The Guard will form the reserve and I will allocate it to move with one or other of the wings according to circumstance.

You will receive your orders from the Chief of Staff and will have full authority over your corps when detached. When I am present I will give orders direct to Corps Commanders . . .

You understand the importance of seizing Brussels for a prompt bold thrust there will isolate the British from Mons, Ostend etc.'

Similar orders were issued to Grouchy, appointing him to command the right wing consisting of Vandamme's III Corps, Gérard's IV Corps and the cavalry corps of Pajol, Milhaud and Exelmans. He was to proceed direct to Sombreffe. Napoleon would be at Fleurus with the Guard between 10 and 11 o'clock and then go onto Sombreffe himself, leaving the Guard at Fleurus. The enemy was to be attacked wherever found. He anticipated that he was more likely to meet with opposition from the Prussians than from the Anglo-Dutch Army. He was, however, well balanced to fight either.

Wellington left the Duchess of Richmond's Ball at 2 o'clock that morning (the 16th). By then most of the senior officers had left and the distant bugles and drums, and the pipes of the Scottish regiments, had begun to furnish an ominous undertone to the music of the dance. He went to his room and lay down to snatch a few hours' sleep; he was not destined to have much rest that night. Dornberg broke in on him at 5 o'clock, having just ridden in from Mons. At the first sight of him the Duke leapt from his bed. Mons was quiet. He told Dornberg to contact Picton and tell him to continue his march beyond Mont-St-Jean to Quatre-Bras. As Dornberg turned to leave, the Duke prepared to dress and go to Quatre-Bras himself.

At about 6 o'clock on a fine, bracing summer's morning that had already begun to grow warm, Wellington rode forward with his staff. He passed the long columns of marching troops and reiterated to Picton that he was to continue to Quatre-Bras. He arrived at the crossroads himself at about 10 o'clock. The Prince of Orange was already there, meditating how he could lay out Perponcher's division to best advantage. Wellington went on down the Charleroi road, going into the dip past Gemioncourt Farm on the left and up to the rise in the road. From there he could see Frasnes about a mile further on. There were a few sleepy-looking French troops about, but nothing much seemed to be happening. He turned his horse and went back to the crossroads. His staff had been preparing for him a statement showing where all his troops should be at 7 o'clock that morning. No reports had been received; the staff simply assumed

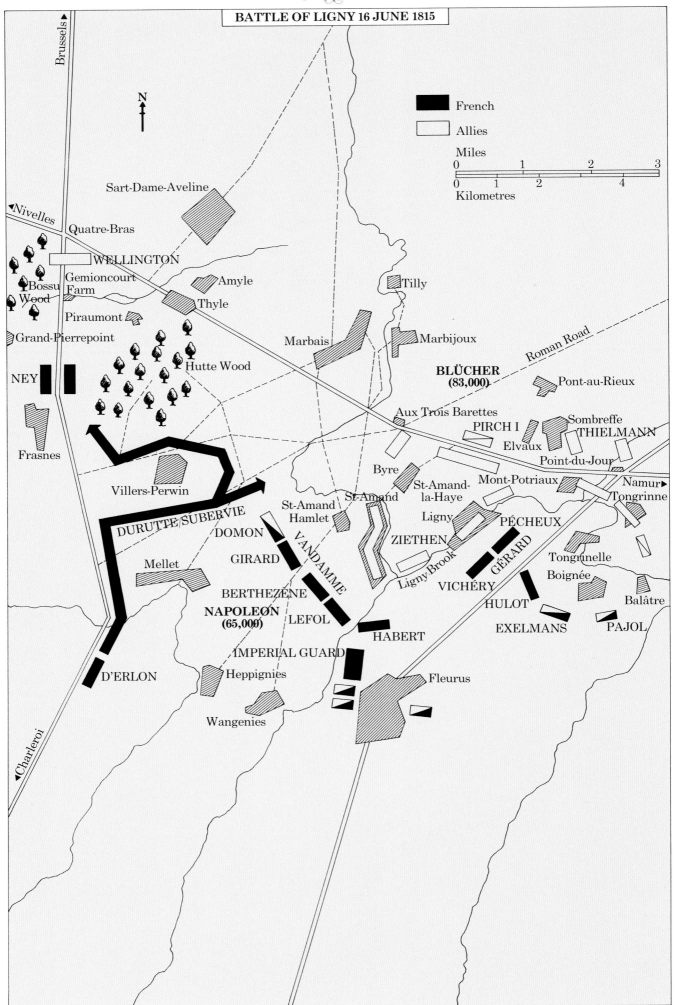

BATTLE OF LIGNY 16 JUNE 1815

French

Allies

Miles
0   1   2   3
0   1   2   3   4
Kilometres

N

Brussels

Nivelles

Sart-Dame-Aveline

Quatre-Bras

WELLINGTON

Bossu Wood

Gemioncourt Farm

Amyle

Thyle

Tilly

Piraumont

Grand-Pierrepoint

Marbais

Marbijoux

Roman Road

NEY

Hutte Wood

BLÜCHER
(83,000)

Pont-au-Rieux

Aux Trois Barettes

Sombreffe

PIRCH I

THIELMANN

Frasnes

Elvaux

Point-du-Jour

Byre

Mont-Potriaux

Namur

Villers-Perwin

St-Amand-la-Haye

Tongrinne

St-Amand

DURUTTE SUBERVIE

DOMON

St-Amand Hamlet

Ligny

PÉCHEUX

GIRARD

VANDAMME

ZIETHEN

Tongrinelle

Mellet

Ligny Brook

GÉRARD

Boignée

BERTHEZÈNE

VICHÉRY

Balâtre

NAPOLEON
(65,000)

LEFOL

HULOT

EXELMANS

PAJOL

IMPERIAL GUARD

HABERT

D'ERLON

Heppignies

Fleurus

Wangenies

Charleroi

that previous orders had been received, passed and acted upon promptly, and then calculated where they thought the divisions would have reached. For the old Peninsular Army their calculations no doubt would have been reasonably correct; for Wellington's present, less efficient army they were unduly optimistic. With much else to occupy his mind, Wellington accepted the statement uncritically. He added to it the progress that might have been expected by noon, five hours later. He then wrote to Blücher that at noon the 5th Division, the Hanoverian brigade of 6th Division and the Brunswick corps should be arriving at Genappe; the cavalry, and the 1st and 3rd Divisions should be at Nivelles five miles to the west. His letter went off at 10.30 am. However, at midday no troops had appeared and he realized that the estimated timings had been too hopeful.

At Frasnes, meanwhile, nothing seemed to be stirring. It was probable that the French would need the whole day to assemble round Charleroi. Wellington thought he might ride over and have a few words with Blücher. He found the old man by the windmill at Bussy, close to the villages of Ligny and Sombreffe and five miles from the crossroads at Quatre-Bras. The old Field-Marshal was in the highest spirits and, as ever, supremely confident. He had deployed Ziethen's I Corps in an arc round Ligny and the Ligny brook. He held Pirch I with II Corps in reserve; Thielmann with III Corps was marching in from Namur. The day was becoming hot and a little close.

Wellington went up to the top of the windmill and looked towards Fleurus; there he found he could see Napoleon himself, marshalling large numbers of blue-coated troops. Viewed dispassionately it was a fine sight. It seemed that a French attack was distinctly possible and he disliked the way that Blücher had deployed his men on a forward slope; but criticism of Prussian dispositions by a Briton was unlikely to be welcome. He suggested that the British, as soon as the troops came up, should push on towards Gosselies. If the French attack materialized, they could take it in the flank. He asked Blücher what he would like him to do. Gneisenau replied, asking him to link up with the Prussian right flank. After some discussion the Duke agreed and started back towards Quatre-Bras.[1]

A little after 9 o'clock that morning Grouchy, in accordance with his orders, told Vandamme to advance on Sombreffe. Vandamme pushed some light troops of Ziethen's corps out of Fleurus, but when he had gone a little farther he saw dense Prussian-blue columns ahead. Grouchy came up to look. The Prussians were much too strong for a single corps to attack. He sent to tell Napoleon, who came up a little after 10 am. Gérard was then far to the south, and the Emperor had plenty of time to make a thorough reconnaissance of the Prussian dispositions. There appeared to be two Prussian corps holding a line extending in the east from the Ligny brook to the south of Tongrinne to St-Amand hamlet in the west. The line was irregular, following for much of its length the Ligny brook. It projected well to the south and was based on a series of village strongpoints. The Prussian left, or eastern, flank included Tongrinne, Tongrinelle and the high ground by Mont-Potriaux, with outposts at Balâtre and Boignée. The centre, still following the Ligny brook, ran south-west with the village of Ligny as a central strongpoint. At the southern end of the village of St-Amand, about 1,200 yards southwest of Ligny, the line turned sharply northwards for about two miles along the western edges of St-Amand, St-Amand-la-Haye and St-Amand hamlet, extending to the high ground at Brye and the estaminet of Aux Trois Barettes on the Namur road.

Ziethen's I Corps held the Prussian centre and right. Pirch with II Corps was deployed along the Namur road in reserve, his 5th Division being placed about Aux Trois Barettes looking westwards to guard Blücher's right and rear from the direction of Quatre-Bras. Thielmann held the eastern flank. Behind the villages the ground sloped gradually upwards towards Brye and the Roman road to form a natural amphitheatre. The villages were some way down the slope and troops supporting the village garrisons had to be deployed in the open on a forward slope. Napoleon observed afterwards that any roundshot missing the front rank would certainly find a target in one of the ranks behind.

Napoleon wanted to push the Prussians eastwards away from the British. He deployed Vandamme's divisions, assisted by Girard's division from Reille's corps, to attack the Prussian right by the St-Amands. Gérard's IV Corps he put with two divisions, Vichery's and Pécheux's, against Ligny village itself while he lined up Hulot's infantry division and the cavalry corps of Exelmans and Pajol opposite the Prussians at Potriaux and Tongrinne. He was unaware that the defenders included Blücher's third corps, that of Thielmann. (Bülow, commanding IV Corps, was still advancing from Liège; it was expected that he would arrive at Gembloux, five miles to the northeast, by nightfall.) The Prussians present on the battlefield numbered about 83,000, the French about 65,000. For the French, it had proved impossible to bring Lobau's VI Corps up in time.

At about 3 o'clock in the afternoon, rather later than Napoleon had hoped, a gun from the Guard artillery spoke crisply three times, then the massive blue and white columns, preceded by a cloud of skirmishers working their way forward in open order, surged across the golden cornfields towards the villages. A fearful and sanguinary struggle developed. The guns kept up an incessant roar, the drums beat maddeningly and everlastingly the *pas de charge,* the grey gunsmoke drifted across the battlefield and above all sounded the crashing volleys of musketry.

As the struggle for the villages grew ever more ferocious, Napoleon realized that he faced most of the Prussian army. At 2 pm he had told Soult to inform Ney that he was about to attack a considerable enemy force, and that he, Ney, should drive away the enemy in front of him, then move across eastwards to take the Prussians in the rear. Now he told Soult to send another message instructing him to envelop the enemy's right and rear by taking the high ground at Brye.

On the western face Ziethen's outnumbered

[1] Müffling states that Wellington added, 'if I am not attacked myself'. At that time he did not expect to be attacked, and the proviso might seem irrelevant. He was speaking to two experienced soldiers; they would not need to be told that he would only come if it was militarily possible to do so. As will be seen, however, the non-appearance of Wellington's men at Ligny caused Gneisenau severe misgivings about his allies.

troops gave back. Blücher fed in regiments from Pirch's II Corps to reinforce them. By St-Amand the battle swayed to and fro. The French secured the hamlet of St-Amand and a foothold in the other villages, but farther forward they could not go. In the centre by Ligny a desperate combat erupted about the Ligny brook, but the French failed to force their way over it. The brook in fact turned out to be more of an obstacle than had been apparent to Napoleon during his reconnaissance. In the east Thielmann, perhaps worried by the sight of the serried ranks of French cavalry, remained fairly quiet, while the heavily outnumbered French were content to remain on the defensive. Some of Thielmann's men were drawn into the fearful combat raging in the centre and right flank.

Napoleon watched the conflict with his usual calm. The Prussian reserves were being pounded to pieces by his guns, but in the villages the combatants had fought each other to a standstill. He decided to change his plan. The time had come to deliver the decisive stroke, and he prepared to make it against the Prussian centre around the village of Ligny.

He had begun to deploy the Guard for this task, when a most extraordinary incident occurred. An anxious-looking ADC galloped up to him from Vandamme to say that a large column of enemy could be seen coming in on their left from the northwest, from the direction of Villers-Perwin. Already some of Vandamme's men had begun to panic. Napoleon despatched some battalions of his Guard to stiffen them and one of his ADCs, General Dejean, to reconnoitre the mysterious column more closely. Dejean galloped away; he returned half an hour later to say that the troops were French and from d'Erlon's I Corps. As they watched, the column shed a division of infantry and one of cavalry, turned about and marched off.

Napoleon had his preparations well advanced for the attack on Ligny and was not prepared to change them. He made no effort to detain d'Erlon. The strange incident delayed the French attack by about an hour. It had, however, an unlooked-for benefit. Blücher, seeing that Vandamme's men had begun to waver, thought the battle won. Storm clouds had come up and darkened the sky, and although it was only about 6 o'clock the old man may have thought night was about to fall. He determined to complete the rout on the French left. He gathered together every available man, two battalions from I Corps and six from II Corps, and plunged with them into the smoke-filled valley. Initially the French fell back, but the detached battalions of the Guard held firm and Vandamme's men rallied. Meanwhile the old Field-Marshal had fatally weakened his centre. Also to Napoleon's joy, the leading files of Lobau's VI Corps had come into view. At about 6.30 pm he gave the order and the veterans of the Old Guard swept majestically forward with Milhaud's cavalry corps and the heavy cavalry of the Guard following behind.

They broke through Ligny and surged up towards Brye. Blücher desperately organized a charge with his 7th Uhlans, the only cavalry left to him, into the flank of the advance. The left-hand battalion of the Guard, the 4th Grenadiers, formed square and received them with a steady succession of well-aimed volleys. The Uhlans recoiled. The cuirassiers of the Guard hurtled down on them. Blücher's horse, mortally wounded by a musket ball, collapsed, badly bruising Blücher and pinning him down by the leg. His faithful ADC, Nostitz, stood guard over him while the French, not knowing who lay at their mercy, galloped on. Eventually Nostitz managed to organize a party to lift the semiconscious Field-Marshal away.

Night had begun to draw on. The Prussian

The Battle of Ligny.
In the right foreground a French column is about to take possession of St-Amand; in the centre,
a brigade column preceded by skirmishers drives forward, and horse artillery gallop across to the left.
Further to the left, Prussian units are falling back in some disorder on their supports; it can be
seen how the ground sloping upwards behind the Prussians' position made them an easy target for the French guns.
In the centre background the village of Ligny is in flames.

Blücher leads his Prussians into action at Ligny. A bad fall later in the day almost led to his capture.

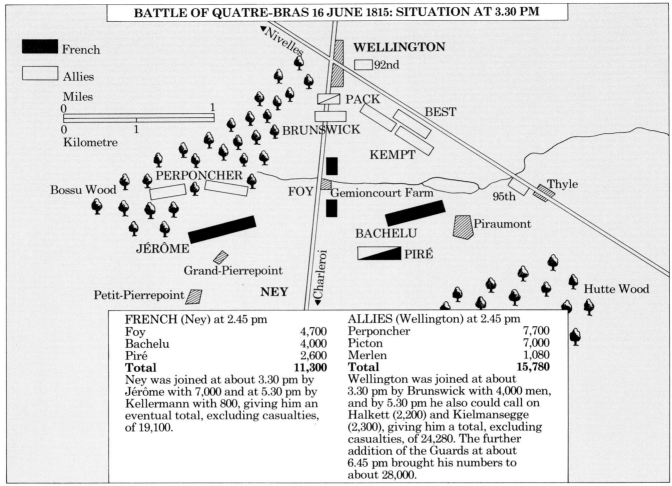

BATTLE OF QUATRE-BRAS 16 JUNE 1815: SITUATION AT 3.30 PM

FRENCH (Ney) at 2.45 pm		ALLIES (Wellington) at 2.45 pm	
Foy	4,700	Perponcher	7,700
Bachelu	4,000	Picton	7,000
Piré	2,600	Merlen	1,080
Total	**11,300**	**Total**	**15,780**

Ney was joined at about 3.30 pm by Jérôme with 7,000 and at 5.30 pm by Kellermann with 800, giving him an eventual total, excluding casualties, of 19,100.

Wellington was joined at about 3.30 pm by Brunswick with 4,000 men, and by 5.30 pm he also could call on Halkett (2,200) and Kielmansegge (2,300), giving him a total, excluding casualties, of 24,280. The further addition of the Guards at about 6.45 pm brought his numbers to about 28,000.

centre had been all but pierced. The regiments had begun to break up and the soldiers streamed away from the battlefield. Blücher had disappeared. Gneisenau, near Aux Trois Barettes, ordered a retreat. Thielmann's 12th Division, which had done little fighting was to cover it. In the face of Thielmann's troops, the pursuit halted – although Clausewitz, Thielmann's Chief-of-Staff, reported that the confusion was enough to turn his hair white.

The exhausted French bivouacked on the battle-field among the wounded, the dying and the dead. The Emperor had won a battle in his classical style. He had kept Thielmann's corps in check with less than a third of its numbers; he had forced his enemy to commit virtually all his reserves while keeping his own intact; he had deceived him about the decisive area, and finally he had driven off in great confusion an army almost a quarter stronger than his own.

As Wellington rode back to Quatre-Bras from the windmill, he heard cannons start to boom from the direction in which he was going. The noise increased. Clearly some form of battle had begun. The crossroads in themselves were of no great tactical importance, as Wellington clearly thought, and as later in the action Napoleon was to tell an infuriated Ney. They were too far north to safeguard Blücher's rear and too far south to be a safe concentration point for the Anglo-Dutch Army. Wellington would have done better to concentrate at Nivelles, as indeed he had wished. Any enemy coming down the Charleroi road would have then found him on its flank and been compelled to attack. But Blücher, by standing at

Sombreffe with only three corps, had given him no choice. If he wanted to help the Prussian, he had to hold Quatre-Bras.

Ney at Frasnes received his written orders from Napoleon at about 11 o'clock that morning. He was to push on to Genappe. He saw no reason to hurry. A few Germans had been reported at the cross-roads at Quatre-Bras. They could be thrown out easily enough. Meanwhile he needed time to disentangle his two corps from the chaos and congestion in Charleroi – d'Erlon still had one division on the far side of the Sambre while Reille's corps had experienced some stiff fighting the previous day at Gosselies, and Girard's division seemed to have wandered off and become attached to Vandamme. Ney felt that his soldiers should have a rest and a substantial meal, particularly if they were to cover the 20-odd miles to Brussels before dawn next day.

Reille agreed with his chief. He had fought the British often enough – he had commanded a corps in the army that Wellington thrashed at Vitoria. Now he pointed to the wooded, undulating country that lay ahead. He thought that the crafty Wellington might well have most of his men concealed there; nor did he fancy the massive Prussian columns forming towards Brye, which could take him in the rear. He strongly advised Ney to wait for d'Erlon and not to move forward until he had his whole wing in hand.

Ney was inclined to agree. But d'Erlon was slow in coming up and he dared not dally too long. At about 1.30 pm he took forward Bachelu's and Foy's infantry divisions and Piré's light cavalry division from Reille's corps to establish himself on the crossroads. As at about 2 o'clock he approached the hamlet by the crossroads, he saw that an enemy force, perhaps a Dutch division, barred the way. He determined to roll it up from the east and thrust down the Namur road to Quatre-Bras. He directed Bachelu onto Piraumont Farm, east of the Charleroi road, Foy to drive down the road with one brigade, keeping the other in reserve, and Piré with his chasseurs and lancers to follow behind, ready to exploit any opening that occurred.

The Prince of Orange had studied his position with some care. The three or four houses of the Quatre-Bras hamlet formed a useful small inner keep on the crossroads itself. To the west of the Charleroi road the large Bossu Wood stretched southwards for about a mile, ending just before the twin farms of Grand Pierrepoint and Petit Pierrepoint. The Charleroi road dipped down after leaving the crossroads, then ascended a low rise with its crest about 1,000 yards away before dipping down again towards Frasnes. On the eastern border of the road, just beyond the small stream in the bottom of the dip, was Gemioncourt Farm. The hamlet of Piraumont lay some 1,200 yards east of Gemioncourt and 200 – 300 yards north of Hutte Wood. About 600 yards east and a little to the north lay the village of Thyle astride the Namur road. The countryside rose and fell in a series of gently sloping swells and troughs which, while being no obstacle to movement, provided a good deal of cover, a characteristic accentuated by the fields of standing corn, up to six feet in height, and the two woods. The Namur road was slighly embanked here and furnished cover to anyone approaching from the north.

The Prince of Orange deployed Perponcher's division with four battalions on his right, in the area of the two Pierrepoints, and two at Gemioncourt blocking the Charleroi road. To watch his left he put some light troops into Piraumont and kept three battalions in reserve in the area between the crossroads and Gemioncourt Farm. The front was wide for a single division but he wanted to create an impression of numbers.

At about 2.30 Wellington road up.[2] Three major developments were in progress. Away to the south thick columns of soldiers with blue jackets and white breeches with drums beating and colours flying were bearing steadily down on the farms at Gemioncourt and Piraumont; cannon were deployed on the flanks of the columns and gaily uniformed lancers and chasseurs rode behind. A few hundred yards away down the Nivelles road he could see the nodding plumes of van Merlen's Belgo-Dutch cavalry brigade; along the road from Brussels a long dark green column steadily approached, while behind it could be seen the red coats and shakoes of Picton's English battalions and the kilts and bonnets of the Highland regiments.

As Picton's regiments marched up, Wellington directed them to turn east down the northern edge of the embanked Namur road. He told the leading battalion, the 95th Rifles, to take Piraumont and anchor his left flank. By the time the 95th arrived, however, the French were there in strength. The 95th contented themselves with occupying and fortifying the hamlet of Thyle on the Namur road.

Meanwhile matters had gone ill with Perponcher's division. Bachelu, having driven the light troops out of Piraumont, swung westwards towards Gemioncourt which Foy with one brigade was also approaching down the Charleroi road. The converging attack was too much for Perponcher's men. They started to move back to the Bossu Wood. The watchful Piré at once swooped down with his chasseurs and lancers. The hapless Dutchmen broke ranks and bolted for the wood with the lancers in hot pursuit. As they rushed by, a number of men in the Prince of Orange's reserve battalions also found the attractions of the wood compelling.

Wellington had detached the 92nd Highlanders (The Gordons) from the rear of Picton's divisional column for the close defence of Quatre-Bras hamlet. Now seeing the plight of Perponcher's men, he went forward with Merlen's cavalry to rescue them. Piré's lancers turned fiercely on the Belgo-Dutch horsemen and overthrew them. The Duke had to ride for his life and seek shelter behind the Gordons. Some of the shaken cavalry rallied and reformed behind the Highlanders, others disappeared into the thickets of the Bossu Wood. The French lancers, themselves disorganized by their series of charges, rallied back.

It was about 3 o'clock. Picton had formed and dressed his line to his satisfaction with Kempt's brigade on the left, Pack's on the right and Best's Hanoverians behind. Now the fiery old veteran led them across the road and a short distance to the south. At the sight of the red coats, Foy and Bachelu checked. The musketry died away to be replaced by the steady roar of the guns.

Ney now held a line stretching from just south of the Pierrepoints to Piraumont and which included Gemioncourt. But Picton's intervention had thwarted his initial attempt to seize the crossroads. It was going to take a fully concerted attack. Jérôme's division had come up from Frasnes. He deployed 42 cannon for a preliminary bombardment. Jérôme was to clear the Bossu Wood with one brigade while another advanced parallel to it along the wood's eastern border. Foy was to launch his division straight down the road at Quatre-Bras, Bachelu to head northwards towards the Namur road while Piré with his cavaliers again followed behind to exploit the slightest sign of wavering.

Wellington waited on events without a great deal of pleasure. Müffling riding beside him afterwards remarked that the Quatre-Bras position was a thoroughly bad one. At 3.30 pm the French gunfire reached a crescendo and once more the blue and white columns strode forward through the fields of rye.

Jérôme's left-hand brigade took the Pierrepoints and burst into the Bossu Wood, driving the bright-green-uniformed Nassau troops before them. As the French columns to the east breasted the tall cornfields, a long red line suddenly emerged before their eyes and the deadly volleys of the British infantry smote Bachelu's men. His columns halted, dismayed, and the weaker members began to turn back. Picton at once detected their hesitation. There was a loud shout of 'Charge!' The bayonets of Kempt's men flashed down and the long line swept menacingly forwards. The French gave ground. Kempt's brigade began to run after them. The French guns opened up and Foy, seeing the plight of his comrade, brought his rear brigade across to

---

[2]Timings are difficult as no two authorities agree. Wellington himself said that he arrived at 2.30 pm. It may have been later.

help him. Its fire checked Kempt's brigade and the British, who had nearly reached Piraumont, retired almost to their original position. Piré's chasseurs hurtled down but the British battalions coolly formed square and repelled them.

And so the struggle continued and the gun-smoke swirled over the area enveloping the contestants with its acrid fumes. Near the Bossu Wood Jérôme's men carried all before them. The Belgo-Dutch regiments disintegrated and found in the wood a convenient refuge. The Brunswick corps had followed Best's Hanoverians up the Brussels road. Wellington ordered them forward to plug the gap that had begun to yawn between Picton's right and the Bossu Wood. As Jérôme's right-hand brigade drove triumphantly forward with loud cries of 'Vive l'Empereur!', the raw young German recruits began to panic. Appalled, the Duke of Brunswick led forward his cavalry, about 900 strong, supported by those of van Merlen's troopers that were prepared to resume the battle. Brunswick fell, mortally wounded by a musket-ball, then Piré's ubiquitous lancers crashed down. A confused mass of battling cavalrymen reeled back towards Quatre-Bras. A few lancers actually reached the crossroads only to be despatched by the 92nd, but most wheeled round behind the 42nd, the Black Watch, and the 44th, later the Essex Regiment, of Pack's brigade. Coming out of the smoke still mingled with the Dutch and Brunswickers, the Highlanders mistook Piré's men for allies. Too late they tried to form square. The lancers were among them, killing their colonel and spearing many of their number as they passed; but the surviving Highlanders refused to give ground. Colonel Hammerton of the 44th saw a little sooner than most what was happening. He realized there was no time to form square. He gave a stentorian shout 'Rear rank, about face! Make Ready! Present! Fire!' The volley took its toll but Piré's troopers inflicted fearful casualties before they rode off southwards into the smoke. The two superb regiments reformed their mangled ranks; they still held their ground

despite the fact that now they numbered less than a single battalion.

Bachelu's defeat had caused Foy to check and Jérôme had been unable entirely to clear the Bossu Wood, now packed with every sort of runaway. By Quatre-Bras Wellington improvised a weak brigade composed of Brunswickers and Dutch, with the 92nd as its core.

And now another long red-coated column appeared, uncoiling itself from the Nivelles road. Halkett's brigade of Alten's 3rd Division began to deploy on the left of the Bossu Wood to replace the Dutch and the Brunswickers. Then came Kielmansegge's Hanoverians. Wellington placed both under Picton's command. Kielmansegge he directed to reinforce the 95th on the left. Ney's great attack had failed.

Of d'Erlon there was still no sign. Then an ADC came up with the incredible news that d'Erlon had taken his complete corps to Ligny instead of sending merely his light cavalry and one infantry division. Ney, wandering round the battlefield like some titan of old, two horses having been shot under him, raged against his fate. He sent d'Erlon orders to join him at once. Then an officer galloped up with Soult's second message. He was to take the crossroads then manoeuvre towards Ligny where the decisive battle was being fought. Quatre-Bras was of no great significance. During the break in the fighting the guns had recommenced their infernal duet. As roundshot hissed past him he proclaimed that he wanted nothing more than for one to hit him. Then the fury of battle once again gripped him; Kellermann, his cavalry held back in case Napoleon should need him, had come up with a single brigade of cuirassiers. Ney ordered him to charge forward and seize the crossroads. As Kellermann looked at the 20,000 men he was to charge with his 1,000 horsemen, he queried the order. Ney, almost demented with passion, ordered him to charge forward and tread the enemy into the ground.

Kellermann turned to lead his men forward.

British infantry in square at Quatre-Bras face a storm of French cavalry.

As they topped the rise from Frasnes he put them into a gallop so that they would be in action before they had time to realize what they were charging.

A tremendous drumming of hooves sounded over the ridge. Picton's weary, attentuated brigades once again formed their squares. The cuirassiers surged among them, unable to break them. For a moment the 28th faltered. Picton's tremendous voice made itself heard. '28th, remember Alexandria!' The ranks held firm. A battalion of Halkett's newly arrived brigade broke under the impact; it was afterwards said that the Prince of Orange had ordered it to remain in line. His own brigade, charged by the cavalry then pounded by the French guns, withdrew into the wood. Some cuirassiers penetrated as far as the crossroads and ran into a vortex of fire. After what they had already endured, this was too much. They broke back carrying away with them Foy's leading brigade that had been forming up by Gemioncourt.

The rest of Reille's corps had followed the cuirassiers but by now the horses of Piré's cavalry were blown and the troopers tired out. Bachelu's division although no longer capable of a sustained attack, sent forward a cloud of skirmishers that descended on the 95th and Kielmansegge's Hanoverians about Thyle. They cut the Namur road but could not penetrate into Thyle itself. By the Bossu Wood a dangerous situation developed for the defenders as Jérôme's brigades drove through nearly to Quatre-Bras. But once again the red-coated columns came pouring up the Nivelles road. Cooke's 1st Guards Division had begun to arrive; at once it was plunged into the struggle. It checked the advance of Jérôme's men, but the French fought with great determination. Slowly and at heavy cost the Guards gained the mastery. By now it was nearly 8 o'clock in the evening, and it was plain to Ney that d'Erlon[3] would never arrive in time and that the odds were stacked against him. He pulled back his exhausted men to Frasnes. At about 9 o'clock Wellington retook Gemioncourt and his men bivouacked on the ground that Perponcher had formerly held. In the fighting Ney lost 4,000 men from his single corps, proportionately more than did Napoleon at Ligny. Wellington lost 4,500 men.

At the end of the day both armies to a certain extent had triumphed. Ney had held the ring for Napoleon. He had prevented Wellington from sending a single soldier to aid Blücher just as effectively as if he had actually captured the crossroads. Equally, Wellington during the remorseless pounding of that bloody afternoon had prevented Ney from assisting his Emperor. Although much criticized, Ney had in fact served his Emperor well. With a single corps, and that without one of its divisions, and one heavy cavalry brigade he had held Wellington at bay. Admittedly the circumstances were different, but had Grouchy done half as much at Wavre on the 18th, events at Waterloo might have taken a different course. As often happens in these affairs, however, Ney received nothing but blame from his Emperor.

---

[3] D'Erlon's troops did not fire a shot that day. Such mishaps were implicit in the speed with which the campaign was conducted. Bülow did not take part, nor did Lobau. Wellington was without half his army. D'Erlon's absence, however, seems the strangest – although his journeying between the battlefields has perhaps received more attention than it deserves. Houssaye in his celebrated account of the events of 1815 quotes 15 authorities to prove that Napoleon called d'Erlon to Ligny but that Ney, to whose wing d'Erlon belonged, over-ruled him. But nothing can overcome the fundamental implausibility of that proposition. No one could over-rule Napoleon, and the extraordinary effect of his intrusion on the battlefield at Ligny is inexplicable if Napoleon had reason to expect him. The most probable explanation is that some staff officer exceeded his authority and took d'Erlon to Ligny, either by accident or design, and that neither Napoleon nor Ney authorized or expected the move. D'Erlon, had he remained at Ligny, might have given an added impetus to the Prussian retreat; but he had arrived too late to do more, and his men were tired. At Quatre-Bras on the other hand he might have forced Wellington to retire to Genappe, thereby anticipating by a few hours what in fact happened next day. But he could not have deployed before about 6 o'clock that evening, and Wellington was far too skilful a general to suffer more than a reverse, after which he would have left the battlefield to the French – as indeed he did on the next day, the 17th.

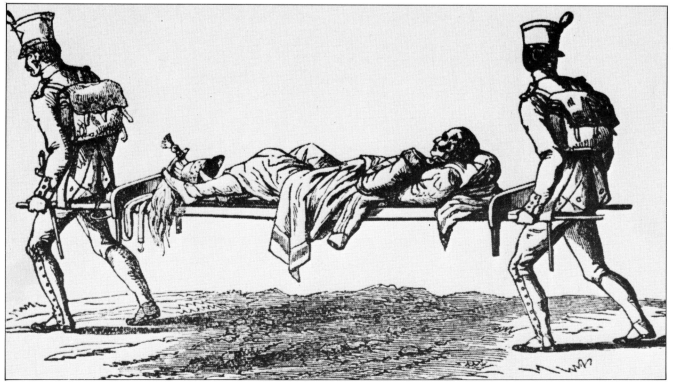

Stretcher-bearers carry off a wounded dragoon.

CHAPTER 12
INTERMISSION

Between 9 and 10 o'clock on the evening of the 16th, Gneisenau sat his horse on the road near the estaminet of Aux Trois Barettes. The musketry that had roared incessantly through the afternoon now was muted and the gunsmoke had cleared. Beside him were Ziethen and Pirch with their staffs. Behind them an enormous disorderly mob of soldiers and troopers, among whom the West-phalians predominated, streamed away to the north and east. Here and there were clumps of men where officers had managed to rally a few of the fugitives. In front, Thielmann still held some steady regiments along the heights of Brye. The French

Ligny after the battle.
Engraving by George Cruikshank.

advance had halted. Gneisenau peered at his map in the gathering darkness. Of Blücher there was no trace. He had to take on his own responsibility perhaps the most crucial decision of the whole campaign, and he had only a few minutes in which to take it.[1]

The generals waited gravely; experienced soldiers, they contemplated the appalling disorder dispassionately, waiting for Gneisenau to decide where they should take the shattered wrecks of their corps for the night. During the night no doubt many men would rejoin the colours. In war things were seldom as bad – or as good – as at first they seemed.

Gneisenau hesitated. If the army fell back down the old Roman road towards Liège, Bülow could cover the retreat, sheltering the shaken regiments while they reorganized. A retreat from Liège towards the Rhine should present few difficulties; thereafter Schwarzenberg would soon restore the situation and draw off the French. On the other hand, such a retreat would almost certainly entail the fall of Brussels; the British army would probably take to its ships, as it had done often enough in the past. Were the British and the Duke in earnest? Although he knew that Blücher thought so and that Müffling agreed, Gneisenau found it difficult to overlook that secret treaty with France. Moreover, despite all his bland assurances, the Duke had not sent a single soldier from Quatre-Bras to help them that afternoon. To wait for the Duke to fulfil his pledge would clearly be an act of folly. But a retreat to Wavre, 13 miles to the north, could be a useful compromise. Brussels would not be uncovered and no irrevocable decision would have been taken. Blücher, if he was still alive, would never forgive him for deserting a friend, and his many enemies in Prussia would pounce on the loss of Brussels as an excellent stick with which to beat him. A new line of communication through Louvain and Maastricht could quickly be improvised. The decision had to be made at once: it was almost night and the bivouac areas had to be suitable for what might be a perilous move next day. Gneisenau made up his mind. The retreat should be to Wavre. Ziethen and Pirch would bivouac between Mellery, Tilly and Gentinnes, two or three miles north of Aux Trois Barettes. Thielmann should hold on to his present positions and Bülow bivouac at Baudeset, near Gembloux.

A little later, at about 10 o'clock, Gneisenau learned that Blücher was lying in a cottage at Mellery. The old man had been carried in semiconscious. He had broken no bones. His limbs were being massaged in a mixture of gin and garlic. He had recovered sufficiently to suggest that an internal application might prove beneficial. By morning he was able to mount his horse.

The Prussian withdrawal started soon after dawn. Their movements shielded by Thielmann's III Corps, Pirch's and Ziethen's men slipped away unobserved. By noon Ziethen was west of the Dyle by Bierges and Pirch between Wavre and St-Anne, a mile and a half to the south. As they went, the old Field-Marshal rode up and down the marching columns and was cheered wherever he went. Despite the defeat and the disappearance of 20–25,000 men from the colours, both he and his soldiers appeared to be in remarkably high spirits.

Once Ziethen and Pirch were well clear, Thielmann drew back towards Gembloux. Here he joined forces with Bülow and came under his command. They held positions on the west bank of a stream, the Orneaux. French cavalry appeared but avoided coming into contact. About 2 o'clock, once the two leading Prussian corps were firmly in position at Wavre, Thielmann and Bülow withdrew to join them. As they went, the black clouds that had been piling up overhead disgorged flashes of lightning followed by torrential rain. The guns and wagons soon churned the narrow, unmetalled roads into a sea of mud. The cavalry and infantry toiled across boggy fields. It was an intensely fatiguing march. Thielmann's last division did not cross the Dyle until 8 o'clock that night, while Bülow's last formations did not get in until two hours later. During the afternoon French cavalry hovered about the Prussian rearguards, but in the blinding rain seemed reluctant to close.

Napoleon spent the night after the battle in the château at Fleurus. He woke to a sunny morning. So far, despite the inevitable mishaps, matters were shaping well. He had driven a wedge between Wellington and Blücher and defeated the Prussians. He was in the position of a chess player approaching the end-game with a clear advantage. He had only to play his pieces correctly and the game would be his. He must avoid making a false move now. On no account should he come to a decision prematurely or on insufficient information. The Prussians had been beaten, but how badly? And where did they propose to go? And what did the Duke of Wellington intend? And where were his own troops? On his decisions that morning probably would depend the fate of the whole campaign. He could continue to screen Wellington with his left wing under Ney while he pursued Blücher with the same ferocity with which he had pursued Sacken and Yorck after Montmirail. But if the Prussians were retreating towards Liège, this would lead him to the east – away from his objective, Brussels. Moreover, if the Prussians were retreating towards Liège or Namur, a hot pursuit would be unnecessary, and might cost him his chance to beat Wellington before they recovered from their defeat.

The administrative chaos caused by the crossing of the Sambre on the 15th needed to be disentangled. Nothing had been heard from Ney, save that he claimed that the absence of d'Erlon had robbed him of a brilliant victory and he had failed to take Quatre-Bras. There was little positive information about the Prussians. Pajol, commanding I Cavalry Corps, reported at 4 am that his vedettes had seen movement and he was following up some troops who had taken the road to Namur and Liège. The news sounded good. At about 7 o'clock Napoleon sat down to breakfast in the château. Flahault, who had been with Ney in Quatre-Bras, rode in to interrupt his meal. He confirmed that Ney had in front of him a large mixed force of British, Dutch and German troops.

Napoleon reflected. If the Prussian army was retreating on Liège, the campaign was virtually

---

[1] Years later Wellington told Stanhope that the decision to retreat to Wavre was only taken after long discussions between Blücher, Grolman and Gneisenau (Grolman had taken over as Quartermaster-General from Müffling). Houssaye maintains that Gneisenau took the decision on his own. This seems the more likely. The bivouac areas had to be selected with the morrow in mind, and Blücher was still sick and shaken after his fall.

over. He could afford a day off to rest and reorganize. He wrote to Ney, 'It is absolutely necessary . . . to complete the military stores, rally scattered soldiers and to call in all detachments.' He added strict injunctions that he was to observe closely all that passed at Quatre-Bras, and if the crossroads was held by only a rearguard he was to attack and seize it forthwith.

At 8 o'clock Grouchy rode in. It was still too early to take any firm decisions. Napoleon led him over the previous day's battlefield; as he went, he chatted with the soldiers that he met and made arrangements for the caring of the wounded. He beckoned to a trembling Belgian peasant and said

he would certainly suffer from hell-fire if he did not look after a horribly mangled Prussian officer lying nearby. He ordered that the wounded should be tended whatever uniform they wore. His tour over, he started gossiping with Grouchy over the social scene in Paris and the activities of the Legislative Assembly. At last Grouchy could bear it no longer. He burst out, 'What are my orders, Sire?' Napoleon snapped back, 'I will give you your orders when it suits me.'

Slowly information seeped in. It was becoming plain that no rest would be possible. Ney reported eight regiments and 2,000 horse on his front, the equivalent of one cavalry and two infan-

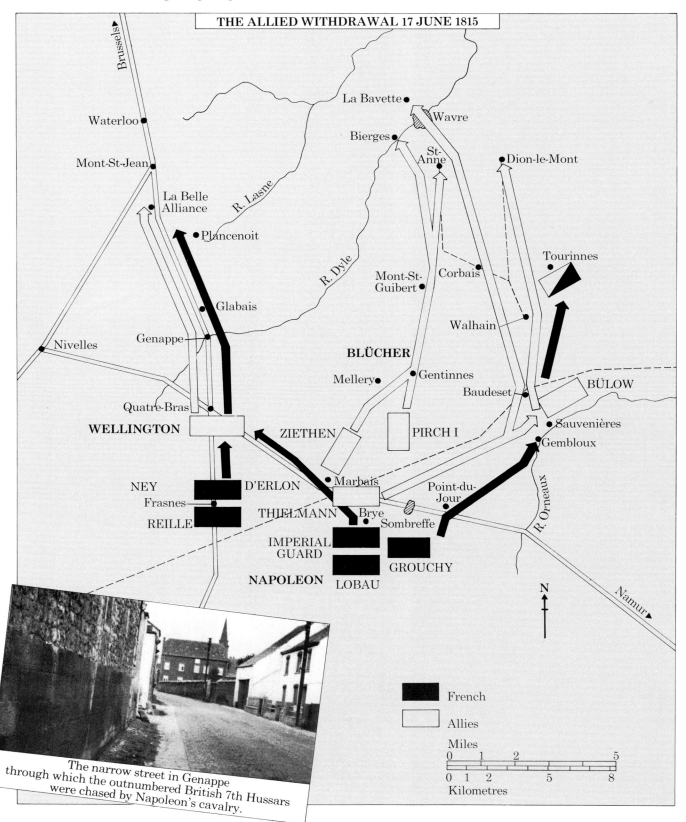

THE ALLIED WITHDRAWAL 17 JUNE 1815

The narrow street in Genappe through which the outnumbered British 7th Hussars were chased by Napoleon's cavalry.

try divisions. From the east Exelmans sent in a message that his leading brigade had encountered a strong force of Prussians at Gembloux; they seemed to be in excellent order. Then a Prussian battery arrived which Pajol had captured complete on the Namur road; but it turned out that the battery had lost its way, and the road forward of it was empty. Blücher might be retreating towards Liège, but in far better order than Napoleon anticipated. It was vital that he worked out the balance of his forces correctly and selected the right objectives. He had to retain under his hand sufficient troops to be certain of beating Wellington, and beating him before the Prussians recovered from their drubbing. At the same time it was painfully clear that the Prussians could not be disregarded. Yesterday, despite certain mishaps, his plans had produced the right results. He returned to work.

If Grouchy with the right wing went to Gembloux, he could follow the Prussians to Liège or Louvain or Wavre, as might prove necessary, and be strong enough to neutralize them for the next few days. There would still be ample resources left with which to dispose of the 'Sepoy General'. By a little past 11 o'clock he had made up his mind and gave Grouchy his orders. He was to take his wing with the cavalry corps of Pajol and Exelmans and go to Gembloux, reconnoitre in the direction of Namur to the south and Maastricht to the east; he was to pursue the Prussian army wherever he might find it.

Grouchy rode away a worried man. It was his first day in command of his wing – Napoleon had commanded it for him the day before. How would the stiff-necked Vandamme, with whom he had had a violent argument on the 15th, and the veteran Gérard, fuming that he had not been made a marshal for the victory at Ligny – how would they take his elevation as their commander? Tact would be essential. He personally told Vandamme to concentrate at Point-du-Jour and march on Gembloux. Gérard was to follow. As Vandamme's corps marched off, the black clouds broke amid thunder and vivid flashes of lightning, then the rain fell like a celestial river in spate.

With two corps moving along a single road, Grouchy's column thinned and stretched out into an immensely long, slow-moving blue and brown snake. The infantry and cavalry took to the fields to leave the road free for the guns and caissons. Mud caked the boots of the infantry; they sank ankle-deep at every step; the horses of the cavalry sank to their fetlocks; the rain lashed down unmercifully. Gérard's rear divisions did not arrive at Gembloux until 9 o'clock that night, then dispersed seeking shelter from the elements. Exelmans's troopers followed Bülow's and Thielmann's corps, but slowly; the rain driving into their faces made it difficult to see ahead. About 6 o'clock that evening a regiment of dragoons struck a Prussian rearguard at Tourinnes, some five miles north of Gembloux and eight from Wavre. The bedraggled dragoons bivouacked for the night near their adversaries. They failed to see them depart. At 10 o'clock a friendly peasant wandered in to tell them that the Prussians had vanished in the direction of Wavre.

Grouchy and his two corps bedded down at Gembloux. They had covered little more than eight miles, but their soldiers were miserably wet and hungry. Grouchy thought it essential to allow them to dry out and cook themselves a meal. He wrote to Napoleon, 'We may perhaps infer that one column is going to join Wellington and that the centre which is Blücher's army is retiring towards Liège.'

After Grouchy's departure, Napoleon turned his attention to Quatre-Bras. At Marbais he concentrated Lobau's corps (exept for Teste's division which had gone off with Pajol), two divisions of the Guard, two divisions of light cavalry and Milhaud's corps of cuirassiers; then he took them down the Namur road towards an apparently somnolent Quatre-Bras. By Frasnes there was no sign of activity.

In Genappe Wellington rose early and rode up to his headquarters, bivouacking in the fields by Quatre-Bras. Around him men had begun to stir. His outposts watching Frasnes reported the French still to be asleep except for foraging parties. From the direction of Ligny there came not a sound. It was strange. He had received no word from Blücher. Probably the French had been beaten off and now was the time to begin an offensive. But he had to know positively what had happened. He sent his senior ADC, Lieutenant-Colonel Sir Alexander Gordon, escorted by a squadron of the 10th Hussars, to reconnoitre to the east of his position.

Ominously, Gordon soon ran into French cavalry vedettes and swung north of them to Marbais. As he approached the village, he came across a party of Prussians who told him that Ziethen was there. He had a brief talk with the General, then hurried back to Wellington with alarming news. The Prussians had been driven out of Ligny and were in the process of going back to Wavre.

Wellington directed a sour and suspicious look towards Müffling who hastened to assure him that he had no inkling of such a move. It turned out that Gneisenau had sent an officer the previous evening to tell Wellington that they were withdrawing, but the officer had been ambushed by some French skirmishers who had established themselves across the Namur road. He had been badly wounded and had failed to deliver his message. His suspicions of Müffling's good faith allayed, Wellington discussed with him what should be done.

The Duke was extremely worried. He had with him by now two Belgo-Dutch divisions, four Anglo-Hanoverian ones, the Brunswick corps, Lord Uxbridge's cavalry corps and van Merlen's cavalry; in all about 50,000 men. Other troops were expected shortly. But he might be attacked by almost the whole of Napoleon's army. It was a very dangerous situation. He meditated ordering an immediate retreat. Müffling counselled delay. The British troops had fought and marched themselves into the ground the day before. He had noticed that during the campaigns in Germany Napoleon invariably allowed his men time to cook and eat a proper meal the day after a hard-fought battle. He thought the French most unlikely to move before 10 o'clock that morning. Wellington decided it was worth risking a difficult rearguard action to allow his men to eat a good meal and start their withdrawal reasonably fresh. He now had a strong cavalry force of his own with which to cover his eventual line of retreat to the north.

He ordered the infantry to withdraw to Mont-St-Jean and to be clear of their present positions by 10 o'clock. Uxbridge was to screen the move, deploying his cavalrymen in three lines across the Charleroi road. Troops still on the way to Quatre-Bras were to turn about and go direct to Mont-St-Jean. At this rendezvous there was a possible position blocking the Charleroi road to Brussels, which Wellington had noticed some time before. The Nivelles road joined the Charleroi road there, and to the north stretched the Forest of Soignies. A series of low ridges ran from east to west and he was confident he could make a sound defensive position out of them. In any case he had no choice if he was going to maintain any sort of touch with the Prussians. If he did not stand at Mont-St-Jean he would have to retire north of Brussels and uncover his line of communication to Ostend. He still felt nervous about his right flank and the excellent road to Brussels from Mons. He ordered General Hill with two brigades of 4th Division, Prince Frederick's tiny corps of one Belgo-Dutch infantry division and Anthing's Indonesian brigade to block that road about Halle.

The guns and infantry marched away without incident. Ney at Frasnes seemed oblivious of this world. Wellington himself stayed with Uxbridge and the rearguard to see that his army got clear away. By about 1.30 pm the infantry were over the River Dyle and through Genappe. The wind had begun to freshen and the skies to cloud over. Suddenly in the distance down the Namur road someone in Wellington's staff saw something glint. 'Bayonets,' he exclaimed. Wellington levelled his telescope. 'Those are cuirasses.' It was time to be gone.

Uxbridge himself with the 7th Hussars and Mercer's troop of the Royal Horse Artillery took post across the Namur road. The ranks behind them began to thin out as regiments withdrew. At about 2 o'clock the cuirasses showed up plainly among the dark masses of horsemen approaching them. Then there suddenly appeared a square figure wearing a cocked hat transversely and a green coat. Mercer recognized Napoleon, trained his guns on him and fired. Wellington would not have approved of such behaviour; he held that generals did not indulge in personalities of that sort. But one shot might have ended the war, and Napoleon was reputed himself to have directed 16 guns on Moreau and mortally wounded his former rival. However, Mercer's shots flew wide. His fire was soon followed by a tremendous roll of thunder, lightning streaked to the ground, then the rain poured down. Despite the rain, a French 8-gun battery came smartly into action and a mass of light cavalry began to form up for a charge. It was already dangerously late. Mercer shouted for his guns to come out of action. The limbers dashed forward; the guns were hooked up and pulled away at a gallop with the 7th Hussars following hard behind. The French cavalry raced after them. It became a wild hunt on horseback with the outnumbered hussars and the guns as the quarry. The gun horses were equal to the occasion, hurtling through the narrow streets of Genappe. On the far side of the village Uxbridge drew rein. The 7th Hussars reformed and turned about. Some French lancers were emerging from the village. The hussars charged down on them but were baffled by a wall of lances and were driven back. A British battery fired a salvo of grape, then, on Uxbridge's command, the Lifeguards deployed nearby hurtled down on the lancers, forcing them back into Genappe. In the pouring rain a wild *mêlée* ensued in

Self-portrait of a gunner in Napoleon's army;
the picture was part of a letter sent to the gunner's father.

the narrow, slippery streets. In the confined space the French lancers with their long weapons found themselves at a disadvantage. They retired from the village; then the Lifeguards in their turn withdrew. After this sharp clash the pursuit was not again pressed.

Soaked by the remorseless rain, Napoleon with his cavalry approached the inn called La Belle Alliance. Behind the cavalry d'Erlon with his corps pressed forward, but the rain funnelled him onto the road and the corps behind could barely start before nightfall. The Guard struck across country to Glabais and then scattered in search of shelter.

Napoleon stared through the swirling rain clouds at the low ridge ahead. He thought he could see flashes of red and the grey of gun barrels stretching away on both sides of the Charleroi road. A battery of enemy guns opened up on his advanced guard. He recalled them and deployed two brigades across the soggy ground to the east. As the long lines of horsemen walked slowly forward into the murk, all along the ridge sudden spurts of flame pierced the scudding squalls of rain. Napoleon estimated that about 50 guns had opened fire. This was no rearguard position; the complete Anglo-Dutch Army must be deployed in front of him. Unbelievably, Wellington was going to stand and fight on his own. It was a stupendous piece of luck. Next day he would thrash him before the Prussians had time to recover from their defeat. Tomorrow should see the opening stages of his campaign come to a triumphant conclusion. He called back the cavalry. Deeply content, he rode south to a farm, Le Caillou, about a mile and a half along the Charleroi road from La Belle Alliance. There he dried his clothes in front of a roaring fire whilst his old faithfuls, the 1st Battalion of the 1st Chasseurs of the Guard, bivouacked damply in the fields around him.

Late that night came Grouchy's despatch from Gembloux. Napoleon read it his satisfaction undimmed. Even if most of the Prussians went to Wavre they would surely be unfit to fight on the morrow. Grouchy could deal with them; his only fear was that Wellington might escape in the night and join hands north of Brussels with a Prussian army that after a few days might have revived. At 1 o'clock on the morning of the 18th he rode all along the ridge that ran parallel to the one held by Wellington. The rain still beat down. On the heights opposite a myriad camp fires still bravely pierced the darkness and the rain, but nothing stirred. Now it would be too late for Wellington to withdraw. The coming day would be the day of decision.

The relentless rain still lashed down, turning the fields into quagmires. D'Erlon managed to have his corps bivouac about Plancenoit, but the greater part of the army stretched away to the north, condemned to spend a hideous night in open marshy fields. Lobau and Reille with their men were still somewhere near Genappe. The weather was bound to delay the opening of the battle.

By Mont-St-Jean Wellington contemplated the next day unsleeping; it would be the moment of truth when, with his heterogeneous army, he confronted in battle for the first time the acknowledged military genius of the age. At 9 o'clock on the morning of the 17th, before he left Quatre-Bras, a message had come from Gneisenau baldly announcing that the Prussians were going to Wavre and asking what he intended to do about it. No doubt there had been little time for consultation, but it was clear that Gneisenau had no intention of indulging in any; it was one way to treat an ally.

Wellington had replied that he would fight before Brussels provided that he might have one Prussian corps to assist him. Blücher replied that evening when it was clear that the retreat to Wavre was not being closely pressed. He wrote with his usual pugnacity that Wellington could count on two Prussian corps, and that he would come with his whole army if circumstances permitted. With 40–50,000 Prussians covering his left flank and his own right strongly posted, Wellington should have been able to rest easy, but no one rested easy when confronted by Napoleon. Even the bull-headed Blücher, in like circumstances, had been known to pause and think.

The old man still felt sick and bruised. But tomorrow he would be leading his army against Napoleon and the French. No prospect could please him more. Gneisenau was not so happy. What was that double-dealing Englishman up to? Might he withdraw next morning and leave the Prussians inserting their heads into a noose from which, this time, they would not escape? Blücher had said that he would support Wellington with two corps. Once the old man had made such a pronouncement nothing would change his mind; but considerable care would be necessary next morning. Gneisenau was probably the most worried of the commanders that night; in effect, he was almost as much a commander as a chief-of-staff, yet lacked the authority to impose his views in the last resort. Even Grouchy, weighed down by an unaccustomed and unsought responsibility, probably lay awake for less of the night.

Lancer of an élite squadron of the 5th Chevau-Légers, who fought with Reille's II Corps.

CHAPTER 13
WATERLOO: THE PRELIMINARIES

Through a wretched, interminable night the rain bucketed down. Then the skies lightened, the rain eased off and spirits began to rise. At about 6 o'clock in the morning Wellington left his temporary cottage home in Waterloo and rode forward to inspect his troops and check their dispositions. He found his men cheerfully engaged in dismantling their scanty shelters of the night before, trying to rekindle their camp fires and dry themselves out, and cleaning their arms and ammunition. All muskets had been loaded for instant use during the night. The simplest way to unload them

Napoleon in 1815, by Carle Vernet.

seemed to be to fire them in the general direction of the French. An irregular popping of musketry fire sounded down the line, to the bewilderment of such French piquets as had not previously encountered this strange British custom.

The evening before, Wellington had deployed his army along a series of low ridges that ran very approximately east and west; in fact the eastern end was noticeably north of the western. On his right was the village of Braine-l'Alleud; the area between the Nivelles and Charleroi roads formed the centre of a possible position, while on his left he had sufficient troops to extend far enough along a road leading to Wavre to avoid any great danger of being outflanked, particularly as the Prussians might be expected down the road by about noon. That road would also have a more immediate use: it ran the length of his position as a sort of artery along which he could move troops swiftly from flank to flank.

Now the Duke had to make his detailed dispositions. After his fashion, he never afterwards divulged on what principles he had based them. However, he must have analysed carefully the problem from Napoleon's point of view. What was the Emperor likely to do? In general terms he seemed to have two major alternatives. He could smash his way through the British position along the Charleroi road, split the British army in two and open the way to Brussels. This seemed a risky manoeuvre, for he could find 70,000 Prussians bearing down on his right flank. Secondly, he could turn the British right flank, or even mask it with an infantry corps and perhaps a couple of cavalry corps, hook round to Turbise and thrust on Brussels by the excellent Mons highway.

To Wellington this seemed a very dangerous possibility. The finely trained French army could outmanoeuvre his clumsy, polyglot divisions without great difficulty, and the battle would be fought well to the west. The Prussians would be late, if they came at all. His first priority must be to safeguard the right flank. He had eight British brigades and two of the King's German Legion. On these he would rely. In particular, in Clinton's 2nd Division, Adam's brigade was composed of what remained of the incomparable Light Division that had served him so well in Spain; these regiments could manoeuvre or fight with the best. They should be placed on the right, preferably in reserve until the moment of decision drew near. There was also the 1st (Guards) Division, his only all-British division, and Mitchell's experienced brigade from the 4th Division: with these he could provide a trustworthy, manoeuvrable core to his right flank. Chassé, with his Belgo-Dutch division, could garrison Braine-l'Alleud itself and turn it into a strongpoint. If he held it against the French with the tenacity with which he had held La Margarita (near Vitoria) for the French against the British, it would make a sturdy pivot for the flank.

If the Duke anchored his right at Braine-l'Alleud, he could extend along the Wavre road towards Ohain sufficiently far to reach the more broken country there, and the Prussians should appear before the battle had been long in progress. His battered 5th Division, supplemented by Best's Hanoverian militia brigade, should be capable of looking after the left. He put the 5th Division, Best's brigade of the 6th Division and the cavalry brigades of Vandeleur and Vivian to watch the left flank, from the Charleroi road eastwards. He added to them Perponcher's Belgo-Dutch division to give added depth, with Prince Bernard's brigade in Papelotte Farm and the hamlets of Smohain and La Haye, and Bijlandt's light brigade across the front, screening the 5th Division. Picton was in charge of the left. All the units had suffered severely at Quatre-Bras, but it should be a quiet flank.

The Duke thought it wise, however, to tell Picton to place his two British brigades on his inner flank with their right on the Charleroi road; he positioned his two fine heavy-cavalry brigades about 200 yards back, one on either side of the road. He earmarked Lambert's 10th Brigade, the missing second brigade of the 6th Division, to come into reserve by Mont-St-Jean when it had marched up from Assche. He positioned Ompteda's brigade of the King's German Legion the other side of the Charleroi road from Kempt's brigade of the 5th Division, telling him to garrison the farm of La Haye-Sainte, which had already been loopholed for defence, with a rifle battalion. In a sand-pit on the other side of the road from the farm, Kempt stationed some companies of the 95th and blocked the road itself with logs of wood. To the right of Ompteda he deployed the rest of the 3rd Division. That left his critical right flank. A château with extensive grounds, the Château and Farm of Hougoumont, stood rather to the south-west of his line. He resolved to bulge the line outwards along a low ridge, so that he could include the château as a strongpoint. This would constrict any attack on his centre. He put his Guards Division on the ridge behind it with all four light companies in the château and its grounds, strengthening them by stationing a Nassau battalion in the woods south of the château and adding a company of Germans.

That formed a useful hinge for his right-centre if he had to change front and face west. Beyond the Nivelles road the ridge turned northwards and there he placed in succession Mitchell's British brigade and Clinton's 2nd Division, giving him four fresh and experienced British brigades, half his British infantry strength, in the area behind Hougoumont. To the west, on the far side of a dip, was Chassé in Braine-l'Alleud. Grant's and Dornberg's cavalry brigades were stationed close to the British infantry, so providing Wellington with a hard-hitting force that he could call upon if Napoleon tried to outflank him to the west. In addition he held the Brunswickers and Kruse's Nassau brigade in reserve.

Between Turbise and Halle, seven miles to the west on the Mons road to Brussels, he had Hill's II Corps consisting of the two remaining brigades of the 4th Division – the 6th British and the 6th Hanoverian – Stedman's 1st Belgo-Dutch Division, Anthing's Indonesian brigade and Estorff's Hanoverian cavalry brigade; one regiment of the latter, Hake's Cumberland Hussars, remained on the Waterloo position where they were to achieve a dubious distinction. The whole totalled about 15,000 men. Their numbers were more impressive than their fighting powers, but by fighting in the two towns they should be able to check and funnel a French advance towards Brussels. Collaerts's Belgo-Dutch cavalry division took post near the angle where the Nivelles road forked from the Brussels – Charleroi highway. Wellington's whole front by Waterloo stretched over about three miles. Buttressed by strongpoints at Papelotte in the east,

Observatory

La Belle Alliance

Hougoumor

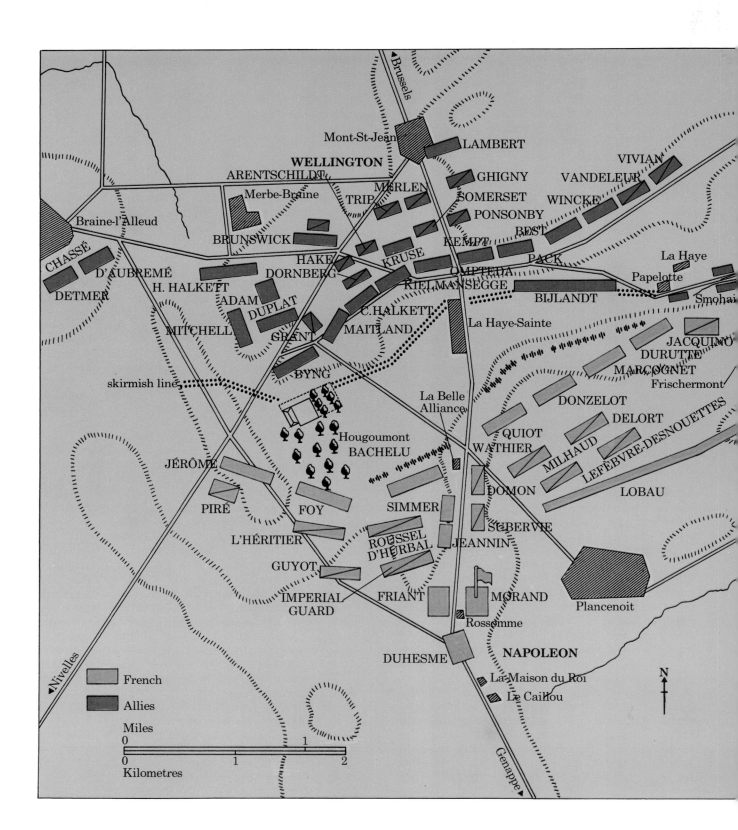

A panorama of the field of Waterloo,
drawn from near the inn of La Belle Alliance a few days after the battle.
The British right-centre extended from Hougoumont to La Haye-Sainte;
the French guns were deployed along the ridge on either side of La Belle Alliance.

THE DISPOSITIONS AT WATERLOO 18 JUNE 1815

ZIETHEN

Ohain

BLÜCHER

ZIETHEN

PIRCH I

BÜLOW
(WITH BLÜCHER)

Lasne

Paris Wood

PRINCE BERNARD

FRENCH (Napoleon) from the left:		ANGLO-DUTCH (Wellington) in brigades:	
		Adam	2,700
		Arentschildt	1,200
		Prince Bernard	3,800
		Best	2,500
		Bijlandt	3,200
		Brunswick infantry	4,400
		Brunswick cavalry	800
		Byng	2,100
		D'Aubremé	2,700
II CORPS (Reille)		Detmer	3,000
Piré	1,500	Dornberg	1,200
Jérôme	6,800	Duplat	1,400
Foy	3,800	Ghigny	1,000
Bachelu	3,100	Grant	1,300
VI CORPS (Lobau)		C. Halkett	2,200
Jeannin	2,200	H. Halkett	2,400
Simmer	3,900	Hake	500
Domon	1,000	Kempt	1,700
Subervie	1,200	Kielmansegge	3,200
I CORPS (D'Erlon)		Kruse	2,900
Quiot	4,000	Lambert	2,500
Donzelot	5,100	Maitland	1,600
Marcognet	3,900	Merlen	900
Durutte	3,800	Mitchell	2,000
Jacquinot	1,700	Ompteda	1,500
IV CAVALRY CORPS (Milhaud)		Pack	1,900
Wathier	1,100	Ponsonby	1,300
Delort	1,600	Somerset	1,200
III CAVALRY CORPS (Kellermann)		Trip	1,200
L'Héritier	1,600	Vandeleur	1,300
Roussel d'Hurbal	1,600	Vivian	1,200
GUARD INFANTRY		Wincke	2,400
Old (Friant)	4,100	ARTILLERY	
Middle (Morand)	4,000	156 guns	6,000
Young (Duhesme)	4,000	**Total**	**69,200**
GUARD CAVALRY		PRUSSIANS (Blücher)	
Lefèbvre-Desnouettes	2,000	I Corps (Ziethen)	20,000
Guyot	2,800	II Corps (Pirch I)	20,000
ARTILLERY		IV Corps (Bülow)	30,000
256 guns	6,000	**Total**	**70,000**
Total	**70,800**		

Note. At Wavre, meanwhile, Grouchy with 30,000
closed with Thielmann's Prussian III Corps (17,000).

La Haye Sainte in the left-centre and Hougoumont in the right-centre, and with both flanks drawn back northwards to make envelopment almost impossible, it was a superlative example of how Wellington's genius could turn an insignificant roll in the ground into a strong, well-balanced defensive position.

As he rode along the front he noted that there was no air of disquiet among his soldiers. The old hands from Peninsular days recalled that a heavy rain storm had almost invariably been the prelude to Wellington's greatest victories. A Nassau rifleman, either by accident or design, loosed off a bullet in his direction, but otherwise all seemed in order. He took up his own post by a large tree close to where the Charleroi road entered the position. There was nothing to do now but wait, and the French were putting on a spectacular display for him to watch.

As the first bars of light appeared in the east and the rain began to slacken off, Napoleon returned to Le Caillou quietly confident about the future. A letter from Grouchy awaited him. Columns of Prussians had been seen, some going towards Wavre and others eastwards to Perwez on the old Roman road to Liège. Grouchy proposed to identify where the main Prussian forces might be, and to follow them.

At 8 o'clock Napoleon sat down in the main room of the farmhouse to eat breakfast off the Imperial silver. A pale sun had begun to break through the clouds and a drying wind had sprung up. He estimated the Allies had about 85,000 men against his 69,000, but he knew that the Belgians were disaffected and the Hanoverians raw and untrained. Wellington had probably fewer than 40,000 troops on whom he could rely with any degree of confidence. He looked round at his senior generals gathered at the breakfast table. 'The enemy army exceeds ours by a quarter but the odds are nine to one in our favour,' he proclaimed.

Ney, who had just come in, with his usual brusqueness replied, 'No doubt, if the Duke of Wellington was simple enough to wait for you; but I come to tell you that already his columns are in full retreat. They are disappearing into the forest.' 'You have not seen aright,' Napoleon rejoined. 'There is no longer time. He will expose himself to certain defeat. He has thrown the dice and our number has turned up.'

The breakfast party had scarcely broken up when some artillery officers sent to reconnoitre the ground announced that it was drying well and could take artillery. Napoleon related in his memoirs, 'I reflected for a quarter of an hour, dictated the battle orders which two generals seated on the ground wrote down. The aides-de-camp carried them to the different army corps who were standing to arms full of impatience and ardour.'

The sun was shining as by 9 o'clock the first marching column swung by the Emperor with drums beating, bands playing, colours flying and eagles held proudly aloft. Originally he had planned to begin the attack at 9 o'clock, but apart from the delay needed to allow the ground to dry out sufficiently to take the guns, Reille's and Lobau's corps were a long way back and their regiments had to cover five or more miles to reach their deployment areas. Nothing would be gained by haste, risking confusion and tiring the troops

before the battle began. Everything should be carried out with the precision of a ceremonial parade; then the splendid army would advance and sweep Wellington into oblivion. There would be plenty of time on that long summer's day.

Reille's regiments of II Corps marched up to their allotted places on the left flank. Piré and his chasseurs and lancers took post just to the west of the Nivelles road. Then to the east of it came in succession the divisions of Jérôme, Foy and Bachelu, each with one brigade forward and the other 60 yards behind it; Girard's division, which had suffered at Gosselies and then even more severely at Ligny, Napoleon left behind to clear up the battlefields. Bachelu's right flank rested on the western edge of the Charleroi road. Some 200 yards behind Reille's corps, Kellermann's corps of cuirassiers jangled into line, its right-flank squadron by the road; behind it came Guyot's heavy cavalry of the Guard.

With its head at La Belle Alliance, Lobau's VI Corps, now of only two divisions, lay in a thick column on the left of the road with Domon's and Subervie's light cavalry divisions in column on the other side. Down the road to the south the three infantry divisions of the Imperial Guard halted and stood at ease around Rossomme.

East of the Charleroi road and roughly level with Reille's corps, d'Erlon's men (I Corps) tramped across the fields of rye before halting and facing to their left towards the ridges by Mont-St-Jean; Quiot's division – he was commanding for Allix, who was away – took post with its flank on the eastern border of the Charleroi road, then Donzelot's, Marcognet's and Durutte's divisions lined across to the east. Durutte formed opposite Papelotte Farm with Jacquinot, commanding d'Erlon's division of light cavalry, on his right opposite Vivian's brigade on the British left flank. About 200 yards behind d'Erlon's infantry, Milhaud's corps of cuirassiers formed in long lines with the flank squadron resting on the Charleroi road. Behind the cuirassiers, Lefebvre-Desnouettes dressed the ranks of his light cavalry division of the Guard.

Ahead of and across the whole front, the gun teams thrust forward with their cannon trailing behind them. Each swung in an arc and halted. The gunners unhooked the guns, then, a little way behind the gun trails, unloaded the limbers and caissons, stacking the ammunition conveniently to hand. The gun teams retired to huddle behind the lines in battery groups. Much of the Guard artillery remained undeployed and limbered up, ready to go into action wherever required.

The miseries of the past night were forgotten. As the regiments, the squadrons and the batteries swung past the Emperor, shakoes were hoisted on bayonets; shouts of 'Vive l'Empereur!' like the roaring of a vast waterfall cascaded over the battlefield. On the ridges by Mont-St-Jean the red ranks watched, silent, impressed, but undismayed as for the last time the pageantry of the *Grande Armée* unfolded before them. It was a scene the like of which the world would never know again.

The long, confident, cheering columns were still striding by when at 11 o'clock Napoleon issued his final orders: 'At the time that the whole army will be deployed, at about 1 o'clock, at the moment that the Emperor gives the order to Marshal Ney, the attack will commence to seize the village of

Mont-St-Jean. Count d'Erlon will begin the attack pushing forward his left-hand division and supporting it as may be necessary by the divisions of I Corps. II Corps will advance as needed to keep level with Count d'Erlon. The sapper companies of I Corps will be ready to fortify Mont-St-Jean at once.'

A long shallow valley divided the two armies. In the west it broadened out into the wooded enclosures and orchard of the Château of Hougoumont; in the centre the Charleroi road climbed the gently sloping ridge, past the farmhouse of La Haye Sainte on the left and the sand-pit on the right, to disappear over the crest. The shallow valley continued to the east, but by Papelotte Farm and the hamlets about Frischermont, its sides became steeper and more rugged. It ended in the tree-covered slopes of the Paris Wood and the broken country about the River Lasne, here little more than a brook.

Napoleon had deployed a heavy phalanx of infantry to gouge out Wellington's centre and left along the line of the Charleroi road. His left flank, facing Wellington's massed right, was his weaker, and Reille's divisions, weary and depleted after their heavy actions at Gosselies and Quatre-Bras, had lost something of their fire. D'Erlon, however, with his four fresh divisions, faced Picton's and Perponcher's men, who, equally, were by no means fully recovered from the mauling they had received at Quatre-Bras. Once again and for the last time Napoleon had deceived Wellington about his intentions. But now for the first time he was to assault a British defensive position.

The action, however, began on the British right. To fix Wellington's attention on that flank, Napoleon told Prince Jérôme to put in an attack on the wood to the south of Hougoumont. Jérôme's divisional battery of eight guns opened fire on the wood. A British battery on the ridge behind the château replied. Reille unmasked another of his divisional batteries to shoot back. Soon a brisk artillery duel raged. Then at about midday, with drums beating and bugles blowing, Jérôme's leading brigade thrust into the wood.

Over by Wavre matters progressed slowly. Blücher had pledged himself to send Wellington two corps and to come with his whole army if he could. Gneisenau doubted the wisdom of the whole project, but a pledge had been made and had to be kept. He still dreaded that Wellington would retreat, that the Prussians would find Napoleon in front and a strong French force behind. He persuaded Blücher to agree that initially the two leading corps should move only as far as the height above Chapelle-St-Lambert, just east of the River Lasne and about a mile and a half from Ohain. If the Anglo-Dutch army was engaged with Napoleon, the two corps would strike at Plancenoit, four miles to the south-west, and come in on the Charleroi road, encircling the French.

French cavalry had been identified at Tourinnes, four miles to the south, probably the advanced guard of a much larger force. A flank march across its front would be dangerous and need extreme care. Gneisenau proposed to concentrate the Prussian army west of the River Dyle. Bülow, whose IV Corps had not yet fired a shot, was farthest to the east. He was ordered to move first, filing through Wavre while Pirch I (II Corps)

covered the move from his bivouacs by St-Anne. Once Bülow was securely across the Dyle, Pirch would follow while Bülow pressed on to Chapelle-St-Lambert. In modern terminology Gneisenau proposed to keep one foot on the ground while the other was moving. The two corps should be at Chapelle-St-Lambert, about four and a half miles from the crossroads at Mont-St-Jean, by noon, in plenty of time to intervene if a battle was being fought round the Charleroi road. If the move was not pressed from the south, Ziethen and Thielmann (I and III Corps) could follow behind. Possibly Gneisenau was over-cautious and in no great hurry to carry out the Prussian commitment to Wellington; but to accuse him of bad faith in the terms used by Fortescue[1] is as untenable as the German accusation that Wellington showed bad faith at Quatre-Bras by failing to send any help to Blücher.

Bülow's leading division arrived at Chapelle-St-Lambert by noon without difficulty, but the road was narrow and bordered by thick woods, making movement slow and elongating the marching column. Earlier, an unfortunate incident had occurred. While the long column wound its way through the tortuous village street of Wavre, a house burst into flames; the fire blocked the road, trapping most of Bülow's corps east of the village. The Prussians were going to be late. Bülow and Blücher themselves were at Chapelle-St-Lambert. As they waited, over towards the Charleroi road sounded the distant booming of the guns. Blücher, still sick and bruised, vowed he would if necessary be roped to his horse rather than miss the battle.

Grouchy too heard that heavy rumble in the distance. He had intended that Vandamme's II Corps should start marching to Wavre at 6 o'clock in the morning, followed by Gérard (IV Corps) two hours later. However, difficulties arose over the distribution of rations. The head of Vandamme's leading brigade did not step off until well after 7 o'clock. The French too suffered from a narrow road with muddy verges. Grouchy was reportedly breakfasting at Walhain – it must have been a singularly late breakfast – when the deep-throated mutter could be heard over towards Waterloo. Gérard, who was with him, claimed that he pressed on Grouchy the need to 'march to the sound of the guns'. Grouchy demurred. He knew that Wellington might well be fighting a battle that day. His duty was to prevent the Prussians from intervening. He was confident he could do this at Wavre. If he marched towards Waterloo by those terrible by-roads, he would not arrive with his leading corps much before 6 o'clock that evening; in doing so he might well emulate d'Erlon's feat on the 16th and fail to bring his wing of the army into action at all. Moreover, Gérard's motives are suspect. He bitterly resented Grouchy's having been appointed over his head. Quite possibly he hoped to join Napoleon and escape from his vassalage to one he deemed his inferior. Equally, Grouchy could not tolerate advice from Gérard. The advance to Corbais and Wavre continued.

Near the crossroads by Mont-St-Jean the drama had begun to unfold. The Duke rode over to the ridge behind Hougoumont. The sun was shining as, preceded by a cloud of skirmishers, Jérôme's division plunged into the wood south of the chât-

---

[1] John W. Fortescue, *A History of the British Army* (13 vols).

THE BATTLE FOR HOUGOUMONT

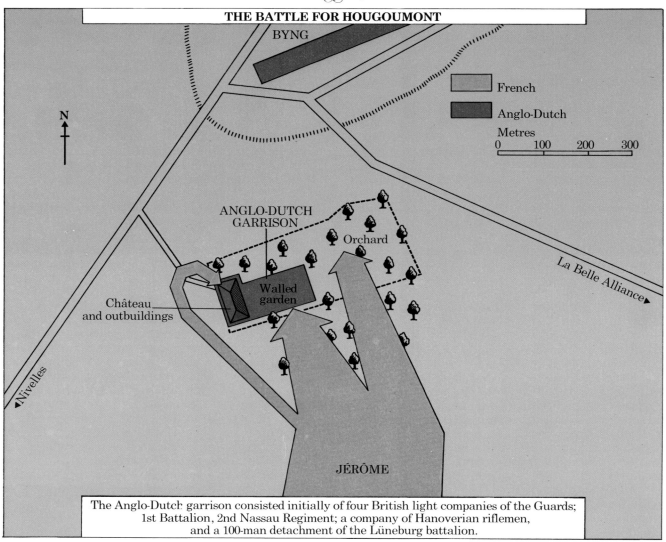

BYNG

N

French

Anglo-Dutch

Metres

0   100   200   300

ANGLO-DUTCH
GARRISON

Orchard

La Belle Alliance

Château
and outbuildings

Walled
garden

Nivelles

JÉRÔME

The Anglo-Dutch garrison consisted initially of four British light companies of the Guards;
1st Battalion, 2nd Nassau Regiment; a company of Hanoverian riflemen,
and a 100-man detachment of the Lüneburg battalion.

The beginning of the action.
The columns of Prince Jérôme's leading brigade, preceded by skirmishers, are beginning to
penetrate the woods by Hougoumont; a battery has come into action
firing over the heads of the advancing infantry. The French are trying to isolate
the château from the main British position to its rear, marked by smoke
from the British guns. The houses on the ridge behind the poplars are at Merbe-Braine.
In the left foreground Jérôme's second brigade, drawn up in line, is waiting
in reserve. Behind it can be seen Piré's light cavalry.
To the right some cuirassiers, probably from L'Héritier's division, seem to be changing position.

eau. On the far side of the Nivelles road, Piré's brightly-clad lancers and chasseurs walked their horses, keeping them level with the advancing infantry. The drums beat incessantly, the bugles blared and with a great shout of 'Vive l'Empereur!' the French forced their way through the wood towards the château. The Duke watched impassively. He could see a great mass of infantry menacing his left between the Charleroi road and Papelotte. He was not to be tempted to any premature reactions, even if the attack against his right flank, which he had expected, seemed to have begun.

Among the trees the crackle of unseen musketry moved steadily northwards. The triumphant French pressed up towards the orchard and walled garden that lay beyond the wood. Before reaching the walled garden they were abruptly checked by a ride 30 yards across, bordered by a solid six-foot masonry wall; this had been loopholed and a firestep embanked behind it. Through and over the wall projected a steady row of muskets held by the light companies of the Guards. The wall became coated by billowing white smoke. Well-drilled volleys smote the leading ranks of the French. Those who tried to rush across the ride and climb the wall were remorselessly shot down. Their advance was checked. Jérôme sent in more troops. Wellington fed forwards reinforcements with a niggardly hand. Jérôme's men fanned out and swarmed all round the château. With astonishing boldness they penetrated between its north face and the ridge, little more than 200 yards away. The great château gate had not been barricaded, so that supplies and reinforcements could come down from the ridge. An enormous French subaltern, Legros of the 1st Léger, hacked the door open and rushed in, followed by a number of his men. For a moment it seemed that Hougoumont must fall to the French. Then the garrison of the Guards turned on the intruders; Colonel Macdonnel with the aid of some sergeants forced the gate shut. The audacious French were shot down where they stood.

Four companies of the Coldstream Guards under Lieutenant-Colonel Woodford descended on the château, driving the attackers from its north face; a battery of howitzers shelled the French in the wood and orchard. The French drew back, but only to reform and begin again a deadly struggle that was to last all day. Although on several occasions the orchard changed hands, the British were not to be evicted from the château and walled garden.

While this combat raged, a French grand battery of 80 guns lined up on the rising ground running eastwards from La Belle Alliance on the Charleroi road. Shortly after 1.30 pm the last gun was in position. Napoleon gave the word and with a fearful crash the guns opened a fire that was to continue at intervals throughout the long afternoon and evening. Soon the acrid fumes were drifting over the battlefield while the air whistled and cracked with round-shot and shell. At this time the Anglo-Dutch guns on the ridge stayed silent, reserving their fire for an actual assault; the soldiers lay down behind the ridge and the soft ground muffled the effect of the bombardment.

The first great clash of the Anglo-Dutch and French armies was clearly imminent and the Duke regarded it with some uneasiness. Who would have believed that the Emperor would attack his left flank when the nearest Prussians were bivouacked a mere six miles away? On the other hand, was Blücher still in a position to send the two corps he had promised?

A Red Lancer. Napoleon raised two Guard lancer regiments from among his Polish and Dutch allies.
Troopers of both regiments wore the square-topped Polish lance cap, the *czapka*, and carried lance pennants in the Polish colours of red and white.

CHAPTER 14
THE GREATEST BATTLE

Towards 1 o'clock the Emperor had ridden over to the mound just north of Rossomme, which he had selected as his command post, to tell Ney to begin the attack; he had appointed Ney the battlefield commander. As he joined the brilliantly

Ney's skirmishers advance in the second attack on La Haye-Sainte.

uniformed group of officers on the mound he found them all looking intently towards the wood by Chapelle-St-Lambert some four miles to the northeast. Something was moving in the trees. A dark stain began to spread out from them. Telescopes were levelled. The Prussian blue was difficult to distinguish from the French at that distance. Was it Grouchy displaying a prescience verging on the miraculous? Napoleon felt doubtful. He ordered Domon and Subervie to take their divisions of light cavalry over to Paris Wood and reconnoitre forward to Chapelle-St-Lambert. But as the generals were issuing their orders, doubts were resolved. A patrol brought in a captive Prussian; he said that Blücher himself was over by the wood. A chill hush greeted the news. Napoleon appeared unmoved. He told Lobau to take his two infantry divisions to support the cavalry. Although Wellington did not know it, the Prussians had already subtracted four divisions from the army facing him. Soult wrote an order to Grouchy telling him to manoeuvre towards the right flank of the army. Grouchy did not receive it until 5 o'clock, too late to act on it effectively. Soult could have saved himself the trouble.

On his ridge Wellington could see a tremendous mass of blue-clad infantry forming up, preceded by the normal cloud of skirmishers. They began to scale the gentle slope towards him, treading the rye flat. He rode over to the tall elm by the crossroads just north of La Haye-Sainte. It was too late to call on any infantry, but he alerted his two heavy cavalry brigades, the Household Cavalry under Lord Edward Somerset, and Ponsonby's Union Brigade. The latter formation had acquired its name because it consisted of the English Royal Dragoons, the Scots Greys and the Irish Inniskilling Dragoon Guards. Wellington kept his cavalry commander, Lord Uxbridge, later the Marquis of Anglesey, close by his elbow.

D'Erlon adopted an unusually concentrated formation for his attack. He knew the deadly British musketry of old and probably thought his best hope was not to attempt to match it, but rather to burst a way through the British line by the sheer impetus of his advance. Quiot's division was on the left: his troops marched in two brigade columns, and his battalions, in a line of three ranks, followed one behind the other about seven paces apart. One brigade column marched west of the Charleroi road, the other to the east of it. Travers's brigade of cuirassiers, in a long column, walked their horses on the left to guard that flank. Some 200–300 yards to the east came Donzelot's division, and a similar distance from him strode Marcognet's; both were in a formation like Quiot's, but the second brigade in each followed closely behind the first; they formed bayonet-fringed wedges of men about 200 yards across and 80 yards deep and consisted of some 4,000 closely packed men. It would only be possible to deploy from such a formation on the order of the brigade commander, a fact that was to cost d'Erlon's men dear. It would be wrong, however, to assume that a commander of d'Erlon's experience made a mistake through ignorance. Clearly he did not intend his men to deploy until they had broken through the long thin lines ahead of them. Away on the right Durutte advanced against Papelotte in battalion columns which were as deep as the other two divisions but infinitely more flexible; the broken country he had to cover prohibited too rigid

a formation. To his right, positioned thus in order to watch his flank, walked Jacquinot's division of light cavalry.

It was an awe-inspiring sight: the blue-coated phalanxes passed through the golden fields of corn, the French guns fell silent, and the smoke drifted away so that the sun was revealed. Then the ridge ahead blossomed into a cloud of white smoke. Roundshot and grape tore into the serried ranks, but they only pressed the more fiercely onwards. They brushed Bijlandt's light troops aside. On the left Quiot's men broke through the orchard at La Haye-Sainte to assault the farmhouse. But here the rifle battalion of the King's German Legion under Major Baring, undaunted by the numbers of their assailants, opened a destructive fire. The French swept round the building and isolated it from the ridge. The brigade on the east of the Charleroi road hurled the companies of the 95th out of the sandpit. The situation on the road looked grave. Kielmansegge sent forward his Lüneburg *Landwehr* battalion to succour the beleaguered farmhouse. Travers's cuirassiers swooped down and trampled them into the ground.

East of the road a ferocious combat developed. Picton had been wounded at Quatre-Bras but had refused to give up his command. Now he sternly led forward his division to check the columns of Marcognet and Donzelot. The British volleys roared out, up and down the line. The French, heavily smitten, hesitated. When they tried to fire back they were hampered by their cramped order. Nonetheless, they continued to press forward. Picton at the centre of his line fell dead, his last words, 'Rally the Highlanders.' An irregular wedge of Frenchmen penetrated between Kempt's and Pack's outnumbered brigades. To those watching from Rossomme it seemed that already a lodgement had been made on the lip of the ridge.

Then from the hard-pressed British line there came a thunder of hooves and the wild, high shouts of horsemen. Wellington had seen the crisis arising. At precisely the right moment, when the cuirassiers were still disordered by their charge and the ranks of the French infantry had become confused during the combat, he loosed on them his two heavy cavalry brigades. Behind the cavalry he brought up Lambert's 10th Brigade from Mont-St-Jean, backed by Ghigny's Belgo-Dutch cavalry brigade.

The impact of the British cavalry was tremendous. By the road the Household Cavalry rolled over the cuirassiers and raced on to Quiot's men, who were scattered about La Haye-Sainte. Here their arrival was a complete surprise: the French were helplessly ridden down before they could close their ranks. The horsemen careered madly on into Donzelot's and Marcognet's divisions, but by now they were quite out of hand. They were joined by Ponsonby's Union Brigade which had thrust through the ranks of Picton's 5th Division.

The French masses heaved and reeled under the fearful and unexpected impact of the galloping horsemen. The men in the rear ranks, flung helplessly against each other, found difficulty in using their arms. They fell into hopeless disorder. The cavalrymen and their mounts were seized with a berserk frenzy. They rode through the unhappy infantry, flailing left and right with their swords, galloped over two French batteries and plunged on wildly into the heart of the French position.

Napoleon's dispositions were well judged to meet such an attack, and here retribution overtook them. In the east Jacquinot's lancers wheeled back and crashed into the flank of what was now little more than a disorderly mob of excited horsemen. In front, Milhaud's cuirassiers charged home while west of the Charleroi road a brigade of Bachelu's division blasted them in the flank. Vivian and Vandeleur, on the British left, took forward their two light cavalry brigades a short distance to help extricate their comrades, but avoided becoming tangled with the large masses of French cavalry opposite them. The Household Cavalry, which had kept a small reserve, escaped complete destruction, but Ponsonby's Union Brigade was virtually exterminated.[1]

It was about 3 o'clock in the afternoon. Müffling had wandered over to the British left flank to liaise with the Prussian formations he fondly expected to see arrive at any moment. When he saw d'Erlon's broken formations stumbling backwards towards their start line, he urged Vivian and Vandeleur to charge, asserting that they would bring back at least 6,000 prisoners. They both refused, saying they could only charge when Wellington authorized them to do so. Müffling marvelled at the iron control the Duke exercised over his subordinates. Later, under somewhat similar circumstances, Napoleon was to find his control, so he afterwards asserted, to fail.

Now there was a lull and the artillery took over. The discharges of individual cannon merged

---

[1]The difficulties experienced in operating over the muddy ground and the hedgerows east of the Charleroi road have been remarked on by several commentators; but neither appeared to affect the charge of the Union Brigade.

into one continuous ear-splitting pattern of sound. Smoke rolled over the battlefield, and began to collect in hollows. Ney, with some of Bachelu's troops (who were still suffering from the terrible hammering they had experienced at Quatre-Bras) and some of Quiot's men, made a half-hearted attempt to capture La Haye-Sainte; in the face of the guns on the ridge and the steady German riflemen in the farm the attack petered out. The companies of the 95th Rifles re-occupied the sand-pit. By Hougoumont the volcano seemed in full eruption, sucking in Jérôme's division and some of Foy's men. Nearly the whole of Byng's brigade of Guards had joined the defenders. Duplat's brigade of the King's German Legion from the 2nd Division guarded the back entrance and stood ready to lend assistance. Napoleon personally directed a howitzer battery on to the château and its outbuildings and set them on fire. Some of the wounded of both sides were burnt to death. But the defenders never wavered and the terrible duel continued with unabated fierceness.

Elsewhere, however, there was a pause as both sides braced themselves for the next fearful round. Wellington, now it was clear that Napoleon was concentrating his attacks on the centre and left of his position, drew in the troops from Merbe-Braine. Hougoumont became the right of his position. The Brunswickers replaced Byng on the ridge to the west of the château while Halkett's brigade of Hanoverians from Clinton's 2nd Division lined up behind them and Maitland's Guards to act as a reserve. The Duke had lost his heavy cavalry but otherwise his position was intact. Nevertheless, he was beginning to wonder what could have happened to the Prussians.

Napoleon too had begun to feel anxious. Time

The Scots Greys, centre, are shown at the end of their glorious charge.
In the foreground French cuirassiers are charging them from the front;
on the right more cuirassiers and Jacquinot's light cavalry, armed with lances,
are charging them in the flank.

An episode during the cavalry battle.
Uxbridge leads the 15th Hussars in a charge against Lefèbvre-Desnouettes' Red Lancers of the Guard
in an effort to relieve pressure on the infantry squares.
Painting by Denis Dighton.

The picture, painted by Lieutenant R. P. Read and published in 1817,
shows the battlefield a little before 3 pm as d'Erlon's great infantry attack reaches its climax.
On the left, the Charleroi road runs from La Belle Alliance, in the background,
to La Haye-Sainte, in the foreground. A British battalion, probably of the 32nd, has formed square to
repulse an attack by Travers's cuirassiers. On the left, the rest of Kempt's 8th Brigade is advancing in line,
and a wounded Highlander is being carried out of the action. By La Haye-Sainte,
Ompteda's regiments of the King's German Legion are hotly engaged. The wood south of Hougoumont,
background right, after being shelled by Wellington's howitzers, has gone up in a sheet of flame.
Congreve rockets, depicted overhead, seem disproportionately large.
The picture clearly shows how packed was the field of battle, and how difficult to control.

The Prussians have descended in thick columns from Paris Wood
and are waiting for their leading units to clear the way ahead.
The church spire is presumably that of Plancenoit.

was running out. For the time being d'Erlon's corps was completely out of action. Most of Reille's was locked in the never-ending struggle to capture Hougoumont; the only infantry he had at his disposal was Bachelu's division, weary and weak after its trouncing at Quatre-Bras. Moreover, an infantry assault could be enfiladed from Hougoumont unless the château was neutralized. On the ridge Wellington, seeing his men falling like ninepins in their ranks before the blistering bombardment from the French grand battery, pulled them back behind such cover as the crest of the shallow ridge could afford them. Through the drifting smoke Ney thought he saw the red-coated line retiring. The moment to strike had arrived. He ordered Milhaud's cuirassier corps over to the left. Milhaud was unenthusiastic. He pointed out that the ground was soft and a charge in his judgement was premature. No one argued long with Ney. The cuirassiers trotted over to reform their lines west of the Charleroi road in the valley in front of Kellermann's corps. Lefèbvre-Desnouettes' light cavalry of the Guard followed, although normally they only moved on the direct orders of Napoleon. Possibly he himself authorized the charge, though later he denied it. Some 4,000–5,000 horsemen, splendidly uniformed, dressed their lines in the valley south-west of La Haye-Sainte where they could find some shelter from the guns of the British.

The front on which they were charging, funnelled by Hougoumont on one side and La Haye-Sainte on the other, extended for scarcely 1,000 yards. Their objectives were guns and infantry, and they moved in depth and in open order. In successive waves, 300–400 strong, they rode up the ridge, crossing the standing corn at the cuirassier's slow trot. As they approached, the British guns blasted them, first with roundshot then with grape, tearing great gaps in the leading squadrons. For a moment or so they hesitated, then with a great cry of 'Vive l'Empereur!' they broke over the British gun-line like the wave of an incoming tide. The British gunners ran back and sought shelter in the silent British squares ranged in a chequer-board formation on the far side of the crest. The horsemen raised a great cheer as they overran the guns; then they saw the squares beyond. However, to Napoleon at Rossomme it appeared that they had captured the ridge.

But now the musketry volleys rang out and the gunsmoke rolled down. Spur their horses as they might, the French cuirassiers could not persuade them to impale themselves on the bristling hedgehogs of bayonets before them. They could only discharge their pistols, generally harmlessly, at a square, then ride on to the next, to be greeted by searing volleys from the rear two ranks of the four-deep squares. The defending infantry welcomed the cuirassiers; at least they gave them some respite from the guns of the French. The cuirassiers, angry and frustrated, saw their comrades fall to little purpose. Wellington, as ever, judged his time well. When he saw the fire had gone out of them, he directed Uxbridge to charge from the wings with the light cavalry–he had no heavy at this time. Milhaud's shattered squadrons rode back down the slope. The Allied gunners ran to man their pieces and speed their departure. It was now nearly 5 o'clock, but the battle was far from ended.

Over by Chapelle-St-Lambert, Blücher and Bülow had been waiting impatiently for the rest of IV Corps to arrive. There could be no doubting the Duke's determination to fight. At about 2 o'clock Blücher could wait no longer. With the division that had arrived he pressed on towards Plancenoit. The road was narrow, wooded and muddy; the guns stuck; the bridge over the Lasne forced the column to contract, adding to the delay. Blücher rode up and down it, pleading with his men, 'We must get on. I have given my word to Wellington, you would not have me break it.' The soldiers responded as always to the old man, and tugged at the guns and wagons that had stuck with renewed energy; but it was not until 4.30 pm that the corps began to emerge from the Paris Wood and not until 5 o'clock that it mustered sufficient strength to commence an attack. Then two divisions, supported by the cavalry of the corps, attacked Lobau's troops at the mouth of the woods. When they came up, the other two divisions hooked round Lobau to the south and headed straight towards Plancenoit. As they surged through the narrow streets of the village, they were only about 2,000 yards from Hougoumont; the whole of the French army was in danger of being encircled. Napoleon detached Duhesme's division of the Young Guard to hold the Prussians in check. A furious struggle flared up in Plancenoit, particularly round the church. Duhesme's men would not be denied and the Prussians recoiled. For the moment the Prussians were held.

Meanwhile on the ridge the battle was renewed. Napoleon had seen his cuirassiers wandering round the ridge, apparently its master, and Ney had succeeded in rallying some of d'Erlon's scattered regiments. He told Ney to launch Kellermann's corps of cuirassiers after those of Milhaud. As they turned and started to trot up the fatal ridge, Guyot with the cuirassiers of the Guard, with or without orders, joined in and the remnants of d'Erlon's corps prepared to follow after. It was a little after 5 o'clock and the battle was about to reach a peak of almost unparalleled ferocity.

Once more the French cavalry burst through the British gun line, the ordered volleys sounded and the grey gunsmoke rolled down over the ridge, as thick as an old-style London fog. Out of that fog horsemen would suddenly appear, spurring madly towards a square. Some would fall and the others sheer away down its fire-breathing sides. The squares and the squadrons pursued their independent destinies, unmindful, even unaware, of what happened elsewhere. Men lived for the moment. Events became blurred and unreal. Relief might come to a square momentarily when a mounted battle erupted round it. But still the cheering French squadrons spurred over the crest and on to the squares. One or two of the squares swayed dangerously, but none collapsed. The Duke was everywhere, encouraging the faint-hearted, taking refuge in a square himself when a tide of horsemen threatened to engulf him. Occasionally some Allied cavalrymen charged forward to free a square, but some were chary of plunging into battle against their armoured adversaries; Wellington's superb heavy cavalry had been destroyed and Vivian's and Vandeleur's veteran brigades were now away on the left flank, where Jacquinot's cavalry and Durutte's infantry threatened an attack. Some French cavalry had penetrated on to the ridge and Best's brigade formed square; but the invasion turned out to be little more than a large reconnaissance and the horsemen rode away at the

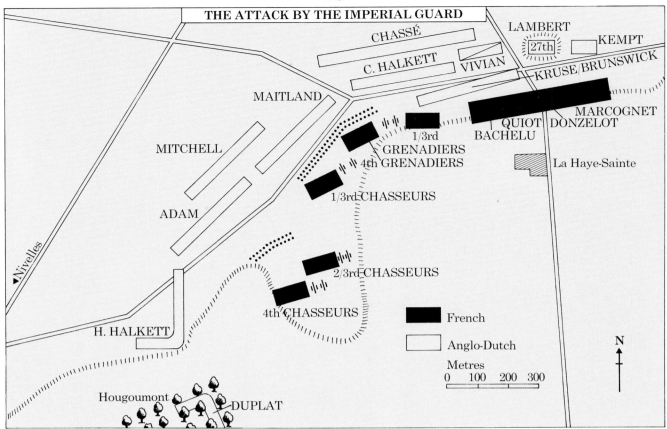

THE ATTACK BY THE IMPERIAL GUARD

CHASSÉ

LAMBERT

27th

KEMPT

C. HALKETT

VIVIAN

KRUSE/BRUNSWICK

MAITLAND

MARCOGNET

MITCHELL

1/3rd GRENADIERS

QUIOT DONZELOT

BACHELU

4th GRENADIERS

La Haye-Sainte

1/3rd CHASSEURS

ADAM

2/3rd CHASSEURS

4th CHASSEURS

French

Anglo-Dutch

Nivelles

H. HALKETT

Metres

0   100   200   300

N

Hougoumont

DUPLAT

sight of steady infantry. Down by Frischermont and Smohain, although Bijlandt's brigade had left the fray, Prince Bernard's fought on. In the centre the Cumberland Hussars distinguished themselves by refusing to charge and then galloping off to Brussels to announce that Napoleon had triumphed.

Both armies were locked in a death-grapple. One had to break soon, but it was by no means certain which it would be. Kincaid, with his riflemen evicted once more from the sand-pit, wondered if there had ever been a battle which no one survived. Or would this be the first? Napoleon rode almost alone down the length of the battle line. He told Ney that La Haye-Sainte must be captured and the British centre by the Charleroi road broken. Ney led all the infantry he could rally forward on either side of the Charleroi road. This time they moved not in solid masses but in huge clouds of skirmishers, working their way forward in twos and threes. He himself led an attack on La Haye-Sainte. The riflemen, who had made so undaunted a defence, began to run out of ammunition. Ompteda on the ridge behind went forward with his 5th and 8th Battalions of the King's German Legion to succour them. A mob of cuirassiers suddenly burst out of the fog. They smashed into Ompteda's infantry. Ompteda himself was killed, his 5th Battalion badly cut up and his 8th almost annihilated. Baring and his gallant riflemen tried to break out. Most were cut down.

The French occupied La Haye-Sainte and pressed on to the ridge. A gap yawned in the centre where Ompteda's brigade had been. It was a time of deadly menace for Wellington. The ridge swarmed with French cavalry who at any moment might appear, charging out of the fog. Wellington's infantry had to remain in square, but were then an ideal target for the muskets of the *tirailleurs* now infiltrating everywhere. The French began to run

up light guns with which to pulverize the squares. Lambert's 10th Brigade, holding a mound just behind the crossroads, was blown to pieces. The 27th the Inniskilling Fusiliers, lost more than three-fifths of its strength. Incredibly, the few survivors kept their formation. An officer with the 30th in Halkett's brigade, which had closed in to its left, recounted, 'At about 6 o'clock I perceived some artillery trotting up the hill . . . I hardly mentioned this to a brother officer when two guns unlimbered within seventy paces of us and by their first discharge of grape blew seven men into the centre of the square. They immediately reloaded and kept up a constant and destructive fire. We would willingly have charged these guns, but had we deployed, the cavalry that flanked them would have made an example of us . . . As he [the Duke] came near us late in the evening Halkett rode out to him and represented our weak state, asking him to afford us a little support. "It's impossible, Halkett," he replied. Our general replied, "If so, Sir, you may depend on the brigade to a man." '

It was vital to plug the gap west of the Charleroi road. Wellington piled into it every soldier he could lay hands on. Kruse's brigade was already hotly engaged there. He pushed in the Brunswickers and Chassé's division. The remnants of Kielmansegge's brigade tried to close in to their left. Then came welcome support.

Over towards Ohain Ziethen's corps had started to arrive. It had been delayed, waiting for Bülow's and Pirch's corps to clear the road. Wellington's plea for the immediate loan of a brigade met with a blank refusal; Ziethen said that he was not prepared to dismember his corps. He could hardly be blamed. The wounded, their supporters and the faint-hearted were streaming away from the ridge in such numbers that Ziethen, convinced Wellington was retreating, turned his men about and prepared to join Pirch. Müffling,

The last stand of the Imperial Guard.
A British officer calls in vain for their surrender. Painting by R. Hillingford.

horrified, galloped frantically after him and persuaded him that Wellington still stood fast.

A Prussian battery went into action and started to engage Durutte in the neighbourhood of Smohain; it also unfortunately engaged Prince Maurice with his Nassau brigade, until it was stopped by hurried expostulations. Vivian and Vandeleur saw that the left was now safe. Without orders, but on whose initiative it is uncertain, they took their brigades over to the crucial battle raging in the centre. Their arrival enabled Wellington to rally the raw troops of the Brunswick Corps, who had given way. The Duke personally led them back while the long ranks of the cavalry formed up behind them boot-to-boot so that, whether they wanted to or not, they had to stay. They took fresh heart from the cavalry regiments behind them, but these at first had to sit helpless on their horses while the *tirailleurs* shot them down. Nevertheless, the line held and the great crisis was nearly over.

Ney sent urgently to the Emperor for more troops. The Prussians at this time were nearly across the Charleroi road. Duhesme had been forced out of Plancenoit. Napoleon strung his two remaining infantry divisions of the Guard in squares down the road from La Belle Alliance to Rossomme. To Ney's request he responded with rare irritability, 'Where do you think I can get them? Do you think I can make them?' But at this moment his last chance of victory slipped away. The 1st Battalion of the 2nd Grenadiers and the 1st Battalion of the 2nd Chasseurs of the Old Guard plunged into Plancenoit and Duhesme's soldiers rallied round the superb veterans. The Prussians, almost overcome by the thought of facing such men, fell back. For the time being Plancenoit was safe. Napoleon turned back to the main advance of the Guard. But there were now no cavalry to support them. The Emperor bitterly regretted that Guyot had joined Kellermann and now was lost to

view with his cuirassiers somewhere on the smoke-veiled ridge.

Pirch with his corps was *en route* to join Bülow at Plancenoit. From Papelotte to Plancenoit the Prussians were closing in on Lobau's hopelessly outnumbered divisions. The light was beginning to fail and the drifting gunsmoke cloaked a scene becoming every minute more confused. The remnants of Bachelu's division and d'Erlon's corps, exhausted by their last great effort, lay on the lip of the ridge, unable to penetrate farther. To the west, survivors of Kellermann's and Guyot's cuirassiers, sullenly conceding defeat, were drifting away from the fatal ridges. By Hougoumont, Foy had joined Jérôme in the remorseless struggle against a rock-like defence. Duplat had joined the defenders with his brigade, backed by Hew Halkett with his Hanoverians, while Adam's light brigade linked the château grounds with Maitland's brigade of Guards. The French skirmishers could not stay where they lay; they had to go forward or back. They could not go forward; perforce they went back. Only by La Haye-Sainte did a gallant handful refuse to retreat.

The battle was all but lost and in his heart Napoleon knew it. Ever-increasing Prussian masses were crowding in from the east. Now was the time to withdraw, but to what end? His own fate was irretrievably bound up with that of the battle. A reverse would be as catastrophic as an outright disaster. He reacted by ordering forward the Imperial Guard for one of those final attacks that had so often brought victory in the past. In Europe it had become almost a ritual. When the bearskins of the Guard hove into view, the party was over and it was time for the guests to depart. This time, however, the guests were determined to outstay their welcome.

On the French right the Prussians had driven Durutte out of Smohain and his troops were withdrawing in disorder. Lobau's hard-pressed divisions had begun to break up. If the attack was to be made at all it had to be made at once, and somehow the incipient panic in the east had to be checked. It was about 7 o'clock in the evening. Some 11 battalions of the Guard, each numbering between 400 and 500 effective men, remained uncommitted. He told Ney to take the leading six and launch an immediate attack. The remaining five, still marching up, would be needed to stiffen his right. To Ney's disgust he sent an ADC round the regiments telling them that Grouchy had arrived on the battlefield. Every man, on horse or foot, was to support the attack, but although one or two squadrons rallied and followed the Guard forward, there was no proper formation of cavalry to support them.

As Ney advanced, d'Erlon's gallant few by La Haye-Sainte redoubled their fire, but over by Hougoumont Jérôme's and Foy's men had shot their bolt. The 2nd Battalion of the 3rd Grenadiers formed square by Rossomme, to establish a firm base, but Ney's remaining five battalions, perhaps numbering a little fewer than 3,000 men, strode forward to retrieve the battle almost unaided.

The declining sun broke fitfully through the gunsmoke, a blood-red ball glowing above Braine-l'Alleud. The corn lay trampled and stained with the marks of battle. The Imperial Guard strode forward in impeccable order. Every minute counted. To avoid delay it deployed on the march into battalion columns, stretching from the Charleroi road almost as far as Hougoumont, each with a two-company front. On each inner flank two light guns were deployed, making up a battery of eight. As each battalion column swung clear of the one in front, the Guard became echelonned back like the steps of a gigantic ladder. Napoleon himself tried to lead, but he was restrained and the death-defying Ney took command. Drums beating, the generals in front, the Guard went steadily forward through the smoke to its doom.

A deserter had forewarned Wellington of the attack half an hour beforehand. Quietly he prepared for the shock. Duplat's brigade had joined the garrison of the orchard at Hougoumont. Hew Halkett's men watched the northern approaches to the château while Adam's light brigade had withdrawn to the ridge on the right of Maitland's Guards. Colin Halkett's battered brigade continued the line towards La Haye-Sainte, which was ringed by Brunswick and Hanoverian troops backed by Chassé's Belgo-Dutch division, and held in place by Vivian's and Vandeleur's light cavalry. Mitchell's brigade, the only representative of the 4th Division, supported Adam and Maitland. The battalions formed four-deep. There was a pause in that part of the battlefield filled only by the infernal noise of the guns and the roar of musketry in the east. For the most part the men lay down. All was in order, in good time.

Then out of the smoke loomed the bearskins of the Guard. Since it was in echelon, the Guard struck the British line in succession not in one great blow. In the smoke-filled valley it had lost some of its immaculate order. What happened now will never be known for certain. It seems that the 4th Grenadiers joined the 1st Battalion of the 3rd Chasseurs to form one column, while the 2nd Battalion of the 3rd Chasseurs and the 4th Chasseurs formed another some distance behind it. The leading battalion, the 1st Battalion of the 3rd Grenadiers, strode on ahead and hit the British line by Colin Halkett's now-skeleton brigade. In this part of the front most of the British guns were out of action. The 3rd Grenadiers advanced with tremendous fire. Colin Halkett's men staggered back. Halkett himself snatched up a colour to rally them,

Napoleon's empty carriage is seized at Genappe by Prussian cavalry in the pursuit following the battle.

but fell severely wounded. Chassé deployed a battery of his guns to blast the Grenadiers in the flank at point-blank range. Halkett's men rallied and, with Detmer's brigade of Chassé's division, surged forward. The 3rd Grenadiers, overborne by numbers, dropped back down the slope. Chassé, in later years, was to claim he defeated the Guard single-handed.

On the left of the 3rd Grenadiers, the 4th Grenadiers and the 1st Battalion of the 3rd Chasseurs, though ravaged by gunfire, gained the crest of the ridge. As they reached it, the gunners ran back. When they saw the abandoned British guns, the Frenchmen gave a great shout of triumph. They seemed to have broken right through the British line. There appeared to be nothing to their front. A few mounted officers wearing cocked hats were clustered about the far side of a cornfield, 60 or 70 yards away. One spoke a few words. Out of the corn, almost at their feet, a solid wall of red emerged, four ranks deep. The 2nd and 3rd Battalions of Maitland's 1st Footguards barred the way. Terribly thinned by casualties suffered both on that day and at Quatre-Bras two days before, the two battalions probably amounted to 1,300 men, the French to about 1,000. But the French were nine ranks deep, the British only four; twice as many could fire their muskets. For a few moments there was a terrible exchange of musketry. The French tried desperately to deploy. But beneath that deadly hail of musket balls their ranks became unsteady. The bayonets flickered down, the long red line drove menacingly forward. The Grenadiers and Chasseurs fell back down the slope, the 1st Footguards followed hotfoot after them. Suddenly out of the banks of smoke some cuirassiers loomed up. Unscathed, but in some disorder, the 1st Footguards scrambled back on to the ridge.

The Grenadiers and Chasseurs rallied on the column formed by the 2nd Battalion of the 3rd Chasseurs and the 4th Chasseurs (a single battalion since Ligny), who were coming up the hill behind them. The four battalions once more charged the ridge. In front they were met by the steady volleys of the Guards and some of Adam's brigade. Colonel Colbourne boldly led his veteran 52nd Light Infantry, 1,000 strong, down from the ridge almost as far as the orchard by Hougoumont, and his men poured volley after volley into the French flank. By Hougoumont some of Halkett's men and Duplat's fired obliquely into their rear. General Michel probably died at this time and General Friant had already been carried off, severely wounded. Beneath the tempest of fire the Guard shivered, then collapsed. The unprecedented had happened: the Imperial Guard had shown their backs to the foe and fled in disorder. All over the battlefield there sounded the horrified cry, 'La Garde recule.' It was succeeded by other distressed shouts of 'We are betrayed,' and then 'Sauve qui peut.'

Where, before, there had stood a splendid army, in a few moments there was nothing but a demented mob striving to run from the battlefield. Wellington on the ridge saw the chaos below and gave the order to advance to his unbelieving soldiers. Vivian's and Vandeleur's cavalry charged down. The Prussians drove in from the east. Only the Old Guard kept their order and retreated slowly. Napoleon took refuge in one of their squares. Müffling, over on the British left, noted,

'When the line of infantry moved forward, small masses of only some hundreds of men at great intervals were seen everywhere advancing. The position in which the infantry had fought was marked, as far as the eye could see, by a red line caused by the uniforms of the numerous killed and wounded.'

Wellington and Blücher met near the inn of La Belle Alliance. They decided that to avoid further unfortunate incidents in the gathering darkness the Prussians alone should continue the pursuit. And this Gneisenau did with ruthless efficiency. It was reported that when the Prussian cavalry, themselves dog-tired, could go no farther, they mounted a drummer on a horse with a couple of squadrons and these continued the pursuit alone. Whenever the French paused to rally, they would hear the devil drumming behind them and pick themselves up and move on. The Old Guard stayed in its squares: offers of quarter were refused. It perished with the great spirit with which it had lived. Napoleon handed over his army and turned back to Paris.

Grouchy had struck Thielmann near Wavre at 2 o'clock, as the Prussian had been about to move. Thielmann took up positions along the Dyle. A sanguinary combat ensued and Thielmann sent urgent and piteous appeals for help. Gneisenau disregarded them, saying that the battle would be decided at Waterloo. At about 9 o'clock in the evening Grouchy broke through towards Chapelle-St-Lambert. By then the guns at Waterloo, that had roared incessantly through the afternoon and evening, had fallen silent. When he discovered what had happened, Grouchy made a skilful withdrawal. Whatever else he might contrive, he saw that his actions no longer had any influence on events.

A Guardsman protects his eagle, though the day is lost.

CHAPTER 15
AFTERMATH

Napoleon had almost to fight his way through the rabble of fugitives. When he saw his army disintegrate as it had never disintegrated before, the strain of the past five days, of confronting an impossibly difficult situation, became too much for him. Something of Napoleon died with the Old Guard at Waterloo. The magnificent brain still functioned, but the mainspring had broken. He was incapable of making any further decisions.

The face of defeat.

He arrived at Charleroi at 5 o'clock on the morning of the 19th. He went on to reach Philippeville at 9 am, where he was joined by Soult. He issued some instructions designating various towns where the different arms of his army should rally. It was little more than a reflex action. More important than trying to salvage a few fragments from the wreck of his army was the need to fasten Paris in a grip of iron and to rally the nation as a whole behind him.

He arrived at his capital early on the morning of the 21st. During the day it became abundantly clear that the majority in the Legislative Assembly had little use for a defeated Emperor and even less for a war to help him preserve his crown. His brother, Lucien Bonaparte, put the issue to him starkly. Either he staged a *coup d'état* or he abdicated.

On 22 June he issued a proclamation from the Elysée Palace: 'I offer myself as a sacrifice to the hatred of the enemies of France. Perhaps they are sincere in saying that they only desire my person. My political life is ended and I proclaim my son under the title of Napoleon II the Emperor of France.' He withdrew to Malmaison.

Wellington was appalled by the carnage of the battle. Afterwards he said that only a defeat was worse than a victorious battle. Many remarked on his dejected and sombre countenance. Out of some 28,000 British soldiers present on the battlefield 7,000 were listed as casualties, a hideous number for a victorious army; in some units perhaps half those breakfasting on the ridge had fallen by the evening. Almost all had lost a comrade or a friend and had themselves been very close to death. The regiments of the King's German Legion lost 1,500, the Hanoverians 1,300. The Belgo-Dutch

casualty figure has been put as high as 4,000, but this must have included a considerable number of deserters. The Prussians suffered 7,000 casualties, 6,000 of them out of Bülow's IV Corps, showing how fiercely Plancenoit had been contested. Records do not exist for the French. It is thought their losses must have exceeded 20,000, but their whole army crumbled to pieces in a fashion almost unprecedented in modern times. Possibly Napoleon's lie about Grouchy's arrival rebounded, convincing the soldiers that there were traitors in high places; possibly they were prepared to make no more sacrifices for a general whose star had clearly set. Curiously, during the terrible night of 18 June no colours were lost.

On 24 June, although he had learned that Napoleon had abdicated, Blücher refused to cease hostilities. He wrote to Müffling, 'You will direct activities for having Napoleon surrendered to us so that he may be executed. Such is the requirement of Everlasting Justice.' Wellington disagreed. He informed Blücher that a summary execution would be unbecoming to generals of their standing. Unimpressed, Blücher thrust on to Paris, still burning to capture Napoleon, and dragging a reluctant Wellington after him.

Davout, Governor of Paris, had managed to accumulate a sufficient number of troops to ensure that an assault on the capital would be a costly and, in Wellington's view, pointless affair. Largely at his behest the Allies granted an amnesty in exchange for the capitulation of the city. Article 12 of that capitulation stated, 'Persons and property shall likewise be respected . . . Individuals shall continue to enjoy their rights and liberties without being disturbed or made the subject of any inquiries of any kind regarding the function they

A parade of three Prussian army corps through Paris; the Allies entered the French capital on 4 July, Napoleon having abdicated on 22 June.

Malmaison, where Napoleon spent several of his last days
in France.

occupied or have occupied and their conduct and
political opinions.'

On 4 July the Allies entered Paris in triumph,
an experience Wellington had wished to spare the
French. Blücher, who by now was not wholly sane,
demanded an enormous indemnity and two
months' pay for his troops. He enacted a number of
draconian regulations – he thought that any
distinction between Napoleon and the French
nation was meaningless verbiage, suitable only for
politicians. However, when the Allied sovereigns
arrived, they repealed all his decrees. Complaining
bitterly that the clerks and quill-drivers had taken
over, once again the old man resigned. He was
persuaded to stay on until the last French garrison
had surrendered in October, then he retired and
returned to Germany. He spent the last few years of
his life on his estates in Silesia, staying the winter
months in Berlin. He died at the age of 77.

The Duke of Wellington took command of
the Allied occupation force in France and found
himself the most respected man in Europe. In India
he had won his battles with no fuss or publicity, his
countrymen scarcely knew of them. He won fame
in his own country during his campaigns in the
Spanish Peninsula, but the attention of the rest of
Europe was directed elsewhere. Now, after the
Battle of Waterloo, destined to be perhaps the most
famous and most hotly argued-over battle in history, he had every military historian and *savant*
descend on him. Horrified, he did his utmost to fend
them off, pointing to his own, as he thought,
excellent description of the battle, a view not
shared by all. He contended that anyway it was not

possible to describe it. For once he had to acknowledge, with a bad grace, complete defeat. Nevertheless his good sense and moderation made him an
excellent commander of the occupying forces after
the departure of Blücher. He never took the field
again. When later he led his country's Government, however, he was to find that logic and
common sense were not enough. He died in 1852,
revered by all.

Of those who had supported Napoleon, almost all were eventually accorded the protection of
the amnesty and many remained in the Army to
serve their country well. Ney was the most notable
exception. The ultra-Royalists and others among
his enemies clamoured for his death. The good-
natured fat King Louis XVIII, who had waddled
back from Ghent, was in no hurry to act; he said
afterwards that he gave him every opportunity to
escape. But Ney could not bring himself to leave
France, although he knew that his life must be in
peril. He was eventually discovered at a château
near Aurillac under an assumed name, and brought
back to Paris for trial.

It was held that the terms of the amnesty did
not apply to him, for he had led a royal army over to
Napoleon. His offence was clearly against Louis
XVIII, who was not a signatory to the capitulation
which had guaranteed immunity only from any
form of Allied prosecution – a doubtful contention.
Ney's wife, Aglaé, wandered round the chancel-
leries trying to find someone among the Allied
powers prepared to speak for him, but they declared
that this was a matter for France and declined to
intervene. A military court, assembled to try him,
found itself not competent to act. He was brought
before the House of Peers. By a large majority the
Peers found him guilty of treason. At 2 o'clock on
the morning of 7 December 1815 the last peer signed
his sentence – death. He was to be executed at 9
o'clock that same morning. His distracted wife
went to the Tuileries to make a last appeal to the
King for mercy. She was told that it was too early to
disturb him. She was still waiting to see him when
at 9 o'clock a Palace official told her that it was
now too late. By a wall in the grounds of Luxembourg Palace a volley had rung out and Ney,
disdaining a bandage over his eyes, had gone to his
death with his habitual courage. A Russian general
in uniform had joined the group of bystanders
watching the execution. When the Tsar heard, he
had the general's name removed from the roll of
generals. His gesture expressed the view of many in
Europe.

After his abdication, Napoleon stayed a few
days at Malmaison, trying to make up his mind
what to do. He ordered a large library to be
provided for himself, including a number of vol-
umes on America. When the war continued, he
offered his services to the provisional government
as a general. They declined the offer and ordered
him out of France. He went to Rochefort and
boarded a ship in the harbour on 3 July, the day
before Paris capitulated. A British ship of the line,
the *Bellerophon,* commanded by Captain Maitland,
cruised off-shore. It seemed simplest to board it and
allow others to decide his destiny. He surrendered
himself to the Navy that had always defied him.

What should now be done with him? Some in
England wanted to see him executed and to hand
him over to Louis XVIII; but many respected and
admired him. He himself suggested that he should

Napoleon on the deck of HMS *Bellerophon*.
He stared at Ushant from the early morning until it faded from view about noon.

Longwood, Napoleon's residence on St Helena.

Napoleon dictates his memoirs in the garden at Longwood.

be allowed to settle down as a retired country gentleman under the name of Colonel Muiron, after a friend killed at the bridge of Arcola.

Plainly, if he was anywhere near Europe, whether he wished it or not, he would become a potent centre of intrigue. Another Hundred Days did not bear contemplation. The East India Company used a remote island in the Indian ocean, St Helena, as an occasional port-of-call. The island was rocky, and landing anywhere but at the one port was difficult. Some said it was a tropical paradise, furnished with a fine residence where the ex-Emperor could live very comfortably and at a suitable distance from Europe.

Protesting violently, to St Helena Napoleon was sent. A royal Governor was appointed to the island: he occupied the fine residence while Napoleon was accommodated in a small house, called Longwood, that sometime afterwards gave good service as a pigsty. A British battalion garrisoned the island, and frigates cruised in its waters while the new Governor, Sir Hudson Lowe, British liaison officer with Blücher in 1814, plastered it with gun emplacements to guard against the mythical prospect of invasion.

Lord Rosebery, in his *Napoleon, the Last Phase* (1900), suggested that Napoleon had no real desire to leave the island. He might well be right, but it would have been a dangerous assumption for the Governor to make. Lowe was undeniably a narrow-minded, unimaginative man, a poor choice for a difficult and invidious task. Not all his difficulties were of his own making. He was instructed to treat Napoleon as a retired general who had reached the end of his useful career. He had not the wit to modify instructions that were obviously inappropriate, even when he was a reasonably safe distance from Whitehall.

Napoleon preserved what he could of his old Imperial state. He forbade Lowe his house, and the gaoler-governor found himself in the unusual position of being responsible for the safety and well-being of a prisoner who was apparently prepared to shoot him if he tried to enter his house.

Napoleon was now concerned solely with his legend. A devoted little band of followers rendered him Imperial honours. But he who had once started his day at midnight now started it at midday, and then spent much of it reclining on a sofa. All testified to his kindness and charm. For his last four years he hardly stirred from his little residence, for he could not tolerate the presence of an English escort, but not long before the end he took up gardening with great gusto. When he went sick, Lowe suspected a ruse to enable a return to somewhere nearer civilization. Then on 5 May 1821, three months before his 52nd birthday, he breathed his last. He was delirious for nine days before he died. Occasionally, during periods of marked depression, he wondered if his countrymen would forget his great achievements and remember only that he had failed at the last.

Immediately after his death an autopsy was held, and it was announced that he had died of cancer of the stomach. A political motive lay behind the finding. Britain did not want the odium of contributing to his death, for it was known that a liver complaint was endemic on the island. The verdict of the post-mortem was at once queried in France, and the best medical opinion now seems to be that he did die of a liver complaint, aggravated by his habit of eating his meals so fast that he frequently finished before others had had time to begin. He was also found to have been suffering from tuberculosis, the disease from which Josephine and his son both died. He was buried in St Helena after a simple ceremony, and in 1840, as a gesture of goodwill, he was taken to France to be re-interred.

Although, medically, it might be necessary to conclude that he died from some specific disease, it is probably truer that he died from insufferable boredom. As an emperor and a legend he was already, in all but name, numbered among the dead that fell at Waterloo. The news of his death, even in distant St Helena, still shook the world. The poet Shelley, soon himself to die in Italy, wrote a poem suggesting that the Earth was overbold in asserting the chains of mortality on one such as Napoleon, while Beethoven remarked that he had written Napoleon's funeral march in the second movement of the Eroica Symphony.

Lord Rosebery, who studied his last days, may well have the last word. He wrote, 'Authoritative democracy, or in other words democratic dictatorship, the idea which produced the Second Empire in France, which is still alive there and which in various forms has found favour elsewhere, is the political legacy, perhaps the final message of Napoleon.' He added, 'He raised himself by the use and ruined himself by the abuse of superhuman faculties.'

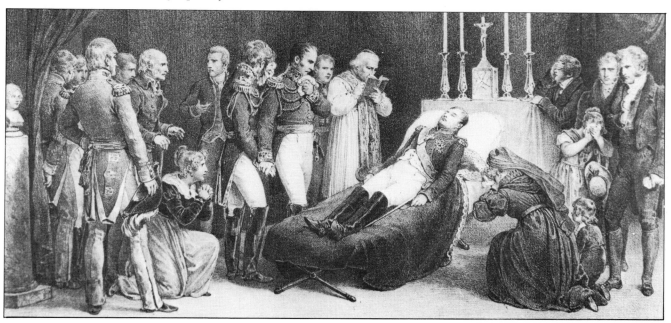

The death of Napoleon, on 5 May 1821.

APPENDIX: A CRITICISM OF THE HUNDRED DAYS

First it is necessary to criticize the critics. An immensely powerful searchlight has been beamed on the events of the Hundred Days; almost everyone has been found wanting at some time, some almost all the time. It might seem that the campaign was waged by three imbeciles, incapable of rational thought, who commanded gangs of lazy good-for-nothings, reluctant to rise in the morning, anxious only to return to their couches as early as possible in the evening. Prince Kraft zu Hohenlohe-Ingelfingen, the 19th-century Prussian general suggested that in much military criticism the critic failed to understand the complexities of military operations. There are several possible reasons.

First there is the *post hoc propter hoc* fallacy, that since events took a certain turn they were bound to take that turn. Second, all too often the normal human attributes of the soldier are ignored. A football manager, for instance, who refused to allow his men to eat on the day of a crucial match, and then took them for a 10-mile cross-country run before leading them on to the football field, would be looked on as somewhat eccentric. It is a truism that battle is the ultimate test of a man's physical and mental capacities. A general then, like any other team manager, should clearly aim to bring his men into battle fresh, at their peak of mental and physical fitness.

When marching from Brussels to Quatre-Bras, that very experienced general, Picton, halted for three hours to allow his men to cook and eat a meal. He has been criticized for being slow. Halkett's brigade of Alten's division, on the other hand, marched continuously that day with no halt for food. The men arrived on the battlefield tired and hungry. Sir John Fortescue, that normally lenient critic of the British Army, censured its performance, although two days later at Waterloo the regiments fought with admirable constancy. Of course, on occasion, a general would have to make an equation and balance effectiveness against speed, and perhaps decide that speed was all-important.

In addition, the soldier was no automaton. He might feel happier and more courageous one day than the next. Even the most valiant, when their regiments suffered heavy casualties, lost some of their fire. They would see their friends struck down, some perhaps dead, others writhing in agony; they would themselves have felt death brushing their shoulders. After a few days the death of a comrade might be dismissed as 'Poor old Tommy handed in his dinner pail,' or by some such euphemism, but for a few days the performance of the unit would be adversely affected.

The influence of the mechanics of movement is sometimes disregarded. It could be great, particularly where, for any reason, movement off roads had become difficult. Distances measured off on a map with a pair of dividers can be misleading. A man with a stick and a dog, who knows that a friendly inn will offer him refreshment and a night's lodging, can cover distances that bear no relation to what a formed body of troops could cover.

A corps column with its cavalry and infantry, its guns and ammunition wagons, its baggage and even, in the French Army, its ambulances, would have to be carefully marshalled at the start of a move and allotted separate dispersal areas at the end. As it stretched out along a road, those behind might have to wait some hours before stepping off. As an extreme example, cases occurred in East Africa during the First World War where the leading men in a battalion, marching in single file down a jungle trail, arrived at the new camp-site before the rear files had left the old. On 17 June 1815 Belgian peasants reported that Prussian columns marching to Wavre took six hours to pass. The shorter the distance the greater the disproportion between a column and an individual. In this campaign, to censure very experienced generals for being slow is merely to misunderstand the problems they had to resolve.

All three armies were somewhat hastily thrown together, and the staffwork left something to be desired, but Napoleon courted the confusion of 15 and 16 June. He crossed the Sambre on a narrow front, fully aware that such a move would cause congestion and chaos if carried out at speed. He could be sure that in the long run this would be to his advantage. If, instead of attacking the Prussians at Ligny at 3 o'clock on the 16th, he had waited until the morning of the 17th, all three armies would have been neatly and correctly deployed, the military critics satisfied and all hope of a French victory banished. As it was, by the evening of the 16th Napoleon had secured a strategic advantage which, against lesser opponents, would have proved decisive.

No campaign against worthy opponents goes through as planned. Luck inevitably affects the issue. On balance it would seem that luck favoured the Allies. The misunderstanding with d'Erlon on the 16th cost Napoleon a vital hour, although it also misled Blücher, and the rain on the afternoon of the 17th deprived him of time at Waterloo. On the other hand, the fire at Wavre restored to him his chance of a victory. It could be said that luck was only marginally adverse to the French.

It is time wasted to criticize troops for failing to cover distances at speeds impossible under the conditions then ruling, to censure Wellington for failing to jump to conclusions on 15 June or Napoleon for a similar fault on the 17th. A wrong decision taken on insufficient evidence is the most time-consuming of all.

On 15 and 16 June Napoleon's speed and boldness undoubtedly surprised Wellington, and against such an opponent, particularly with the political restrictions placed on patrolling into France, it would have been wise for the Allies to make their initial deployment further north, perhaps at Mont-St-Jean. But Blücher hated to retreat; it was a part of his temperament and made him a splendid ally on the battlefield. Wellington therefore had to deploy too far to the south, or the British would have been accused of bad faith. In fact it did not save them from that accusation by Prussian critics anxious to denigrate British achievements.

In the early stages Gneisenau possibly made two of the most vital decisions of the campaign. The first was taken on 14 June, when he ordered Thielmann to move his corps from Dinant to Namur on the 15th, thus enabling Blücher to concentrate much of his army. Then on the 16th he took what Wellington subsequently described as the most critical decision of all when he ordered the Prussians to retreat on Wavre, and organized the retreat so skilfully that the French were fatally late in divining his intentions. Typically, some critics prefer to deride the French rather than praise the Prussians.

After the initial surprise, Wellington handled his army with his usual flawless skill. It was no easy army to handle. The quality of units was decidedly uneven. It was a situation he had known in Spain, but never to the same extent. He could not guess how the Belgo-Dutch units would behave. They did not emulate the Saxons at Leipzig and change sides in the middle of the battle, but their attachment to the Allies was certainly lukewarm; many, like van Merlen, an ex-colonel of the Imperial Guard, had learnt their soldiering with the French and might well have preferred to support Napoleon. If a soldier is to fight well he must be committed either to his cause or his general, preferably to both, and be well trained. Among the Hanoverian troops the conduct of the King's German Legion was beyond criticism, but some of the *Landwehr* units, the militia, were noticeably shaky, and the Brunswickers were young and inexperienced. When to that is added an unpractised staff, it is clear that Wellington had much to cause him

anxiety. It was a measure of his skill as a general and his power to inspire his men that he kept most of his polyglot army in action to the end; when Napoleon threw in his Guard in his last desperate attack Wellington had one infantry brigade, Mitchell's Peninsula veterans, as yet only slightly committed and exactly positioned to sustain Maitland's Guards, where the main weight of French attack fell, should such have been necessary.

Wellington has been criticized for placing too much of his strength on his right when the first great French attack came on his left. To fail to predict Napoleon's actions was not unusual for any general, and the power to concentrate on a particular portion of a front is one of the advantages of possessing the initiative. But to suggest that Wellington was necessarily incorrect is another matter. Taking into account the final result of the battle, Wellington might seem justified in thinking that Napoleon would do well to contain him with, perhaps, one infantry corps and some cavalry divisions while with the remainder he pushed on for Brussels. Moreover Napoleon, the supreme pragmatist, the man least the slave to preconceived ideas, might have taken the Mons road to Brussels had it been undefended. He aimed to defeat the British and Prussian armies separately, but he also aimed to capture Brussels. Perhaps one of Napoleon's mistakes was not to appreciate what a clumsy army he had in front of him, or how vulnerable it was to manoeuvre. His oft-quoted statement that Wellington was a bad general was probably no more than a typical effort to boost the morale of his own generals. It is noticeable that on his left wing he had placed d'Erlon and Reille, both with long experience of Wellington in Spain, and that his Chief-of-Staff was Soult, who had fought the British more than any of his generals. Ney, too, had been repulsed by Wellington, at Busaco. It is more than likely that Napoleon weighed these considerations before selecting his method of attack at Waterloo. In short, he probably regarded Wellington with more respect than he thought it politic to admit.

Of the others, most of the criticism arises from prejudice rather than rational judgment. Ney at Quatre-Bras showed all his great powers of leadership and tactical ability. He was opposed by one of the greatest exponents of tactics of all time. That he did not succeed was no disgrace. And at Quatre-Bras with a single corps he held the ring for his master at Ligny. Even if he had captured the crossroads, or occupied them earlier in the morning, he could have done no more. At Waterloo he performed magnificently. Again, he had no hope of worsting Wellington tactically, but he came close enough to doing it. He is accused of ordering the first cavalry attack prematurely. At this time to pass judgment on such a matter would presume an impossibly detailed knowledge of the conditions.

Grouchy, the general who did nothing right on the 17th and 18th and nothing wrong on the 19th or 20th, seems to suffer from schizophrenia – at least that is the impression the critics give. Pitchforked into high command over the heads of two veteran and resentful corps commanders, possibly he might have been rather more dynamic on the 17th, and have marched to the sound of the guns on the 18th. It was a maxim the Prussians applied to good effect in the Franco-Prussian War of 1870 – 71. In this particular instance, had he done so he would have arrived too late to affect the course of the battle. His duty was to fight a holding battle, as Ney had done at Quatre-Bras. He had good reason to think he would be able to do so.

The most obvious points of criticism relate to the unglamorous subject of organization. If Napoleon intended to act with his army in two wings he should have organized it in this manner before it arrived at Charleroi. In battle an officer may suddenly find himself exercising high command at very short notice to replace a casualty, but he will have a staff to tell him how matters are, and with any luck he will have established some degree of mental superiority over his subordinates.

Ney took over his wing at 3 o'clock on the afternoon of the 15th and was hotly engaged on the 16th. He had no form of staff at all to pass his orders. At least with his towering personality and prestige no one would dare to question them. With Grouchy it was different. He had no such prestige. No doubt Gérard's wound at Wavre eased his problems of command, but it would have been better had he been appointed even two days earlier. Napoleon had much else to occupy his mind in Paris besides the campaign in the Netherlands, and left his plans for it a little late.

For the Allies the mistakes in organization are glaringly obvious, although that does not imply that they were easy to correct. The two headquarters should have been sited close together with a supreme commander to coordinate the activities of both armies. With the hostility existing between Britain and Prussia, politically speaking such a move was impossible. Further, while British interests centred round the Channel ports, the Prussians were concerned about their newly acquired territories on the Rhine. The two had nothing in common except a resolution to defeat Napoleon.

This led to the second great mistake. The communications of both armies ran parallel to their fronts and in opposite directions, Wellington's to Ostend, Blücher's to Liège. In 1944 the communications of the British 14th Army ran parallel to the Japanese. They attacked along the lines of communication, as Wellington feared Napoleon would do, cut off 4 Corps in Imphal and, but for a massive airlift, might have inflicted a major disaster. As in 1815, the error partially arose from the British intention to take the offensive, when the handicap would have been of less importance as the offensive progressed. If in 1815 Wellington's line of communication had run north to Antwerp and Blücher's through Wavre to Louvain, and perhaps Maastricht, Napoleon might possibly not have attacked. The reasons for the errors were largely political and reflected the hostility with which the two powers regarded each other. Fortunately Blücher cared little for politicians and liked Wellington, while Wellington admired the Prussian. Their personalities remedied a situation that with others might have proved disastrous. But the subtle influence of a correct organization cannot be overemphasized, particularly as its results are almost always indirect, and often overlooked.

To conclude, a comparison between Napoleon and Wellington is almost unavoidable. It is a fascinating one, for they were the antitheses of each other, Wellington the cool, dispassionate, calculator of the odds, Napoleon the man who would bend them in his favour. It is tempting to dub Napoleon the supreme strategist, Wellington the supreme tactician. But to suggest that Napoleon was anything but a supreme master of tactics, when he won more battles, often against heavy odds, than any other general, seems to be flying in the face of the evidence; equally no one who consistently out-thought and out-fought the best of the French marshals, as Wellington did in the Iberian Peninsula, could be anything but a superb strategist. Any other verdict does the French marshals an injustice. In minor tactics Wellington may have excelled Napoleon in his later years. His experiences in India, confronting vastly large armies with a small, very professional one, taught him to use ground to protect his troops in a way not then understood in Europe. As an infantry soldier – although he did spend a short time in the cavalry – he made certain that the British musketry was the finest in the world. These two factors combined to give him a considerable advantage; but in the higher levels of tactics, in the handling of cavalry, infantry and guns in combination, Napoleon was probably more skilled than any general since Alexander the Great – even though Alexander was born long before the discovery of gunpowder or the stirrup. It is probably sufficient to say that no one but Napoleon could have attempted his campaign in the Netherlands, and no one but Wellington could have frustrated him. J. P. L.

INDEX

Page numbers in italics refer to illustrations

ACKNOWLEDGMENTS

ROXBY PRESS WITH TO THANK THE FOLLOWING INDIVIDUALS AND ORGANIZATIONS FOR PERMISSION TO REPRODUCE ILLUSTRATIONS APPEARING IN THE BOOK:

MUSÉE DE L'ARMÉE; MUSÉE ROYAL DE L'ARMÉE & HISTOIRE MILITAIRE, BRUSSELS; DOCUMENTATION EDITIONS ARTHAUD; BIBLIOTHÉQUE NATIONALE, PARIS; PHOTOGRAPHIE BULLOZ; DOCUMENTATION PHOTOGRAPHIQUE DE LA RÉUNION; MARY EVANS PICTURE LIBRARY; JOHN R. FREEMAN & CO; ANNE HORTON; LAUROS-GIRAUDON; JAMES LAWFORD; PETER MYERS; NATIONAL ARMY MUSEUM; PARKER GALLERY, LONDON; PHOTO VIOLLET; ZIOLO/PHOTO NIMATALLAH.

THE MAPS WERE DRAWN BY DAVID POCKNELL AND MICHAEL CAVERS.

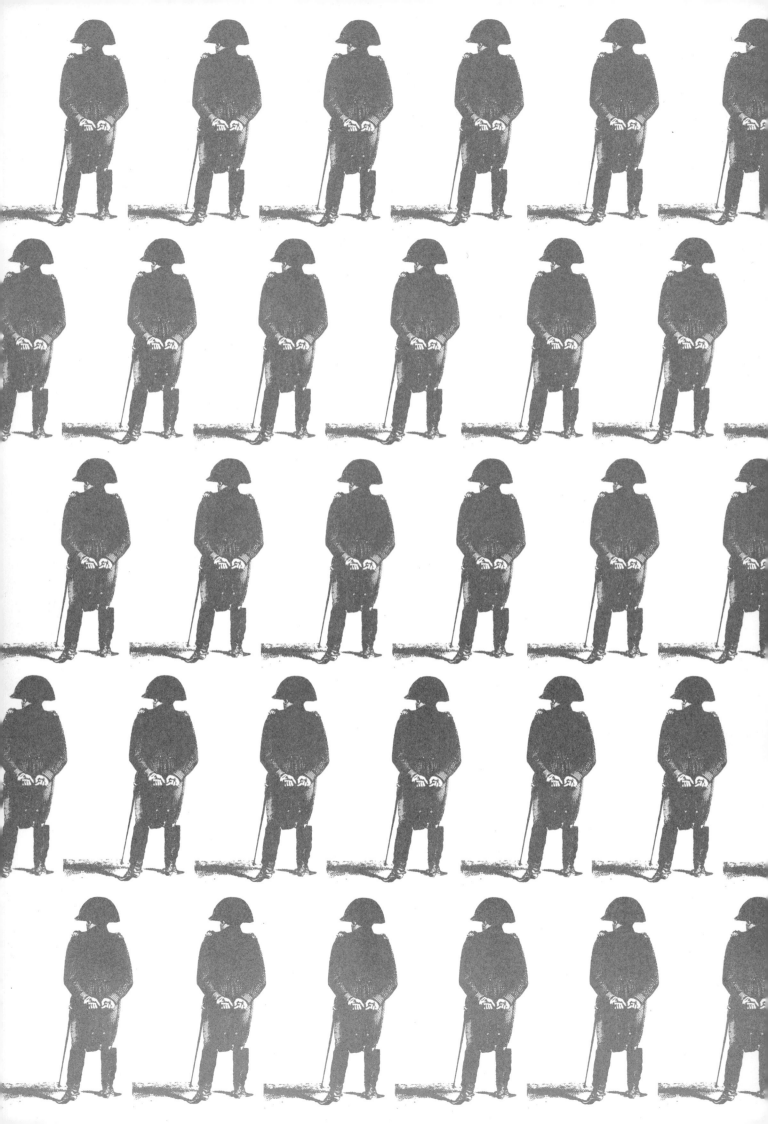